Confessions of a Psychic

CONFESSIONS

OF A

PSYCHIC

Susy Smith

The Macmillan Company, New York, New York
Collier-Macmillan Limited, London

The Macmillan Company
866 Third Avenue, New York, N. Y. 10022
Collier-Macmillan Canada Ltd., Toronto, Ontario

Library of Congress Catalog Card Number: 78-156993

Second Printing 1972

Printed in the United States of America

Confessions of a Psychic

Chapter 1

EVERY MATURE MIND eventually looks for an inner serenity with which to meet life. I believe myself to be on the road to achieving this serenity. I did not reach this state without a vast amount of effort—and even considerable danger—but the results are so rewarding that they should be passed along to others. Of course, the fact that my work has involved what is commonly referred to as "spirit communication" may make my search for inner peace seem a bit far out to some of my readers. To others, who are willing to travel whatever strange roads present themselves in order to learn new techniques for living, my quest may prove exciting and stimulating.

To most of us, life is such an ordeal that we are lucky to come out of it alive. But that is just what we do . . . and that is my secret. Without benefit of formal religious faith, or of naïve un-questioning acceptance, I have become convinced that there is no death. I have gone through many traumatic experiences while learning this. As a matter of fact, during my entire lifetime I have had more than my normal share of difficult challenges to meet alone. If I seem to have conquered them in recent years it is primarily because of this philosophy that has come to me through my experimentation with survival research—that and the fact that I come from a long line of stubborn Scotsmen, some of whom profess still, invisibly, to be helping me.

As to the process of acquiring this philosophical material—it is done by what is termed "automatic writing." Can you imagine how it feels to sit at your typewriter and have your fingers type information which your mind does not consciously instigate and which you don't even know? That is what I've been doing off and on for the past fifteen years.

Naturally I have questioned the source of the material, argued with it, and even fought with it. Does it really come, as it purports to, from surviving entities now residing in spirit dimensions of life? Or have I somehow tapped the universal unconscious—if there truly is such a thing? Might it be possible that my subconscious mind, with strange unfathomable powers, has gathered together brief bits from my purposely very limited reading of philo-ssophical or occult literature, compiled, coordinated, reconstructed, and embellished it with a great deal of additional information, and then poured it forth as automatic writing? To confound this theory is the fact told me by three well-versed Swedenborgians, one a minister: that a vast amount of the material written through me parallels exactly the accounts given in the eighteenth century by Emanuel Swedenborg, whose works I have never read.

In *Believe It or Not* Robert Ripley said of Emanuel Swedenborg, "No single individual in the world's history ever encompassed in himself so great a variety of useful knowledge." The eminent Swedish scientist led a life largely devoted to studies covering practically the whole field of science. He traveled widely, and was knighted by his queen for his achievements. He published many volumes on mathematics, geology, chemistry, physics, mineralogy, astronomy, anatomy, etc. This fantastic man gave up the study of worldly science at the age of fifty-six because he had become so psychic that he made daily trance visits into the spiritual world—or so he believed. He wrote numerous works giving descriptions of the conditions he discovered there, and these became the basis for the Church of the New Jerusalem, which was founded after his death in 1772.

Now, without having the benefit of Swedenborg's information, ever since the year 1956, I have been receiving data very similar to his. Eventually I just had to face the fact that nothing I have ever thought or conjectured about could possibly have produced from my own mind anything half so sensible, or in any possible way so inspiring, as the material that has flowed through my fingers onto the typewritten pages. Let me give an example of what I mean by this:

"Each man is an original creation. From the moment of its inception in your body, your soul (or consciousness, or spirit) lives forever. Your life on earth has a purpose, a goal, a meaning —to individualize you as a person, to begin your character development, and to teach you to coexist successfully with your fellow men. Nothing occurs to anyone which cannot be a lesson, no trouble which may not produce understanding, no unhappy experience which cannot be turned into rewarding usefulness. Thus, while a pleasurable life is a gratifying goal, the acquisition of wisdom is more important. There is plenty of time later when you will be gloriously happy. This is because each soul who is ever born must eventually return to the state of Divine Consciousness from which he came; and he must do so by his own efforts to improve himself to the point of perfection. Whatever progress is not made on earth must be accomplished after death, in spirit spheres of the universe. Eventually each individual achieves unity with the highest, blissfully filling, because of his own special talents, capabilities, and individuality, a place which no other spirit can fill in what might be called the Great Mosaic of Ultimate Perfection."

From the time I was twelve years old I have been trying to find answers to life's eternal enigmas. I can well remember lying in bed many nights during high school, praying—to whom I had no idea—and then demanding hotly, "Oh, God, whoever or whatever you are, please let me learn the *truth*!" Many of my readers have probably done the same thing, and so I am sure you will find similarities in our thinking in this report on my lifetime of searching.

I was living in San Antonio, Texas, during those years when I first began to question the realities of existence—sitting out at night in the yard under those stars that really are as big and bright as the song says. There the immensity of the universe was so startling, the insignificance of man in proportion so apparent, and the questions so overpowering that I was always bewildered. What was especially bemusing to me was the fact that everything in life has a definite origin and conclusion, excuse for being and reasonable explanation—everything, that is, except the greatest and most profound questions of all.

I have always been a rationalist, never a credulous believer in anything since giving up Santa Claus and fairies and Sunday School. I maintain that you do not need to be a scientist to try to look at everything, yourself included, in an introspective and investigative manner. My lifetime, of course, has been right in the middle of what somebody described as "that dank void of Godless intellectualism" that has gripped our civilization for so long; and so eventually I decided that mental maturity was evinced by disbelief in all the creeds of the common man.

I had attended churches of almost every denomination in my search for God, but most of the descriptions given of Him were unacceptable to me. It seemed to me that Christians belittled their God the way they interpreted Him. Could a God who had the intelligence and love to make a man who was shocked and horrified at the idea of eternal damnation or original sin have devised eternal damnation or original sin Himself? Could God be any less humane than the kindest man who ever lived? In college, while I was in a period of further mental controversy, a history teacher said, "Man makes God in his own image." To me, at first hearing, it seemed a most profound and original statement, and my agreement with it was my final step toward becoming an agnostic.

Without an organized religion, then, I developed a philosophy of life which seemed to me adequate. I usually behaved myself, more or less, because it was sensible to conform to the mores of my era, not because of the expectation of winning in the hereafter any loving cups for achievement. But I eventually brainwashed myself to the point that my slogan was, "Always expect the worst so that you won't be disappointed." I was not disappointed. The worst always happened. And I didn't have a very high opinion of life.

I had no hope of a hereafter, either. I truly believed that existence on earth was unfair to most people and could have no excuse whatever without some kind of immortality. Yet no orthodox picture of immortality was in the least acceptable to me. I could not see myself lounging on a cloud giving harp recitals if I had been good nor sharing a barbecue spit with Beelzebub if I'd been naughty. Neither did I hanker after being resurrected in my same old worn-out body at some unnamed future date. Yet there was no appeal to the ideas of survival in an abstract and impersonal form as Aristotle conceived it, or merging my individuality into a Nirvana state with the occultists. My aggressive mind wanted no part of anonymity. Yet if anyone had even suggested my taking any of the premises of Spiritualism seriously, I would have hooted at him. The idea of complete oblivion after death, although not in the least bit enticing, came to be more acceptable than any of those other concepts which did not make sense to me.

What I did, and what most people may do when they reach a like impasse in their thinking, was to stop allowing myself to be involved in conjectures of any kind, managing to keep my mind busy with work, with reading, and with pleasure. For a period of about twenty years my quest for truth was completely sidetracked as I reached instead for any and every palliative to replace serious reflection.

My psychical research just kind of happened to me. After I became interested in it, I argued with it for years before finally allowing myself to admit that it was entirely convincing. It would seem to be a difficult subject to be matter-of-fact about—and in truth many of its followers are dreamers or mystics—yet there are few imaginative cells in my body and I've always had a distinct distaste for superstition. Luckily, early on I discovered scientists at work in this area of research and learned from them how to observe each significant incident carefully and record it immediately.

So I plugged away at it, adding bits of what seemed to be evidence to my record day by day, but fighting it all the time. I have been delving into this area of interest since 1955, yet it took me eight years to give in and allow myself to be persuaded completely that spirits had been communicating with me. In the fall of

1963 I finally conceded: "This is ridiculous. You know you believe; why continue to fight it as you do?" Only then did I wholeheartedly begin to accept it.

When automatic writing began flowing through my fingers whenever they were placed loosely on the typewriter keys in an effort to receive communication, much of what was said seemed rational enough to appeal to me. For the first time in all my life and all my searching, I was reading information that to me made sense. The fact that it was coming through *me* was disconcerting, but eventually even that idea has become acceptable. How are you going to continue interminably arguing with statements like the following?

"Man lives his life on earth for one reason, and one reason only—to individualize himself and establish his identity and character. Creation continues eternally from the highest levels, entirely in accord with system and order. The consciousness that enters each unborn baby on the various inhabited planets of the universe comes from Divine Consciousness. Starting from life's experiences on earth and continuing in spirit planes after he leaves earth through the transition of death, each individual is in a process of evolution, and he must eventually improve himself to the point of sublimity. He is created for one purpose—to return in a perfected state to augment the nucleus of Supreme Power. In other words, the expanding universe is controlled by an expanding God Consciousness which is increased by the constant addition of perfected human consciousnesses."

Once I began the research for the numerous books I have written about psychical phenomena, I became involved in all manner of weird occurrences. I have tracked ghosts to their lairs and bearded poltergeists in warehouses and housing developments. I have sat in pitch dark séances where the craziest things were going on. I have traveled all over the United States and many other countries. And I've had, among other things, the time of my life.

Although this book will tell of these and many other of my personal experiences, it is designed primarily to follow the lead of my communicants, who want me to give their philosophy a very good airing. Let us begin, then, with the words of the entity who calls himself James. He is the one who has provided most of my information. The material from the book he has written through me will be excerpted from time to time in this present work. Here is his brief resume of what his messages are all about:

"I want here simply to give you this startling—to sophisticated contemporary man—idea that you do survive death and therefore that how you live on earth is important. I will also of necessity try to show the reality of communication with those who have preceded you into the afterlife, and how to use the assistance they offer you. If I can put nothing more than these data into this book so that they are acceptable, I will have accomplished a modern-day miracle.

"If you have true knowledge of who you are and why you are here, you will have respect for yourself and for others; and you will be better able to adjust to the conditions of your world. When you understand that life is not just an accident, a cross one must bear for no logical reason if death brings extinction, then it will be possible for you to live more comfortably and think more successfully about yourself and the role you must play.

"Life is by no means an accident, but a design instead; and the design is so perfect that it almost stuns you when you realize it. Prepare yourself to be stunned!"

Chapter 2

ACCOUNTS OF MY PARENTS' youth have been gleaned mostly from their own few reminiscences . . . or from the yarns their families have unraveled for me. That is why it can be said with some slight assurance that almost the first thing my mother reached for was a hammer. I personally can testify that she kept one in her hand frequently during the rest of her life, for until the day she died she loved carpentry. She was always making shelves and cupboards for our numerous homes; and although she was no Duncan Phyfe, it is doubtful if anyone ever had any more fun with a do-it-yourself kit.

This tomboyishness of hers has always been attributed to her father's intense desire to even up his collection of offspring by the addition of another son. To say that Grandfather Otto Hardegen was dismayed by the arrival of this red-haired girl is an understatement. Then his wife died the next day of childbirth complications. On top of all this, the Johnstown flood swept in and inundated the whole town of Piedmont, West Virginia, where they lived.

But a child has to be named no matter what the elements have scheduled, and so word went across the deluge that the new Hardegen baby was going to be christened Sunday come hell or high water. And she was. His wife's parents, known familiarly as "Grandma" and "Grandpa" Anderson, took over arrangements for Grandfather Hardegen, so they get the blame for all the names Mother received. It was only because Great Aunts Annette and Wilhelmina couldn't wade through the flood to the christening that Mother wasn't called for them too. So she only got Elizabeth Maude Anderson Hardegen, which was ample, especially when she later added Smith to it. I was to be glad for all her names when my efforts to communicate with invisible entities first began, because there were enough of them that an "intruder" pretending to be Mother could never seem to remember them all.

Now that my grandfather had his new daughter named, what was he going to do with her? Alone to raise three older children, Algernon, Ivy Lorraine, and Mabel, how could he contend with the tiny newcomer too?

"There's no reason we can't take her," suggested Grandpa Anderson, looking questioningly at his wife. This little new one had batted her eyes at him and already he was hers.

Fortunately Grandma agreed. "She's only thirteen years younger than Charlie," she said. "We could easily raise her as one of our own."

So Mother's father, relieved, took the older three and went West and was never seen again in our parts. And Mother was raised by her grandparents in Oakland, the county seat of Garrett County in the mountains of Western Maryland.

We might as well spend a few lines now getting acquainted with my Scotch great-grandfather—the one known in the family as "Grandpa"—because we'll be contacting him again later in this story . . . in considerably different circumstances. He is said to be one of my invisible "guides."

But at the time of which we now speak, he was a very active family man and the superintendent of the coal mines at Corinth, West Virginia, seven miles from Oakland. I know he had beautiful, wavy, auburn hair because we have a picture of him which shows it. But you can't tell much about the rest of his face because of his chin bush. Grandpa wore a gold watch chain across his stomach and insisted that the B & O, whose trains he rode back and forth to work every day, maintain its schedule in exact conformity to his watch. His name was Robert Ingram Anderson.

His wife, Jane Thompson Anderson, was as firm and uncompromising as the proverbial dour Scotswoman. Mother loved her grandfather dearly, but Grandma was no fun at all to live with. Most of the stories Mother told me about her childhood involved her many pranks and the intricate and unpleasant punishments Grandma devised to keep her in line.

The Anderson children, besides Mother's mother, who had also been christened Elizabeth, were Nettie, Maude, Anna, and Charlie. They were all old-maid types when I knew them. Even Charlie.

I have seldom been to a medium in recent years who has not given the name Charles or Charlie as being with me. I am not particularly delighted with this, because unless Charlie has changed a lot since his death, he is a terrible bore.

As Mother grew older her baby curls turned into carroty braids, and she was always into mischief. She was smoking cigarettes at six. Every summer she had access to the company store at the mines; she would slip in early in the morning when no one was there and fill up a large paper sack with candy and tobacco. She and her little playmates didn't need to smoke corn silk behind the barn like other kids, they had real makins' in steady supply. From the age of six to twelve Mother made smoking a habit during the summertime. As a young woman she was smoking incessantly long before it was fashionable, and until many years later, when the doctor forced her to stop, she usually had a cigarette in her mouth. My father was just as bad, so it is little wonder that I never adopted the habit.

Mother had one endearing quality that was unique—she could sneeze a real honest-to-goodness sneeze whenever she tried. So when she was a girl if she had something she particularly wanted to do outside of school, she'd put red pepper in the corner of her eyes to make them smart and then she'd sneeze, and sneeze, and sneeze. Gullible teacher always excused wheezy Elizabeth from school to take her *grippe* home to bed. But home she didn't go. She went out and bellywhoppered her sled down the hills and into the snowbanks instead.

I used to love to hear about these pranks of my mother's . . . all the naughty things she would never let me do. I had it in me to be a redheaded dickens, too, but it was squashed out of me. I sort of made up for it, though, after I grew up.

Grandpa, whom Mother adored, died suddenly of pneumonia the year she finished grammar school. I think it was difficult for the family to live in Oakland after that, since every memory had Grandpa in it; so Grandma claimed Elizabeth's schooling as an excuse and moved to Baltimore, buying a house there and keeping the Oakland place as a summer home.

With another of those changes a few years' growth can effect, Mother's hair had become soft, auburn waves by the time she was seventeen and her tomboyish mischievousness had toned down to a fun-loving personality and a twinkling eye. Mother was never what you would call pretty, but she was definitely a handsome woman. Plans were to send her to normal school as soon as she was graduated from high—but the occasion for Mother's future education never arrived because Merton Smith did.

Like my mother, my father had trouble retaining his family. His mother and a baby brother died when he was ten and he and his older brother Maurice were raised by his big sister Mabel and his father, Sanford W. Smith, who was a high school principal in Washington, D. C.

When Merton was twelve years old he was hit on the leg with a rock while playing. Soon his knee became stiff and swollen and painful and a doctor diagnosed his trouble as osteomyelitis. It was explained to Grandad Smith that osteomyelitis is a purulent inflammation of the bone, and if the leg wasn't removed the infection would travel to the rest of his son's body and kill him.

Little Merton thought he'd just about as soon be dead as to have his leg cut off. He thought about it all day and way into the night before the scheduled operation. Then he decided to take action. He sneaked out of his hospital bed and surveyed the situation.

Peering from the window, he decided the side of the building couldn't be as steep as it looked and that there were enough vines on it for a foothold. Then he found his clothes in a closet, but he didn't want to take time to put them on for fear a nurse might come in and catch him. So he made a bundle of them and dropped them out the window, then climbed over the sill and started down.

Hospital gowns, of course, are bare behind, and so was my father as he descended the wall. It wasn't easy with his sore leg, but when he reached the ground he was so thankful he just ignored the pain as he grabbed up his clothes and started running.

Over the fence he went and down the alley. Near the corner he found a trash can big enough to hide behind as he dressed. Then he dragged his aching limb homeward.

What are you going to do with a boy who doesn't want to have his leg cut off? Grandad Smith didn't quite know. But as he procrastinated, trying to decide what steps to take, he learned of an old German doctor who had developed a new theory of treatment for osteomyelitis. For months my dad made regular visits to him, and each time the doctor split open the tibia just below his knee, spread it apart, and scraped out the marrow. He eventually got rid of all the infection that way. Painful as it was, it was worth it, for my father ended up with nothing worse than the front of one knee enlarged and an occasional slight limp on rainy days.

When his big sister Mabel got married, Merton went to live with her in Detroit, attending high school, doing a great deal of reading, and secretly writing a novel. In this manuscript he was Lionel, the brawny, rugged stalwart he'd hoped to become instead of a slender blond youth with a game leg. Lionel had lots of romantic adventures with beautiful maidens . . . and he foiled villains . . . and he . . . .

If I'm to give you a true insight into my father and also into some later developments in my own life, I'll just have to come right out and say that my Aunt Mabel was a woman mighty hard to get along with. Dad was scared of her. He was always one for peaceful relations and so didn't answer back when she bossed him, but it built up inside him over a period of several years.

"Aha, here's that powerful Lionel," she greeted him one evening when he came home from school. He realized she'd discovered the secret hiding place of the manuscript of his book.

"Heave your manly chest at me, Lionel," Mabel teased.

"I don't know what you're talking about." He wasn't going to admit anything incriminating.

"Where've you been?" she taunted, "kissing the curl at the nape of Eloise's neck?"

Merton didn't say another word, but he turned and left the room. Aunt Mabel's twitting followed him.

"Don't flash your steely blue eyes at me, Lionel," she snickered.

Dad was seventeen then, just the age to take his book, and himself, very seriously. Anyway, he'd been looking for a good excuse to run away. So he packed his clothes into a small suitcase, slipped out of the house, and headed for the nearest railroad track. He was comparatively wealthy—had saved up all of $25— but hopping the freights was the romantic way to travel in those days. So he catapulted himself into the door of an empty boxcar heading west, and settled down to sleep . . . and to dream about the exciting adventures he would have in Colorado or California . . . or Hawaii . . . or even Australia.

During the night somebody pulled a switch on him, for he woke up the next morning in a freight yard in Pittsburgh. And thus the greatest venture of his life was sidetracked. But Merton rolled with the punch. Since he was that close to Washington he'd just drop in for a visit with his dad before completing his Great Western Expedition.

And yet without being aware that he was undertaking anything in the line of high adventure, he had two momentous experiences before arriving at his father's home. He spent one entire night closed in a boxcar with two huge empty telephone cable spools which rolled back and forth from one end of the jouncing car to the other. He couldn't pause a second to rest, and so danced a rigadoon hour after exhausting hour in his constant efforts to escape the careening monsters.

I was sitting in a house trailer in Daytona Beach, Florida, in 1956 when the above paragraph about my father was first written. I had just begun my attempts at automatic writing on the type-writer and was suspecting, but not convinced, that I might be communicating with my deceased mother from time to time. It was she who had encouraged me to begin my autobiography while there was time, because, she said, "Someday publishers will be requesting it." She promised she would help me when it was nec-essary; and so, as the preceding paragraph was being written, I asked her for a word. I had wanted to describe some kind of a short, lively dance but needed an obscure word that would not intrude too much. I thought of "gavotte," "schottische," "fling," "jig," but rejected all of them as too commonplace. I even looked up the word "dance" in my ever-active Roget's *Thesaurus* and out of the sixty-one entries there was nothing that exactly suited me.

Finally I paused in my efforts and laid my hands lightly on the typewriter keys.

"Mother," I said aloud, "could you please give me a word that would be appropriate here for a little dance step of some kind?"

Immediately my hands wrote the word "rigadoon."

"Do you mean 'brigadoon'?" I asked. "That's not a dance."

"Look it up," typed my hands, and so I did. The dictionary indeed produced "rigadoon," a word so little known that it is not even in Roget's. It is defined as: "a lively dance . . . with a peculiar jumping step; it is no longer popular." Well, it's popular with me, because it was one of the first of those instances that have become increasingly more frequent—where automatic writ-ing produces something I could hardly have known normally.

The night after my father danced the rigadoon to keep from being crushed by the telephone cable spools, he rode on top of a load of logs on a flatcar. This was even more dangerous, as he was soon to learn. The first time he nodded with weariness and loosened his grasp on his precarious perch he almost fell off. Thus he became aware of the desperate peril he was in, for one good-sized doze would have found him pitching off into the great beyond. So he lived through that night only by forcing himself to stay awake . . . reciting aloud every line of poetry he could remember . . . singing all the songs he knew . . . telling himself jokes . . . laughing at them. . . .

"Hello, son, how'd you get so dirty?" was the casual reception he received from his father when he arrived in Washington, but the handclasp was warm; and somehow Merton never did bother any more about going west. He stayed with his dad and completed his education and then went to work. He was toiling as a book-keeper for a biscuit company when he was sent to their Baltimore office, and there he met a lively high school girl named Elizabeth Anderson.

Chapter 3

MOTHER WAS SEVENTEEN and Dad was twenty-five when they were married. He was fairly short and slight, a quiet man with a brilliant mind and a shy disposition. She was taller than he, vibrant, energetic, and she probably exhausted him with conversation.

They soon moved to Washington, where my father went to work for the United States Government. He was always a Government career man after that, and for a time an Army officer. He and Mother, who will henceforth be identified as Betty Smith, had an apartment near Rock Creek Park; Dad loved to go there every evening after work and week-ends to play handball with those of his boyhood friends who were still about or to sit in the cool woods and read. Mother wouldn't go with him because she didn't like to read and she wouldn't sit on rocks and joust with bugs. We never went on picnics when I was young because Mother didn't enjoy the outdoors all that much, and this is one of the things I held against her for a long time.

At home alone, she missed her new husband. So when Dad came back she lit into him. It didn't do her any good, for Dad just spent more time in the woods, so she learned eventually to curb her temper. By the time I knew her she had the sweetest disposition imaginable.

They both liked to tease and we always had fun at home for this reason. Actually, my parents were quite companionable except for Dad's habit of merging with a newspaper or book the second he came into the house and having to be coaxed from it. (I'm exactly like that.) Mother, however, learned how to cope with us. She became a wonderful cook. That lured him—or me when I later put in my appearance—out of any book, no matter how interesting. And then she got a sewing machine. From then on she was content, sewing hour after hour. She liked best to stitch on heavy materials, claiming that working on dainty things made her nervous.

One dainty thing she enjoyed working on, though, was me, and I arrived in June five years after they were married. Halley's Comet was peeking in Mother's window, she says, most of the time she was carrying me; but what astrological influence that may have had on my life is yet to be learned.

The first thing I reached for when my crawling around began was nothing like a hammer. It was, of all things, the *Koran*. I began systematically removing every book from the open shelves every time Mother allowed me out of my crib for toddling practice, and the small Mohammedan bible became my pet. It may have been written in Arabic or in an English translation; I couldn't have told the difference. But its size was right for my size and my hands yearned for the feel of it.

Since it was a book that had little influence on anyone at our house but me, Mother finally allowed me to have it for my own; and for several years I ran around much of the time with the

Koran in my chubby paw. All this has no significance whatever, except that books have continued to have the same fascination for me all the rest of my life. But not the *Koran*.

"Why?" was my most continuous and most aggravating phrase all through my childhood, and it has been my life's theme. So when my father wasn't around to give me answers, or when he made me scramble for my own, books were my main source of enlightenment.

My name was Ethel Elizabeth Smith. I liked the Elizabeth, if it could have been shortened to Betsy, Betty, or Beth, but Mother wouldn't hear to that because those were her names. So I was stuck with the cold crisp Ethel Smith that always somehow sounded to me like a school teacher calling me down. I encouraged nicknames from my friends, but Mother put a quick stop to Ethie, Essel, Smitty, or any others I managed to acquire—and maybe it's just as well. Finally, during my college days Dad started teasing me with "Susy," a friendly name which snuggled to me. After that I always told everyone my name was Susy, and later on even made it stick legally. As for the last name, I'm a Smith who married a Smith. Ever since I got my divorce I have been afraid some other man named Smith would propose to me. I'd be just fool enough to accept him so as to be the only three-time Smith in history. Fortunately, no Smith who has happened to be marriageable has become interested in me, so I have escaped that fate—so far.

But all these considerations are further on in my story. First we'd better observe the molding of this little vessel known as Ethel on the potter's wheel of existence to learn if she will be shaped strongly enough to hold life's headiest potions without turning into a crackpot.

My lifelong habit of lonely peregrinations began when I was two and we lived in Front Royal, Virginia, where my father was Chief Clerk at the U. S. Army Remount Depot. Mother came down with typhoid fever and Dad moved next door to a boarding house with me so we wouldn't catch it. I can remember, and it probably did intense and hidden things to my little ego, crouching alone on a big dark stairway there, somehow in my baby mind wondering what I had done that was so bad that my mother had gone off and left me.

Sensing my misery, Dad took me to Baltimore to stay with friends until Mother was thoroughly well. With a characteristic that has been lifelong, I bounced back from my initial unhappiness and was soon spouting Mother Goose rhymes prolifically to the apparent edification of all concerned. In later years these friends loved to tell me about how delighted they had been with me and how they had wanted to adopt me; but my father would not hear to that when he came for me after six months and took me back to Front Royal.

At home was this strange pale lady without any hair who wore fluffy white boudoir caps all the time. Talk about your bright kids—I didn't even know my own mother. I loved the lady in the white hat and wanted to be with her all the time, but didn't recognize her as Mother until her hair grew back.

I really was supposed to be precocious, though, for all that. In fact, a doctor warned Mother not to teach me anything in addition to what I normally was learning at the time, there being some current theory about it damaging a child's brain to learn too much too soon. But as I grew older the problems of social adjustment at school took care of my precocity. Becoming increasingly eager to be like the other children, I eventually subdued any brilliance to the point that it practically went away.

Perhaps I shouldn't go into too much about the odd little emotional shocks of my childhood or the reader will think, "This woman didn't have a chance. She was bound to be neurotic from her earliest days, so naturally she's ready to believe she hobnobs with spooks."

What I have in mind instead is to suggest that because I had these rebuffing experiences in my youth and overcame them to the point of becoming a fairly well-adjusted adult, I was better able to keep from breaking down under the more violent mental pressures that occurred when my attempts at spirit communication started.

My father was commissioned a captain in the Army when I was about six and soon we were transferred to Washington, where we lived in a boarding house until we could find a home. Dad almost immediately got pneumonia and pleurisy and was taken to Walter Reed Hospital with a temperature of a hundred and six degrees. He hadn't been there a week when Mother caught the flu. She was put into the room across the hall from him. I stood alone on the sidewalk in front of our lodgings and wept when they took Mother away in the ambulance. I stopped crying after a while, and my main memory of the rest of that two-week period until Mother returned is that the twelve-year-old girl whose family ran the boarding house made me help her with the dishes every day, an imposition not lightly forgiven.

Convalescing after his near demise, my father was sent for a month's rest in Florida; and Mother came home from the hospital to find that I wasn't feeling so well myself. Within a few days I was down with something terrible in my throat. The doctor at first thought it was laryngeal diphtheria, since I was choking to death. Soon the ambulance came and I, too, was taken to Walter Reed Hospital, with a condition so severe I was just moments away from a tracheotomy. The doctors finally settled on a diagnosis of acute laryngitis and gave me steam inhalations all that night. These relieved the breathing problem, but I was left without any voice. As my quiet recovery began there in that same hospital where my family had just been favored patients, I really got the royal treatment.

You see, if a child is ingenious enough she can achieve all the goodies her parents do!

From the material I have since received by automatic writing concerning the potency of the mind, I can readily see how my thoughts and intense unconscious desires worked to effect my illness. The communicant who calls himself James is always very serious when he discusses the power of thought. To him, from his vast knowledge and experience, the mind is the strongest force in the world. It is particularly potent in its relationship with our own bodies.

"Many aspects of bodily function can be changed by your thinking," he said, "and you can be sick or well because of it."

According to that, it would seem logical to suspect that my numerous illnesses and operations throughout my life may have been basically, at least in some part, caused by this original episode, when the height of achievement became the acquiring of some kind of a disability that would get me to that same shrine where my parents had been when they went away from me. My friend Bill Hanemann was later to say of me, "Susy goes to the hospital like anyone else goes to the supermarket." It seems obvious to me now that my childhood trauma was partly responsible for this. It is also true that in my twenties I had a streptococcus blood poisoning that led to many subsequent debilities, so my problems have not all been psychosomatic by any means. Still I know that even until recently I was unconsciously holding the concept of a nice cozy hospital room as a place where nurses take care of you, doctors pay lots of attention to you, and you can retreat from the cares of the world.

A sort of a womb with a view, you might say.

"Consciousness controls everything," James has recently written. "All matter, which is composed of energy in a constant state of activity, is directed by mind, the overall regulating principle of the system through which it functions. If you consistently think positive, constructive thoughts, your entire anatomy tends to operate normally. Negative thoughts cause the opposite reaction. So keep yourself well by thinking happy thoughts and not causing your cells conflict.

"You can cure illnesses by the proper positive thinking because when you firmly believe that you are well, your body is motivated to begin to act that way. Watch yourself over a period of time and see if this is not true. There is nothing more effective for good than the constructive thoughts held strongly in your mind."

Oddly enough, the primary scientific corroboration of the power of thought is coming today from Russia, where extensive ESP research is being conducted by leading academicians.

Dr. Lutsia Pavlova, electrophysiologist at the Physiology of Labor Laboratory at the University of Leningrad, and her colleague, the mathematician Dr. Genady Sergeyev of the A. A. Uktomskii Laboratory run by the Soviet military, have uncovered impressive data on the value of thought power. They have learned, according to Sheila Ostrander and Lynn Schroeder in *Psychic Discoveries Behind the Iron Curtain*,* that "negative emotions have a bleak effect on your physiology as well as your psychology. Cheerful 'positive thinking' helps the body itself recoup."

The Russians know that thought can reach right down into our

* Englewood Cliffs, N. J.: Prentice-Hall, Inc., 1970.

blood cells. In 1956 Drs. S. Serov and A. Troskin of Sverdlovsk demonstrated that the number of white blood cells rose by fifteen hundred after they suggested positive emotion to patients. After impressing negative emotion, the white cells decreased by sixteen hundred.* White blood cells, or leucocytes, are one of the body's main defenses against disease.

My spirit communicants had been one hundred percent in agreement with this long before I read anything about the research being done to prove it. I can only hope American parapsychologists and psychical researchers soon begin to spend as much time and effort on it as their Russian counterparts. With proper proof, future generations can be raised knowing the value of constructive thinking.

Instead of such affirmativeness about our health or anything else, most of us—my generation at least—were programmed with all the old negative adages. My mother's Grandma used to say, "Don't sing before breakfast or you'll cry before supper" and so Mother said it too. Although stoutly maintaining that I'm less superstitious than almost anybody, even today if I catch myself singing before breakfast, I stop. This is one instance of early indoctrination that has stuck with me, no matter how hard I've tried in recent years to adopt James's and Norman Vincent Peale's positive thinking. It isn't easy to change the thought habits of a lifetime.

That's why my communicant is so set on starting the youngsters out right in the first place. He writes:

"If you would teach your small children, as soon as they learn to speak, to begin each day with an aphorism for health and happiness, their lives would be much more successful in every way. The child should learn to say each morning when he opens his eyes: 'Today I will be healthy and happy all day long.' Nothing else is necessary. He must learn to say it, not as a rote, but as an affirmation as important in the morning as his prayer at night. If he begins this very early, even before he can talk plainly, it will be such a part of his life's pattern that he will not think of it

---

* *Psychotherapy in the Soviet Union* (Ed. R. Winn). New York: Grove Press, 1961.

as a chore but as a normal routine. His life will be immeasurably improved because of it."

James is undoubtedly right, and it will be easier for children raised this way to conquer the vicissitudes of the world because of their positive attitudes. But what about those of us who didn't have the opportunity to learn it in our youth? Even though I had read Dr. Peale's book on the subject and had consciously tried to practice it, I'd had no luck. Now James was going on the same way.

"It's easy enough for you people to propound these fine phrases," I complained to my invisible associate after a few futile efforts to practice his teachings. "But just plain folks like me are the ones who have to do it; and you haven't made it a bit clear how we're supposed to go about it."

James's reply was immediate: "You consciously deny every negative thought that comes into your mind and substitute a positive one for it. Do not make a big issue of the denial. A negative thought repressed is harmful. Merely toss it out, instead; then substitute a positive thought in its place. For 'I can't do that, it's too difficult,' think, 'That's untrue, of course I can do it, and I'll be successful.' This might not sound as sensible as it really is, but try it. You will discover that it works. That's the important thing —it works!"

We must not only deny each negative thought when it appears, but we should prepare ourselves in advance by a daily recital of constructive aphorisms. James suggests, "Start every day with the statement that you are a brilliant, stimulating mind living in a healthy, normally functioning body. Let no negative reaction deny this as the day goes forward, and occasionally repeat the statement."

We will have much greater achievement with all our efforts to exist successfully if we will learn this, he says. No one need be poor or unhappy (at least, not for long), no matter how hopeless his case may seem. But you won't achieve success without intense effort. You just about have to practice positive thinking as diligently as you would practice the violin if you wish to become a virtuoso. And it is entirely up to you whether or not you want to bother with it.

"Those who wish to live so that they will have a more success-ful life on earth and a head start in future planes of existence have only so to decide," James states. "When you make up your mind that you will expend the effort to keep your life in a constructive path and maintain your thoughts under control, you will learn to do so. While it is very hard work, it is no more difficult than to give up a bad habit or to learn a new aptitude."

I must say he convinced me. I've spent a number of years now trying to learn to practice what he preaches, and it is a fact that circumstances have changed proportionately for the better in my life. Too bad it came so late or I probably could have conditioned myself to consistently better health as well.

There's no doubt that the little six-year-old tyke lying there unable to talk in Walter Reed Hospital could have had a more successful life in every way if she'd known about such things then. While convalescing I was sitting up in bed reading Charles and Mary Lamb's *Tales of Shakespeare* and basking in the nurses' "oh's" and "ah's" of surprise at how "bright" I was. I was ready, although not eager, to go home in a week . . . without my voice. It wasn't recaptured for a year. Even at that young age I was not the strong silent type, so I never gave up trying to talk, especially when starting into several new schools during that period and feeling self-conscious without speech. When my sound box did gradually begin functioning again I forced it constantly, with the result that I've ever since had a husky voice that carries . . . into all the places it is not supposed to go.

The year I couldn't talk my father was Quartermaster at Ft. Sill, Oklahoma. Because of my illness Mother and I didn't go with him. Later we took the train to Indianapolis to visit Mother's sisters. It was the first time they had met since their childhood, and we enjoyed being with family so much that we never did go back to Washington. When Dad joined us, we bought a new house and stayed right there. But my globe-trotting father, now a Major, was sent to the Philippines—a long and lonely way from Indiana. Mother and I rattled around, alone. I pulled my nose out of books occasionally to play with paper dolls, for whom I loved to draw dresses. Mother kept busy at her sewing machine; but we were disheartened dullards, just the two of us.

Luckily, Aunt Ivy had a friend, a tiny woman named Nina

Sharpe, who was at that moment looking for a place to live. She moved into our hearts when she moved into our home to room and board with us. We never let her leave us again, and she became a miniature second mother to me.

A graduate of the Indianapolis Conservatory of Music, Nina showed me what the piano had been designed for, playing wonderful classical music for us whenever we asked her.

"I want to play wonderful classical music, too," I told her, so she started giving me lessons. But the simple exercises which had to be practiced endlessly were so boring that I gave them up as a bad job. My musical education has continued only as a receptive listener; and my artistic urges were taken out in drawing and painting, for which I had considerably more patience and aptitude.

During our three years in Indianapolis, to make up for the taunts I got in school that "Ethel swallered the dictionary" I tried to be an exceptionally good scout outdoors (away from Mother's supervision), doing positively anything daredevil and adventurous. The boys and I coasted our sleds off high banks or slid them over a frozen pond nearby. We ran all over the highest scaffoldings on the apartment buildings under construction in our neighborhood, playing "banner the leader," swinging from ceiling pipe to pipe in the basement like monkeys, and jumping from porch roofs into sandpiles. Once I fell when trying to leap the width of the sidewalk from a high pile of bricks to the top of a shed. I landed on my back on the pavement; but even that didn't stop my career of good-sportsmanship . . . then.

The Smiths found the Pacific Ocean getting wider with the passing months, so finally Dad snatched back his 201 File from the Government and came home. Reentering the service in the Agricultural Department, he was almost immediately sent to Salt Lake City.

Mother was firm about it this time. "We're going with you," she said, and she put our house up for sale. I pored over pictures of Utah in the geography books, eager for a sight of mountains and desert. But it took nearly a year to sell the house and by then my father had been transferred to San Antonio, Texas. That's where we finally caught up with him.

The beauty of the flowers and trees of semitropical San Antonio enchanted us. I think every child should be raised in sunshine and warmth so he can expand and bloom like a rose. This is just a personal opinion, you understand, but it is very firmly held.

With my usual nonchalance I got sick very soon after we went to San Antonio. The doctor thought things in my interior had been scrambled by my fall while porch-climbing in Indianapolis; and I was put to bed for a year so that they could arrange themselves back in order.

This wasn't the intolerable hardship it might sound. Nina—of course Nina, she was part of the family now and naturally she went to Texas with us—brought me books from the library evenings when she came home from work, and nobody called me away from an exciting chapter to do the dishes. The *Graustark* and *Prisoner of Zenda* type thing were my favorites in those days, and I evolved from them a very refined (and unrealistic) idea of romantic love with which to begin my teens.

Returning to school the next year, I was a class behind; and it was now difficult to adjust to my peers, particularly boys. I'd always enjoyed their company before and they liked me. Why, I was even engaged at six to a boy in Washington named Jerome. (That had terminated rather abruptly when he hit me on the head with a rock.) Now this was all changed, and it took years before I grew to be at ease again with the more exciting sex. Oh, the unendurable longings of an undesired teenager. My ardent aim was to be a blasé sophisticate like the older girls, who were known as "flappers," but I couldn't make the grade.

As the twenties roared out I was roaring into my teens equipped with all the wrong things, it seemed. I had a burgeoning bosom when it was the style to be flat as a pecan praline. I had none of the easy-going, slangy banter necessary to communicate with the manly "sheiks" I wanted to impress. This seems strange because I was a natural chatterbox, quick with a quip; but never, it seemed to me, at the right time or place. Analyzing my every remark at home later, I was quite sure the wrong thing had been said on every possible occasion.

And Mother wouldn't even let me wear *lipstick*! That was the crowning indignity. Inferiority complexes were frequently spoken of in those days, and mine was a biggie. What I've always been, let's face it, is an introverted extrovert.

Thus when my high school annual contained the caption under my Senior Class picture: "A future artist, a girl with talents in many directions and a likeable disposition" it made no encouraging impression on me. Nothing had encouraged me much all the way through high school.

I finished the whole thing off with a flourish of red measles, missing most of my graduation ceremonies and parties.

Chapter 4

THE UNIVERSITY OF TEXAS was a friendly campus—known as the Forty Acres. When I was first there it was dominated by a decrepit but gracious Main Building whose clock tower carillon gave forth with "The Eyes of Texas" every hour. You have to be a Texan to appreciate the song that often; but I was, by then. During my three and a half years there much oil money was converted into new buildings on the campus; but it caused a twinge among us students when Old Main was torn down. My recollections of the university still picture the campus as it was then, with Old Main surrounded in springtime by beds of red poppies intermingled with pastel larkspur.

It was during my college years that I was most critical in my thinking—most divergent from my fellow students because of arguing so much with the status quo. Today that is not unusual, everyone's doing it. Then, my classmates and roommates just thought I was more than somewhat cantankerous. Although there were, of course, many radical thinkers on campus, very few of my associates questioned the orthodoxy of their churches or anything else. I was at odds with everyone most of the time until I finally gave up arguing . . . with my friends or with me, resigning myself to being an agnostic who was very suspicious of life. Even so, jibes at existence were most palatable when served up with a laugh, and so H. L. Mencken and Will Rogers were the two human beings in whom I most delighted.

While cynical about other things, I have seldom been so about men, dearly loving almost all of them with whom I have ever been closely associated. In college I majored in men. Journalism was my ostensible main subject, but dates took precedence over everything else, including grades. I had made the honor roll continuously in high school but never had any fun. Now I made up for lost time. I was engaged to Jack the first year, Richie the second year, and then came Henry. Henry was big and handsome and extra special, and even after all this time he is still recalled with warmth and tenderness. Every weekend toward the close of that school year we would almost run away and get married; but sanity would prevail when I returned to the sorority house each night and begged the girls to talk me out of it. We put it off once too often, for eventually priorities intervened.

We had decided firmly that we were going to get married right after school was out for the summer and go to Colorado to work a goldmine Henry had grubstaked the previous year. But when we went to my home in June my father was desperately ill with malignant hypertension—the highest of high blood pressure. The family hadn't told me how bad he was because they didn't want to worry me, and I'd been so immersed in Henry that I hadn't been home for ages.

Dad was still able to spend a little time daily at his office, but the doctor had forbidden him to drive his car. So I was expected to use my summer chauffeuring him back and forth to work.

"But I'm going to get *married*!" I wailed.

Dad called me by the nickname he'd begun using lately. "I need you, Susy," he said.

So Henry went off to Colorado alone, and I stayed home and wrote daily letters to him. When he received my frantic SOS late in August he started hitchhiking to me . . . and I didn't hear from him for an agonizing two weeks. He finally arrived in September just a few days before my father died.

I really hadn't believed anyone close to me could die. I'd never seen death before, being an only child in a traveling tribe which had never even been intimate enough with other families to attend funerals. I hadn't realized it, but death terrified me. Then the dreaming began and made it worse. I had horrible nightmares every night that we'd buried Dad and then he came back, or that he sat up in his coffin at his funeral and told us he was still alive. Or even that we'd buried him alive. Frequently I'd jump out of bed screaming, sure that a luminous figure had been standing beside me.

With my usual efforts to analyze myself and my reactions, I evaluated the dreams as caused by a guilty conscience because I had been so much more concerned about Henry's being away than about my parent's illness. Now it seems to me more likely that my father, after his death, was trying to get through to me in my sleep that he was really still alive and wanting me to know it. If this was true, he must have eventually realized that, because of my half-reception of his messages (which my subconscious was distorting into something monstrous in dreams) he was doing me more harm than good. And so he stopped his efforts; but not until he had broken up my romance with Henry.

We went back to our fourth year of college, but we didn't get along very well. My ragged nerves caused by my bad dreams aggravated his argumentative disposition, which aggravated my argumentative disposition. Our constant quarreling made me more querulous and him more bossy. So finally we decided on a dramatic separation, hoping that absence would make our hearts grow fonder . . . like in the movies. At mid-term I went out to the University of Arizona, where I'd spent a semester once before; but it wasn't possible to concentrate on lessons or dates with other boys, so I soon gave up and came home. After our big and happy reunion, Henry and I began fighting again. This time Mother came to the rescue with an extended vacation trip. She and Nina and I got into our little Ford and took off for the North and East to visit relatives and friends.

Several months later, while we were in Detroit visiting my father's sister Mabel, I heard through the grapevine that my Henry had married another. My heart torn to minced tenderloin, I decided to be a permanent college dropout and remain in Detroit where I could go into my decline far away from the prying eyes of Texas.

A few weeks after Mother and Nina had returned home without me, I met M. L. (nicknamed "Mo") Smith, and, because Aunt Mabel was as difficult for me to get along with as she had been for Dad those long years before, I married Mo in two months' time. These rebound marriages never work out. I soon learned that Mo's soft brown eyes that sometimes sparkled more often didn't. They shot off sparks instead.

Still, nothing was going to keep me from having an award-winning marriage; and so, never admitting to myself that things were seldom congenial, I set about learning to be a good housewife. It took a bit of doing because all I knew how to cook were cakes and fudge. But my cakes always fell in the unpredictable oven of our apartment. And Mo didn't care for fudge. His technique of showing disapproval of anything was to stop speaking, even for as long as a week at a time. I was to learn later that he and one or another of his sisters sometimes hadn't spoken to each other for years when they lived at home together, so he was in good practice; but it nearly killed me. I didn't know what to do in response. Just feeling hurt, or crying got no results. If I tried not to talk either I almost exploded. Finally it unfolded that the only way to get around his silences was for me to go into such a violent rage that he would have to soothe me in order to quiet me down. I acquired a stevedore's vocabulary and rather enjoyed these outbursts, making a real production of them. But I had to unlearn the whole routine at a later date in order to regain my former good disposition.

We had been enduring marriage together for a year and a half when we decided to take a Texas vacation in August. I became very ill on the trip. It turned out to be a streptococcus septicemia —the most virulent form of blood poisoning. Evidently a bad sore throat I'd had earlier in the summer had been a strep throat, and the germs had gone into my blood stream and lay dormant until the excitement of traveling aroused them. By the time we reached Mother in San Antonio I was almost comatose with a low grade fever that kept me lying without stirring or eating for two weeks.

Then the infection localized in my left hip and the pain became so intense that I screamed whenever the joint moved. Finally life was one long scream to me, no matter how hard I tried to suppress it; and I was taken to the hospital and put in a plaster cast. I breathed that ether greedily; but later coming out of it I seemed to climb for hours a steep icy hill dragging the painful hip and leg behind me.

I tried to pray that night. It was the first real praying I'd ever done in my life and the attack of religion didn't last past the illness; but it carried me through—along with the prayers and love of my family and friends. A neighbor, Bonnie Pitman, kissed me goodbye when I was taken to the hospital; and later, after my return home, she told me it had been goodbye for real, for the doctor had informed her I had no more than one chance in a thousand to pull through. This was in the days immediately prior to the discovery of the sulfa drugs and penicillin, which are effective against strep.

When I went home from the hospital I was put on a fracture bed, for I was in a cast which started at my waist and went to my ankle on the left side and to my knee on the right, its purpose being to immobilize the hip until all the infection was gone. Unknown to me then, it would also stiffen the hip joint so that it wouldn't bend and I would be crippled for the rest of my life.

My days in the cast were not too difficult to endure because Mother and Nina and a practical nurse gave me constant attention. I knitted an afghan, holding my arms up in the air over my head, and even got some reading done—of lightweight books.

It was the nights that were most difficult. Mo had stayed in Texas to be with me, but he was never home. I would seldom be able to sleep until he returned, which was rarely before three in the morning. As I lay awake, the fear of my death, whose imminence Bonnie had revealed to me, was overpowering. I contemplated death and God a great deal—but achieved no satisfactory answers. I was still too agnostic.

I wonder what my thoughts would have been then if there had been even an inkling of the fact that someday, many long years later, I would sit at a typewriter and have a description of God that made sense to me flow through my fingers. It would have been extremely difficult to convince that skeptical girl that anyone who could even make such a statement would not have been completely unhinged. Yet were she to have read such concepts as those of my communicant James, and to have been able to accept them, her entire life from then onward would have had a more rational basis.

James started out the book he eventually wrote through me with definitions of God, whom he likes to refer to as "Divine Consciousness," "Supreme Intelligence," or "Ultimate Perfection."

He wrote: "In our consideration of life we must first speak of what has always been thought of one way or another as God. The initial thing which must be understood is that this is never a man-God, nor a man-like God."

I would certainly have agreed with that, having always argued against any anthropomorphic concepts. So does James:

"Do not at any time confuse the Supreme Intelligence of the universe with man, for man is only one of its many manifestations. It is all-powerful, all-knowing, all-seeing, all of everything. Above all it is Intelligence—inconceivable, incredible, incomprehensible Intelligence. Nothing that we can in any way imagine can limit God's perfection. Everything in the universe has its origin in it and of it. Man, himself, is an integral part of Divine Consciousness, always has been, is now, and always will be."

Man's spirit, or soul or consciousness (the terms are interchangeable) had its origin as what might be called a "Thought" from Ultimate Perfection. James says that William Wordsworth expressed it correctly and beautifully in "Intimations of Immortality" when he wrote:

". . . trailing clouds of glory do we come
From God, who is our home . . ."

If we could always maintain awareness of this fact—of our complete oneness with God—our lives would benefit accordingly. But no human being is quite able to accomplish this while on the earth plane, no matter how saintly a life he lives. The time eventually comes after his death when he does completely realize his true conscious unity with God. James says, "After eons of time (as you understand time) and after unbelievable personal progress each man will eventually return to a condition of complete and absolute unity with Divine Consciousness. But at the same time he retains his conscious awareness of his own individuality, never melding into the God state so that he loses himself."

It seems to me that it would be impossible for any sane person on earth today to consider himself in his present state worthy of such a great destiny. James explained, however, that by the time man is ready to attempt to attain the heights he is able to understand and appreciate what his place, his powers, his abilities, and his uses will be after he has perfected himself. Then the idea of eternal life as a functioning individual component of Divine Consciousness is totally inspiring and challenging . . . and acceptable.

To me at the time of which I write, the thought of that extinction which had been so near to me a few weeks before was horrifying. And yet the possibility of existing forever would have been equally appalling. James makes it clear that by the time in the afterlife when we are faced with the actual event, we have learned enough and developed enough that we can comprehend this great concept of eternal existence within a total relationship to God.

"Supreme Intelligence has no physical aspects of any kind, except insofar as it is the basic *cause* of the existence of all manifestations in the universe—physical and mental. Matter is originated by Divine Consciousness, but Divine Consciousness is not matter and matter is not characteristic of it. Matter is Force in a form in which it can be used by all aspects of the Divine, including men.

"All the planets, stars, and galaxies of the universe exist only for one purpose: their usefulness to Man, either by providing him with a place of habitation or as modifiers of the conditions on other planets in order that these others will be habitable. I use the term Man as a generic identification for the residents of all planets which are inhabited. These men may differ in their physical bodies according to the conditions on the planets on which they exist; but the same type of consciousness that is in earth's men is in the denizens of all other worlds. Some, of course, are much more highly advanced than you are, and some are less so. The body, no matter what form it takes, disintegrates at its death and is used no more. The consciousness of each man survives the body at death. In its first phases in the spirit world the consciousness has a nonphysical body which is a duplicate of its former physical self. As the spirit progresses upward his successive bodies become more and more refined. There is only one life for each person, but once it begins in a physical body on earth it lasts forever in continuous conscious existence.

"The entire universe follows systems and laws which are the same as the natural laws which apply in your world. (And about many of which you are still woefully ignorant.) Nothing in nature occurs by chance. Nothing occurs by accident or in a haphazard manner. Natural laws, including the law of cause and effect, are always in operation. System always prevails. Even those things which seem to be chance happenings are definitely the result of some cause, although on many occasions you are unaware of what the cause is. When you learn more about the law of cause and effect you will see that each event that occurs has a definite reason. Each action, a specific reaction. The great instigating power of Ultimate Perfection conceived the laws and set everything in the universe in operation in accordance with them. Order is constantly maintained. Patterns are invariably conformed to.

"Each man is a separate entity with conscious existence apart from every other man, and he will remain so," James writes. "He will eventually progress to such heights of greatness that he achieves unity with all other men in the state of Divine Consciousness; but this is unity in the way that members of an orchestra perform in unity, or a choir sings in unity. Souls never merge into one another or into the whole. Each spirit is always a unit which knows itself to be one and individual, yet at the same time it is a functioning, self-operating, cooperating, working unit in the overall Consciousness."

I am grateful for the information that man will be busy after death with interesting and inspiring activity. I would be as unable now to accept anything less than that in the name of Heaven as I would have been when lying in my cast worrying and wondering. James sympathizes with us who ponder such things; but he assures us that the ultimate reality for man is as perfected as every other aspect of the miraculous universe in which we find ourselves.

"The pattern for man's existence, then, is this," he sums up: "A consciousness originally conceived as a thought from the Universal Nucleus of Consciousness is placed in a physical body forming in the uterus of a mother on an inhabited planet. It is born, goes through its life cycle learning what it can from the experiences it encounters, dies to the physical body and emerges as a spirit in whatever stage of personal character development it has achieved up to that time. No matter how poor a start this entity has, it will someday learn how to uplift itself and begin its joyful advancement. Eventually by its own efforts at self-improvement it will progress to a state of wisdom and love so superlative that it enriches and increases the universe with its peace and perfection."

Chapter 5

WAS RELEASED from my plaster prison after three months, and then, at first, I felt insecure without it. It is odd but true that one can get used to almost anything—except extreme pain, and I'd had enough of that to last a lifetime. I was allowed to get up on crutches every day after that, and set about learning to live with a stiff hip—which wasn't particularly pleasant.

During all this time Mother and Nina spoiled me with loving care. Mo occasionally lent a hand, if he could spare it from his girl friends. I was still on crutches the next September when it was revealed to me that much of the time I'd been told my husband was out of town on business he had been in town on monkey business. So I got a divorce, on the grounds of incompatibility. It was uncontested and I didn't ask for alimony, so in a month it was all over. After two and a half years of miserable matrimony I was free.

It was just as exhilarating as getting out of a plaster cast.

It was the same month of the divorce that I happened to see a wooden photograph album with a Mexican design on the cover. I said to Mother, "Bet we could make one cuter than this."

She agreed and immediately went to her workshop and produced one. Nina stained it dark oak, and I painted the decorative figure. Then we decided to personalize it with a name. Soon our house was overrun with albums and scrap books with our names on them, and friends were ordering them for every member of their families. By then we were so enthralled with our productivity that I took samples and walked down the street with them to canvass the neighborhood. So many were sold in the first block that we were kept busy until Christmas.

In January I showed the books to the manager of Joske's Department Store in downtown San Antonio. He suggested that a demonstration table of them might be put in the gift shop for a week . . . and after a year it was still going strong. My days were spent there and my evenings were spent painting figures for the books Mother and Nina had produced during the days. The following year we hired a girl to maintain our Joske's demonstration and I went out on the road, suspecting the books could do as well in other cities. Neiman Marcus in Dallas agreed and sold them; so did Ticht Gittinger, where I put in a demonstration that stayed for months. The same procedure was repeated at Rich's in Atlanta and Holmes in New Orleans, and in stores in several other southern cities.

Then, as much as anything because traveling was such an ordeal with my physical incapacity—how, for instance, can your toes be washed when you can't bend your hip in order to reach them?—I went to a hospital in Missouri to have an operation designed to restore motion to my stiffened hip.

One day Dr. Earle stuck his head into the door of my room and said, "I need an intern."

"Sorry, there's none to spare," I answered sassily, for an intern was standing at the foot of my bed at that moment and another was sitting on the chair alongside. They'd been telling jokes, which I was trying not to enjoy because there isn't room in a cast for a belly laugh.

"I call this the club room," the physician said, as both young doctors jumped at his beckoning. "Whenever I need an intern I know where to look." He wasn't really objecting, though, which was good because I needed their company. Having come on the train alone all the way from Texas for my arthroplasty, I was glad that many on the staff spent some of their leisure time keeping me from being lonely.

My main topic of conversation with the medics was surgery, for it completely fascinated me, and I had developed an abiding admiration for surgeons. They had told me that in time I would be allowed to watch operations, and it was an incentive to improve rapidly. But when I was finally up on crutches wandering around the halls and Dr. Earle, Jr. said one day, "There's some interesting surgery scheduled today, Susy, you'd better come in and watch," I shook my head vehemently and said, "Oh, no, not yet. I couldn't stand the smell of ether so soon."

"You're chicken," he taunted. So naturally I went into the operating room. The interns put a cap and robe and mask on me and showed me to a row of seats behind a railing. And then so much exciting activity began that ether had been permeating the air for some minutes before it impinged on my consciousness. The smell doesn't bother one, apparently, when she has something as fascinating on her mind as watching a double mastectomy and then a thyroidectomy.

After that I went into the operating room every day, and my admiration for surgeons increased to hero worship as actual observation revealed to me what great skill their work requires.

Being so interested in everything going on at the hospital, I didn't want to leave when the hip was finally well enough that I could go home alone on the train.

"I don't want to go," I told Dr. George. "It's too entrancing here."

"Then just stay around. We don't mind," he answered.

"I can't afford it." My father's Veteran's Insurance was going fast. "I've studied stenography . . . why don't you let me help out around here?"

So we arranged a deal for me to stay there and do part-time secretarial work for the doctors in exchange for my meals and treatment. I lived reasonably in a nearby student rooming house and, in my spare time, sitting around in the hospital halls waiting to be called for duty, I read medical books. Gray's *Anatomy* was my text, the whole thick volume. Then in the evenings on dates with the interns and medical students I made them explain the functions of the various organs and bodily processes I read about during the day. Then we'd drink beer and hike home, sometimes each using one of my crutches if we felt silly enough.

I constantly observed operations at the hospital and also got up at any hour of the night when the phone call came, "Surgery in the pit," hurrying to the medical school with the students who streamed out of dormitories and rooming houses in various stages of undress to watch emergency surgery. I saw babies born, appendectomies by the dozens, gall bladders, tumors and breasts removed, and even endured one man's leg being cut off.

I went to the vats in which the "stiffs" were stored until needed for dissection, and to the lab where the students learned anatomy by cutting and slicing these cadavers. It wasn't just morbid curiosity. It was a detached view of a subject which interested me deeply. The prognosis was excellent that I might have a future career as a medical secretary, or even a medical artist. And curiously enough, as life hands out its little surprise packages, a medical secretary is exactly what I did become briefly some twenty years later, when, on the basis of my knowledge of the terminology, I took a job in the Pathology Laboratory of Lenox Hill Hospital in New York City.

At the time now under discussion, however, something unpleasant started happening to my hip and it began slipping out of the socket. I'd probably been running around too gaily, thinking it was almost well. So that nasty ether was sprinkled on me again and I was poured back into plaster of Paris. This time it was an ambulatory cast which held the left leg out stiffly at an angle, but was not on the right leg at all. A narrow band of it went around my hips, and moving about on crutches was possible after a few weeks. Then work for the doctors was resumed, although the ungainly cast stuck with me (and to me) all that hot summer.

About the time they took those plaster pants off me, more unpleasant things began to occur. One day I watched a hip operation exactly like the one that had been performed on me, and that finished me with surgery. After they had chiseled and pounded and hacked on the bone of that poor woman's hip for several hours my nerves began to fray, and I walked out of the operating room, realizing that I wasn't entirely scientifically uninvolved after all.

As was my usual habit when in the company of a group of nice men for any long period of time, I had taken the opportunity to fall in love with one of the medical students. It turned out to be a rather fruitless endeavor, and it began to seem to me that, taking it all in all, my course had run at the hospital so I went back home to Texas.

There I got involved immediately in another cross-country junket. Mother was selling the Cape Cod cottage she and Dad had built several years before he died, and we were going back to her old family home in Oakland, Maryland, which she had just inherited. Mother and Nina planned to rent rooms to the tourists in that mountain resort town.

We arrived in Maryland to find a decrepit, doddering oldster all of whose nine rooms and exterior area needed every trick of modern rejuvenating plaster surgery to revive it. Energetic Betty Smith considered it a personal challenge, and she directed a crew of carpenters as they roofed, plastered, papered, puttied, and painted. Even after the workmen were finished she was still building shelves and cupboards, keeping that hammer in her hand much of the time. When there was nothing else she could add to the house, she continued spending a great many hours in her basement workshop, enthusiastically constructing desks or tables or scrapbooks with her electric power tools. And, unfortunately, putting more pressure than she realized on a weak heart.

I occupied myself with books, oil painting, and anything else that didn't take much physical effort. I was on crutches for my first two years in Oakland, and it took over four years to recuperate fully from the hip surgery. I'd had a remarkably successful restoration of motion; but the infection had eaten away so much of the bone that there is only a very shallow hip socket and a tiny head to the femur left. This does not even fit into the socket, but sits at the outside edge of it somehow, held in place only by scar tissue and muscles. Because this no-hip deal gives a bit each time I step on the left foot, the support of a cane has continued to be needed when walking. But a cane really isn't so bad once you've made friends with it.

I realize that in the effort to move this book along quickly to my psychic experiences I may have to pass lightly over periods of deep emotion. But how can I, without seeming maudlin, go into the thoughts of one in her twenties suddenly facing the fact that her life would henceforth be compelled to move at a considerably slower pace? I still thought of myself as a rather diverting young thing, yet one day overheard a little boy walking by the house say to his companion, "This is where that crippled woman lives." To see ourselves as others see us can be an anguish not easily exposed to print.

Still, my friends profess to think of me as Susy, one of whose small conceits is that she affects a walking stick. Who can object to that?

Chapter 6

MOTHER, NINA AND I all delighted in getting acquainted with changing seasons again in Western Maryland, where Fall was a flaming rowdy striding gaily across the mountains. But Winter moved its white self in on us early and dared us not to enjoy its long wearying visit. Spring never seemed happy to arrive and she wept during her entire stay, and Summer hardly got there at all. I spent the next nine years trying to figure a way to get back South again, for I was seldom free of aches and pains in that climate.

Yet it was nice to live in a small town while convalescing, for it was much easier to get around; and I relished the new experiences offered. Mother's girlhood friends and their families welcomed us cordially, and we joined the Methodist Church and attended regularly, even though I argued in my mind during all the services. We became active in circles, Sunday School classes, and I even added my uncertain second soprano to the otherwise excellent choir and found it completely rewarding. I joined the Civic Club, the Business and Professional Women's Club, and the American Association of University Women and any other clubs going. I went in for rummage sales, bake sales, home shows, amateur theatricals. Church and club work were all new to me and I had much enthusiasm to offer if only a limited amount of physical stamina.

Mother and Nina were considerably more successful socially than I, however. My breezy Texas humor made me stand out among the staid Marylanders and West Virginians like a penguin in a flock of Plymouth Rocks, and it took me quite a while to realize that my pleasantries weren't always accepted as such.

So I fooled around there in Oakland for several years without accomplishing much more than getting better and having a moderately good time; and then my insurance money ran out. I contemplated leaving home to go to work.

I was always contemplating leaving home for one reason or another, because, much as I loved Mother, she was just like other "moms" who indulged in "smother" love. She had never realized I was grown and continually kept trying to run my life for me. She even told me which spoon to stir the gravy with and exactly how to thread my needles. For some reason these little things annoyed me more than bigger decisions she was also determined to make for me.

(My dear friend Mary Elliott, who, with her husband and children are more like family to me than anyone else and are one of the main reasons I enjoy returning to Oakland again and again for visits, recently told me, "You know, Susy, you never really matured until after your mother died."

I knew she was right. But it wasn't for lack of trying.)

I contacted the Maryland Vocational Rehabilitation Service for job placement, and they very kindly got me what seemed to be an excellent position in Baltimore. I was to be the secretary to the Director of Nursing at one of the newest hospitals. My shorthand was never very good, but my knowledge of medical terms and hospital routines was excellent, and so I was well-enough qualified. Unfortunately, it was one of the most trying experiences of my life because of the arrogance of the head nurse for whom I worked. It turned out that the reason I had been hired for the job was that no one else would remain in it. Nonetheless, I determinedly stuck it out there for a year. Once during this time I became so unendurably miserable that I attempted suicide; but the report about that will fit better in a later chapter.

Then I got the mumps. Where was I after they slunk away? Right back home in Oakland convalescing again.

Finally I was lucky enough to find fascinating work right at home. The *Mountain Democrat* newspaper had been closed during the war, and when it reopened they hired me as a reporter. So far, one thing or another had always kept me from practicing my college journalism, but it was still my goal. It became evident during my three years there that with my gregarious nature newspaper work was what I'd been designed for. Well, good thing some use for me had been discovered. For a long time I had been feeling completely unnecessary. But the same bright shiny comments that had been difficult socially were considered friendly and not too forward in business. I soon learned to know a large percentage of Garrett County, and was invited to nearly every meeting, banquet, and luncheon that occurred. (Small town newspaper people are a well-fed crowd.) I wrote everything from front page news stories to Personals, Weddings, and Funerals; and there was a "Shopping with Susy" column that was quite popular. I even did makeup of the front page when the editor was sick, and helped run the press on publication day. This was the first challenging work I had ever undertaken and I thrived on it. I also acquired an enduring love for the "dear hearts and gentle people" in that only small town of my experience.

But, oh, those winters in the Maryland mountains were cold! I was plodding my rounds through snow and ice, dressed in ski pants, sweaters, fur coat, fleece-lined boots, fur-lined gloves, wool headscarf, and ear muffs. Sometimes even in red flannel longies. And constantly in fear my cane would skid and flatten me and I'd have to do another stretch in casts and hospitals.

So I secretly yearned for warmer climes, but only secretly, for Mother was becoming increasingly ill and I could not more than dream of leaving.

The Christmas of 1947 Mother gave me a musical powder box which played "Susanna Don't You Cry." But even though it admonished me not to, every time I raised its lid and the tinkly tune started, tears came to my eyes because I knew by then that

Mother was going to die and hearing that melody always called attention to the fact.

After working overtime as she had wrestled with the chores of the big old house for eight years, Mother's heart had begun to fail rapidly. She was satisfied that she'd lived an active life to its most complete fulfillment; but now she was bedridden all the time, her difficulty in breathing causing the most discomfort. Nina and I gave her devoted care, and in some ways there was compensation in it for me. For the first time in my life I was able to do things for my mother in return for all the affection she had given me.

She was never cross, never complaining, even though during her entire last year she sat up in bed and gasped for breath. She wasn't afraid to die, confident she was only being separated from us for a while; but to me her assurance was a groundless thing. It was nice that Mother and Nina had it, but their faith was no help to me, for I had no belief in a hereafter.

Mother waited until spring to die, leaving us on the twenty-first of March, two months before her sixtieth birthday. She told us that day that she wanted to be taken on the train back to San Antonio so that she could be buried beside my father, and so that Nina and I would have a few weeks among our friends there. She even made jokes with us the day she left us—little efforts to raise our spirits—and as we gently teased with her we found inspiration in her bravery.

The doctor had shown me how to give a hypodermic to relieve her discomfort, and I gave Mother the first one at 11:30 that night. She died at 11:45 and I was afraid the hypo had killed her until the doctor explained to me the next day that administering it at just that time had probably made her death much easier. I had put away the syringe and then kissed Mother good night. She thanked me for my gentleness in using the needle, she repeated her love and appreciation to us, then she had a sudden spasm. She said, "I wish somebody would tell me where I am," and then, "Don't leave me." And suddenly she went away.

My little music box had sat on my dresser neglected for months because its tune brought tears to my eyes every time it played. And now it remained alone, along with the house, while Nina and

I took Mother to Texas for burial and stayed for two weeks of visiting.

About four o'clock one morning shortly after our return, the powder box began to play. I awoke alarmed, and then somehow comforted by the strains of "Oh, Susanna, don't you cry for me." Although it momentarily seemed like a direct message from Mother, I almost immediately began to try to figure some natural means by which the lid could have become jarred loose. There were no vibrations in the house, we did not have mice—what other thing could have caused it normally? That I wasn't able to conceive of any possible way it could have happened did not convince me it was anything other than a physical phenomenon free of any supernatural origin. But . . . what you profess to believe and what you secretly hope could be true are two different things. It was consoling at least to consider the possibility that Mother was taking this means to tell me she was still around.

I was too pushed by business to spend much time pondering this, however, being involved in my first attempt at super-salesmanship. Oakland was to have its Centennial that summer, and the minute Nina and I returned from Texas the Committee had asked me to take charge of selling $8,000 worth of advertising for the Centennial program. I'd make a good commission and be able to occupy my mind, so the opportunity pleased me.

Turning in Mother's small car on a bigger one, I drove every day to Cumberland, Baltimore, Pittsburgh, or other neighboring cities, selling $50 ads here and $25 ads there and $100 ads another place, and after nearly three busy months, sales went over the top.

Then the Centennial was over, Oakland settled back into its routines, and Susy struggled out of her rut, as impatient as a whistling teakettle to flee away South.

· "You'll have to go alone. I can't possibly leave my piano pupils," Nina told me, for she had music classes she delighted in. So we turned half the house into an apartment and rented it so she would have company; then I packed my car with all my favorite personal possessions—even to a chairside phonograph and several hundred symphony record albums—and hied me away to Florida . . . to sit under a coconut tree.

Chapter 7

MY FIRST THREE YEARS in Florida were a period in which I learned to face life without any kind of parental domination and it was good for me. With no mother to run home to when things got tough, I had to square up to each situation and make my own decisions, for better or worse, and I responded adequately. I had loved my mother. She was the most wonderful person I'd ever known. But in a way I welcomed the challenge of trying to make it on my own without her. There were many problems and lots of grievances in doing it, and the results could hardly be called successful; but neither did they signify failure.

Back in mockingbird country once again, I rejoiced as their melodious tunes made merry with the atmosphere. The blue ocean sparklingly invited me for a dip. The glistening palm trees suggested I sit for a while in their shade. And the sunshine wanted me to bask in its warmth. I cooperated fully. The look and the feel and the sounds of the Sunshine State made me happy, and it was the first time happiness had lived with me in a long, long while.

I applied for a newspaper job in every city I came to while touring the state, but in September, 1949, nothing was going on in Florida but the autumnal equinox, and nobody was hiring anybody. I eventually ended up back on the East Coast in Daytona Beach, selling radio advertising and putting on a program called "Shopping with Susy."

I also learned to be "mommy" to a new puppy. Well, I'd discovered that living alone wasn't to my liking. Obviously what I needed was someone to wag his tail when I came home evenings.

Fortunately, just two months before, a miniature dachshund had been born with the intention of becoming mine; so when I went to the kennel he immediately stuck his head out of the basket of rolling and tumbling puppies and claimed me. I picked him up—the pee-wee of them all—and said, "I'll take this one. He's a redhead, too, and it's the style for dogs to have owners to match."

From then on wherever I went the little sausage named Junior wobbled and spilled along beside me. He helped me to sell advertising, for even people who find it easy to resist a woman salesman can melt to jelly over a dachshund pup. The little fellow was to be my constant companion for twelve years. Who could dream that after his death he would be the object of one of my most compelling psychic experiences?

Just about three months after I went to Daytona Beach my radio job was mutually terminated because I couldn't leave the ocean alone. Beachcombing is an occupational hazard of the tropics, you know. In Daytona one drives his car on the flat beach, and I'd route myself via the ocean when making my business calls around town. But the piled-up clouds, the festoons of flying pelicans, and the capering waves were so irresistible that I became compelled to frolic with them on my lunch hour. It was one of the most delightful episodes of my life, that balmy first spring in Daytona, as I'd float on my back, rolling with "the slow swinging seas," as much a part of the ocean life as the porpoise scalloping his way through the water.

Somehow the radio station manager wasn't happy when I came in late from lunch because of my swims. Working evenings to make up for it didn't seem to him to be the same thing at all. So we got into a little discussion, and then I went away without a job.

At the time I had only $300 in the bank and a puppy to support, but nonetheless I began to think seriously about an idea of mine—to start a shopping guide. It would be a free throw-away sheet to be paid for by the advertising. Every merchant approached about it encouraged me, seeming to think there was money to be acquired that way. I figured to have fun and make a good living, be able to work the hours I chose and have time for the beach, too.

Well, the only one of those dreams that came true was the fun. *That* I had. Reminiscence now in the light of experience indicates that my health and my pocketbook would have survived in better shape if such a taxing enterprise had never been started. And had hindsight been foresight, I wouldn't have had the nerve to begin. All I knew then was that I could write ads and sell them, I got along well with people, and the merchants of Daytona said they needed a shopping guide. What more was required?

I was soon to find out, as I coped with social security and withholding tax, making collections from tough accounts, cutthroat competition from would-be competitors, hiring and firing employees, struggling with the most uncooperative machine ever invented—a typesetter that (supposedly) aligns type into columns —and trying to produce acceptable radio programs on a tape recorder whose tapes were the wrong width to be played over the studio equipment. Yes, eventually there was a radio program of our own in addition to the weekly paper.

From its initial issue *Shopping with Susy* was a success with readers, if not financially. It was a nice-looking tabloid-size sheet, six pages thick at first, although later it went up to twelve and fourteen pages during rush seasons. It was written with the lightest possible touch, with interesting sidelights about the advertisers, and stories and jokes with local application. It had a different appeal from most shopping guides because of its manner of gently ribbing the advertiser, the reader, and ourselves as well. It was (we thought) fresh and bright, and certainly no one ever knew just what to expect from it or what we were likely to come up with next.

Although we soon went to offset as the easier way to handle the production, at first *Shopping with Susy* was printed at a small independent newspaper shop. There the foreman, Bill Beard, had a large black bull terrier named Lil, of whom Junior was very fond, and watching the big black dog and the small red puppy romping together became part of our daily routine.

One day, when Junior was about five months old, Bill Beard came storming into my office waving the mat of a picture I had asked him to cast in metal so that it could be reproduced in my paper. It was of a Negro soldier returning home from the Korean War. Bill, who had been reared in South Carolina a long time ago, threw the mat onto my desk and demanded to know why I was putting a picture of a "nigger" in my paper.

"If he's good enough to fight for us, he's certainly good enough to have his picture published," I said. "We'll run it proudly."

"Well, I won't set it," said Bill, and he left it on my desk.

A little later I took the mat back to the shop and handed it to Beard, but he still refused to have anything to do with it. Then I got mad.

My pup was at that moment wagging his tail vigorously at Lil and rubbing noses with her.

"Come, Junior," I said, snatching him from the floor. "A nice little red dog like you is too good to play with that *black* dog." And I stormed out.

Bill Beard cast the picture.

Shopping with Susy grew so big so soon that another writer had to be hired, then another salesgirl. Then, in order to protect the paper from its editor's legerdemain (I'd been keeping the records with a clever little triple-entry system of my own devising) the next logical step was to employ a bookkeeper.

If the staff was soon almost too big to handle, it was also competent and charming, and several of the people who worked for me then have remained my fond friends. There was slender, attractive Jean Webber, now wife of the artist Bart Fonda, and short, plump Kitty Silk. There was also Pat Eells, just out of college, with a certain appealing quality of offbeat freshness that makes her very special to everyone who knows her. These girls sold ads, wrote copy, and Pat did an "Inquiring Photographer" column. They did not hesitate, also, to pitch in with the manual labor required to paste up the dummy sample of the paper which went to the photo offset printer each week, frequently working until two or three o'clock in the morning on the night before press day.

In addition, as main contributor to our Wit, Humor, and Entertainment, we had the late, enchanting Bill Hanemann. I will go into some detail about him because several years later he was to become chief confidant, pepper-upper, and ghost chaser when I returned to Daytona Beach with a house trailer full of spooks in tow.

As a nonconformist, satirist, and debunker, Bill was another H. L. Mencken. He was a practicing individualist, even to the point of wearing a bristly moustache and riding a bicycle to work long before they were in style, and doing anything else that occurred to him anywhere he happened to be when the notion struck him; but everyone put up with all his peculiarities because he was so much fun. With his short, stocky figure and his deep, husky voice, he was the most masculine of men, but he often wore a beret in that area of the country where they were looked on with suspicion. I can remember going into stitches once when we were waiting in line for ice cream cones at a Dairy Queen and he decided to illustrate some point we were discussing about Swan Lake. Entirely oblivious to the curious stares of passers-by, he performed several intricate ballet steps . . . almost graceful in his tennis shoes.

Bill and his gracious wife Helen ran Marigold House Restaurant then, but he still found time altruistically to bestow on us his brilliant comment in the form of editorials much too good for our small effort. He did this, he said, not just because he approved of the paper but because I allowed him to write what he wanted to. (And then what he wrote always had to be cooled down, with great argument between us, because he was also ahead of his time in what he thought could appear in print.) But since he used to be a successful script writer in Hollywood—Fred Astaire's "Flying Down to Rio," no less, was one of his—all his largess had a polish and style which lifted the paper into the higher literary brackets.

Shopping with Susy became very popular around town. The theme song of the radio program was "If You Knew Susie" and a record of it was played before and after the show. The paper and program were so well-known that whenever I walked into a local night spot the pianist or band would immediately start playing "my song." I cherished this attention, even though realizing that most of it was in the hope that in a return of professional courtesy I'd emphasize in the paper the latent genius of the entertainer. I usually did.

People knew my face from the picture on the masthead, my voice from the radio, Junior (our mascot) because he wrote a column in the paper, and even my car because it was decked with little *Shopping with Susy* signs fore and aft. And so whenever they saw us they whistled and waved. And I waved back, loving every minute of it.

I didn't have too bad a social life either. For a while I took pleasure in running with the Florida wolf pack—until I learned that in that vacationer's paradise "single" means that your wife didn't make the trip with you. Then I settled down to a few old-standby friends and very few dates. But the paper kept me so occupied that I didn't miss them.

Shopping with Susy never did make any money. If our advertisers had paid proper attention to the bills we sent them, we would have been solvent; but, unhappily, at that time too many small businesses in Daytona were in the same leaky lifeboat. So I mortgaged the old family home in Maryland to give the paper a financial transfusion. And then survive we did—with bannerheads held high—for a while longer.

With all our problems, however, we had much hilarity. *Shopping with Susy* was more like a party than a business, and my home, in which we did our work, was more like a club house than an office. I'm afraid Bill Hanemann's description of it as an amiable madhouse wasn't too far from the truth. It's certain that no one ever knew when he came there if he'd get a kiss or a bat on the head or a Scotch and soda or a peanut butter sandwich. But it was also referred to as a salon of distinction because of the diverting people who congregated there.

Chapter 8

||| T TOOK A LONG SPELL of illness to convince me. I just didn't think it would be possible to live without *Shopping with Susy*—until finally learning I couldn't live with it. But apparently

the pressures I worked under brought my strep infection back in some low grade form the doctors couldn't identify. For months I was in and out of the hospital and lived on sulfa, penicillin, cortisone, and all known antibiotics. Sometimes they'd make my temperature cool off; but it always heated up again soon, and I ached all the time.

Most of the work fell on the staff, and those wonderful people not only kept the paper running but prepared and served my meals, did the marketing and even sometimes the housework. After so long a time this seemed to me just too much of an imposition on them, and even though they didn't complain, I did. So I sold the paper, with tears in my eyes.

I only got $300 for it, but since that was exactly what had been put into it in the first place, it could be said that the deal came out even.

But what to do with myself now? Daytona Beach without the paper was no pleasure to me, and, anyway, it was too damp for my particular condition.

"I'd like just once to get dry enough to dehydrate like a piece of Melba toast," I told Pat, at whose home I was staying. "It would surely make me feel much better."

Just in the nick of that time of indecision, the estate of the last of my great aunts in Washington was settled and I inherited $5,000. With this grubstake I decided to break camp and go West. The thought frequently being father to the action with me, my dog and I were on our way in a short time.

We headed first deep into the heart of Texas, thinking that might be an ideal place to remain; but it soon appeared that San Antonio had spread out during my absence like jello on a warm plate. I didn't feel up to contending with so much city, so after a few days spent contacting old friends, we were soon driving farther and farther westward. And eventually we ended up in the desert country of Southern California.

"Come ye yourselves apart into a desert place and rest awhile," says the Psalm. I accepted the invitation, glad to sit down and relax for a good long four months—if you call having two operations and writing a book about my experiences with *Shopping with Susy* relaxing. Still, after the hurdy-gurdy existence of the previous three years, the thing most necessary for me was a spell of peace and quiet. And that I got in my desert cathedral, its spires the jutting white-domed mountains San Jacinto and San Gorgonio to the west, the pipes of its organ the rolling San Bernardino hills to the north.

Moving into a new, well-built efficiency cottage, I hibernated completely, seeing almost no one, spending my days relaxing in the sunshine hoping the desert air would make me well. Unfortunately, my problems were not climate-curable. My doctor in neighboring Palm Springs couldn't find anything wrong other than a cyst on my thyroid gland and he didn't think that was causing my temperature elevation and shortness of breath; however, he stated that the tumor had to come out sometime because it would never go away of its own accord and might become malignant.

Finally one day I said to him, "Look, if you don't cut my throat I'm going to."

So he did.

I got along fine, but still found it all rather discouraging. I told my surgeon, "All my girl friends go to the hospital and return with babies. I go oftener than anybody and all I ever have to show for it is scars. And most of *them* I can't properly show!"

"I've got news for you, Susy," he responded. "You might as well prepare yourself for another scar you can't show, and that very soon again." Then he explained that their thorough check-up had revealed the necessity of another operation somewhat further south. I went ahead within a month and had that done, too; and there, among numerous cysts and tumors was a little pocket of infection that was the seat of almost all my current problems. After the latter surgery I felt wonderful for years.

Convalescing in my desert retreat, however, was purely lonely. Existence began to seem as parched as the wastelands around me as I lay about doing nothing more stimulating than healing and reading. No phones ringing every five minutes. No people dropping in constantly to talk. No men. Nothing.

My thoughts dwelt so much on the fun in Daytona Beach with *Shopping with Susy* that I decided to write a book about it, so after that all my time was spent at my typewriter.

Junior was also busy. He whiled away his hours hanging around the yard chasing little lizards. Since reptiles do not have a person-ality one can snuggle up to, I preferred them to keep their distance. In fact, I rather insisted upon it. But my dog was having the time of his life.

Have you ever been all alone in a desert with nobody to talk to but a dachshund and an occasional chuckawalla? If so, you can probably see why the thought of home and friends began to creep nostalgically into my mind more often than not. So I told Junior that if the point of boredom ever came when I felt like joining him in his lizard hunts, then we'd go back to Nina in Maryland. And one day in late March, a little over a month after my last opera-tion, I actually found myself wandering out in the sand with the dog saying, "There's one, see him? There he goes under that greasewood bush."

We packed up three days later and started back east.

Growing more and more eager to reach home, I practically hurtled the car through space, seeming not in the least worried about the possibility of ending my career creamed on a mountain top somewhere in the southwestern scenery. But once on a level stretch of road in New Mexico, as the speedometer soared to eighty-five miles per hour, I suddenly seemed to smell a whiff of burning rubber. I immediately slowed down, and within moments the car had a blowout on its left rear tire, which would have given Highway 66 one of its more spectacular statistics if we'd still been traveling at the higher speed.

As it was, a passing Samaritan changed the tire and we pro-ceeded along no worse for the experience. As a matter of fact, I was improved by it, for from then on I had a much greater respect for the speed laws. In contemplating my narrow escape I won-dered how it would be possible for an odor of burning rubber from a rear tire to travel forward to my nose when it was behind me and retreating at eighty-five miles per hour. Anyway, would a tire preparing to have a sudden blowout make a smell of burning rubber? I didn't know . . . and had no possible intimation then that the day would soon come when I would suspect something Guardian Angelish in such an advance warning.

When we left the land of magical panoramas and cactus, we

came into a section of the country that had trees and looked lived-in and loved. It was hard to choose between them as to beauty, for lilacs were blooming along most of the route and redbud and dogwood illumined the Kentucky hills. And Oakland was aglow with fruit blossoms when we arrived.

Nina and the big old house were glad to see my dog and me, even though I turned traitor to the house immediately by putting a For Sale sign on it. But it took a year and a half to sell because my price was too high.

When the time came that our home would be sold, Nina and I both would have to settle somewhere. I had no means of making a living in the little town in the Maryland mountains, and, for that matter, I was still obsessed by the idea that if you had to live at all you might as well live where the weather was warm. But where to go? And until the house was sold, what to go on? Aunt Anna's bequest had nearly all gone on hospital and traveling expenses.

Just when I was most discouraged, a letter came from Salt Lake City, which had always seemed like Paradise Lost to me ever since it had been one of our unachieved goals in my childhood. It was from my friend Margaret Sanders Adams, who had gone there to study sculpture at the University of Utah. Margaret is the daughter of Colonel Harlan Sanders, who was later to become famous as the colossus of Kentucky Fried Chicken. At that time he was just getting under way, having put his first franchise in a restaurant in Salt Lake City.

"It's heaven on earth here," Margaret wrote, bombarding me with descriptions of the ideal climate.

So why not? I started making immediate plans. Nina debated taking an apartment alone in Oakland or coming with me. I would have loved to have her along, being entirely fed up with traveling alone to strange places, and also being very fond of Nina. But I wouldn't urge her. She had to make her own decision. She didn't want to leave Oakland and her music pupils, but neither did she want me to go traipsing off again without her.

"I'll go for the life of adventure," she finally announced; so we agreed to point ourselves westward once more, this time together.

Once our thoughts were focused, events took shape rapidly.

The price of the house was reduced for quick sale and it was claimed in a week; within two weeks more we'd had an auction of all our household goods, packed the car, stored the things we wanted to keep, and we were ready to leave.

Who said pioneering days were over? There was a little seventy-two-year-old woman, small, frail, but valiantly leaving a town and friends she'd grown to love, just to accompany me because I had the roving urge. *That* was a little pioneering woman. And off we started on a cold rainy morning in late September—Nina, Susy, and Junior heading into the unknown once again.

This time it was to bring rewards undreamed of.

Chapter 9

As we drove along toward Salt Lake City, the car piled awkwardly high with all our belongings, I told Nina, "Life would be so much simpler for us if we lived in a trailer."

She squeaked with alarm at the idea.

"We could just take our home with us like a turtle," I went on, the possibilities appealing to me more and more.

My traveling companion didn't like the idea at all. "If you get one, I'm not traveling with you," she said, more prophetic than she knew.

We were following the trail of the Mormons and began to feel like explorers ourselves as we traversed the vast bare expanses of Nebraska and Southern Wyoming and then Utah's golden aspen-glowing mountains. We stopped from time to time to read the roadside markers about the sturdy little band who had made its way across to its promised land. When we came out onto the promontory marked "This is the Place" we were hushed with anticipation as we looked across the magnificent valley, a desert when the Mormons first saw it but now blooming with beauty because of their efforts.

The first thing Margaret Adams and her twelve-year-old son Trigg did for us after we arrived, and the nicest greeting they could have given us, was to drive us out to the foothills in time to see the sunset. We were enraptured. In that sparkling autumn air the view of Salt Lake City, the lake in the distance, and the Wasatch Mountains at our backs, made us sure we'd achieved Utopia at last.

Next day, with my mind so firmly set on a house trailer, it wouldn't have been possible to find an apartment to suit me had any been available. But almost the first trailer I looked at answered all our requirements. On my third trip to observe the twenty-one foot Terry, Nina came along, and after that she seemed resigned to what was about to happen. But she insisted that before any papers were signed I try it out on the highway to see if I could pull a thing so big and bulky. As my car wasn't yet equipped with trailer hook-up and brake, I had to use the dealer's automobile for my trial run, and after he had driven me out to the highway I discovered his car had a clutch and standard gear shift.

"I haven't used a clutch in years," I said. "It will take concentration to remember to reach for it."

Nonetheless, I took the wheel for the return trip. As we started, the car jerked until my left foot stiffly and awkwardly rose to the clutch and I remembered to shift the gear. Almost as soon as the caravan began moving we came to a traffic light. I had to reach for the hand-brake of the trailer, the foot-brake of the car, and the clutch, and then try to keep the car from sputtering as I fumbled around for the gear shift in its unfamiliar position. I was so busy with the mixture of mechanisms up front that I can hardly remember what pulling the trailer felt like. However, I came back right through town traffic at four o'clock in the afternoon. It seemed as if travel with a trailer would be a breeze with my own car.

We planned to live in it, anyway, not tour with it, so until the time came why worry about the eventuality of pulling it? I didn't expect ever to leave Salt Lake City again anyhow . . . it was so delightful and the weather was so invigorating! I secretly intended soon to be married to a uranium king and settled down right there for the rest of my life.

Our mobile home was towed that night to a trailer park not far from downtown; and its new family, with the help of Margaret and Trigg, started moving in. After our nine rooms in Maryland, the trailer put us in mind of living in a small, neat, well-furnished iron lung. But it had a bedroom, a bathroom with a shower, and a convertible bed in the cozy living room for Nina. It also had a big storage space underneath and lots of closets and cupboards inside, so we found room for possessions before we began actually to realize there was plenty of room for us as well.

Still, we always had to make appointments whenever we wanted to pass in the hall.

The kitchen had a big stove and refrigerator both of which ran on propane gas. Because of the tricky lighting system at the back of the underneath of the refrigerator, the various large Utah men (all Utah men are large) who came to connect our gas and show us how to use it and then kept coming back because it took a while to get things adjusted, all stretched out flat on the floor in front of our ice box. Junior was much impressed and watched their activity with great interest.

"He's never in his life lived in a place where so many men lay around on the floor," I told them. After we finally learned the procedure ourselves, I had to place *me* supine to restart the refrigerator whenever the gas went off. It was the only really bad feature of the trailer.

After we moved ourselves into our "Gingerbread House," as we called it, I located a job with the Newspaper Agency Corporation, which handles the advertising for both the *Salt Lake Tribune* and the *Deseret News*, and was set to writing neighborhood shopping columns which appeared in both dailies. I never enjoyed working anywhere for anyone (except myself) as much as I did for the NAC. I was the only woman in retail advertising along with thirteen salesmen who helped me when they could and always were grand to work with. And the numerous bosses were the kindest men in the world.

Now, of course, before we had decided to remain in Salt Lake

City we inquired among many people about the winter weather —and got as many answers. But the consensus was that we would love it. Well, maybe we ran into the usual unusual weather, for it was solid snow and ice from Christmas into March and then it continued to snow intermittently during April.

As I slushed about through this difficult environment each day in my work, it seemed advisable that I start a new fad—sponge rubber bustles. I had snow tires on my car, and snow boots on my feet, but nothing to protect . . . me, in case I fell. Oh, well, I didn't fall.

Nina and Junior rode along as I drove to the suburbs on business. We enjoyed together the powdered sugar mountains, especially liking the days when every bush and tree played snowman. As spring began to thrust out timid fingers of green we rejoiced, and then the flowers overwhelmed us. We didn't know lilacs could grow in so many deeply vibrant shades or in such great profusion. Same with Japanese cherry and pink flowering peach. The blossoms covered every bit of every tree. We admired the many sedate tulips in each yard, dignified of posture and flashy of dress; and when we considered that less than one hundred years ago that country was a treeless desert, we appreciated the show even more.

That old phrase "Shopping with Susy" couldn't stay out of my life for long, and in March a page by that name was started in the Sunday *Tribune* Magazine Section, the idea being that Susy was to case the downtown stores for items of novelty and interest, take photos of them, and write enticing copy extolling their virtues. But to get the pictures I was expected to use a Polaroid camera which developed its films right there. This was an elegant idea theoretically, for the merchant could then see the take to make sure it suited him. However, Polaroid cameras weren't intended for closeups of small articles and weren't equipped for such work— the special close-up lenses not then being available.

I practiced at home a month before the column started, but, still, when I first went into the stores it was sometimes necessary to take as many as six or eight pictures before getting in more than a piece of the strand of pearls or the crystal goblets or the hat at which I aimed. If you've ever stood in a public place and tried to do something as attention arresting as stooping, squatting, and squinting with a camera and flash attachment, you'll know that I was quite disconcerted by having to keep photographing the same piece of merchandise over and over again.

When this job first started, my employers didn't realize just how heavy the case with camera and equipment was for me; but it couldn't possibly be carried one-handed. I hated to admit it, though. So to save any annoyance until it was known whether or not I'd be able to cope with the picture-taking anyway, Margaret donated her spare time to the cause of friendship by lugging the weighty case around for me for a couple of days.

She and I look somewhat alike, both having high cheek bones and the same coloring, so everyone thought we were sisters out on some family project together. We had merry times as we went about shooting the gew-gaws and knick-knacks; even though I was getting frustrated beyond endurance at my difficulties producing usable pictures.

"Susy, why don't you let me try it once?" Margaret asked, for I'd been working half an hour on a silver platter in a jewelry store and the proprietor was getting edgy. If I finally managed to center the whole platter correctly, then the reflections ruined it. So I was perfectly willing to let my helper take the camera, holding the flash gun for her gladly. And the first picture she took was perfect!

Margaret tried hard to be tactful about it but I could see complacency oozing from her; and the jeweler came right out and said it was time *somebody* knew what she was doing.

I told my friend she could just take all the rest of the pictures and my job to boot, while I crawled beneath the glass showcase.

Margaret couldn't get another good picture either when we went to subsequent stores. I wanted the "Shopping with Susy" page to look properly professional, but had to admit to myself a certain relief that she hadn't kept on being successful when I had consistently failed.

Then, at last, when I was finally beginning to learn to allow for the angle of trajectory and starting to achieve acceptable pictures, my boss became convinced that the column had a future and was worth spending some additional money on, so he hired an experienced photographer with proper camera and lighting equipment to accompany me on my rounds. And after that all went smoothly.

I've often been puzzled about why I've so continually gotten into situations where it seemed necessary to overcome some complex obstacle without proper training for it. I've wondered why it was unavoidable that I spend weeks trying to broadcast with tapes made on the wrong kind of recorder for transmission over the radio when "Shopping with Susy" was on the air. Why did I have to run a complicated Vari-typer without anyone around to give instructions? Or try to teach myself professional photography with a camera unequipped for the work?

Sure, I got into those things because of my own ignorance and stayed in them because of my persistence; but they always seemed inevitable, and I never knew how to get out of them without giving up and admitting defeat, which I was too stubborn to do.

Now I'm thankful for this training in perseverance and in enduring stressful situations without help. Because of it I was able to struggle with the difficulties next encountered and not break under the strain. I had acquired determination to overcome whatever problems presented themselves, no matter how confusing they became . . . and it had prepared me well.

Chapter 10

AMONG THE NEW FRIENDS I made in Salt Lake City was Veryl Smith, who frequently improved the shining morning hours with me over a cup of coffee. One night in January she told Nina and me, while having dinner with us in the Gingerbread House, that she'd met a girl who had a Ouija board and said she got frequent messages from the spirit world. Veryl's big gray eyes were bright with anticipation as she said, "I told her to bring her board to my house tomorrow night and we'd give it a try."

"You can't be serious," I laughed. "Why that's just a child's toy. Or, if you take it seriously it's black magic . . . strictly from the Dark Ages."

Nina wasn't amused. She was afraid for Veryl. "You don't know what you're letting yourself in for," she said gravely. Then she told us that she had known a spirit medium long ago, a Mrs. Perkins of Indianapolis, who had achieved amazing results communicating with other realms but had become slightly unsettled in the process.

"I'm afraid you'll run into things you can't handle," Nina warned Veryl.

But when my friend phoned a few days later she had nothing to relate. They hadn't entertained any unseen personages after all.

"No luck, nobody came to our party," Veryl told us, and Nina was relieved.

Several weeks later I saw *The Unobstructed Universe* by Stewart Edward White on the bookshelf of an acquaintance who was entertaining us at dinner and exclaimed, "Why, we had this at home." A relative of Nina's had sent it to us long ago and not one of us had ever read it. I'd given it to the library along with most of our other books when we left Oakland.

"What's this about?" I asked.

"I haven't read it," its owner said, "but it's supposed to try to show that people continue to live after death."

I glanced through it, picking up in passing terms like "receptivity" and "conductivity" and "impetus" and others which meant nothing to me in the context in which they were used.

"How obtuse can you get?" I wondered, but still there was a compulsion to read it for some reason not then understood. So I borrowed it, found that Nina and Veryl were also interested, and the next night we three sat down to peruse it aloud together and discuss it.

Now, the book is supposed to be a true account of messages obtained through a non-professional medium from White's wife Betty, who had died some months before. The well-known author, a man of obvious personal integrity, related several instances when he received information which he was convinced could have come from no one else except his dead wife; and even to skeptical readers it sounded so authentic it made our spines tingle.

After she had established the fact of her continued existence to his satisfaction, White's wife told about conditions after death, first trying to impress him with the *hereness* of immortality. When a man dies, she said, he merely sheds his body like an overcoat. Then his conscious spirit continues to exist at first in the same world right along with us—but without being hampered by things that to us are obstructions like doors and walls. Or even time and distance.

"Consciousness is the only reality," White writes, "and consciousness is in a state of evolution."

At a later date James gave a general summary that parallels, adds to, and somewhat clarifies the material in Stewart Edward White's books. Among other things, he wrote:

"The first phase of life after the experience called death has been described adequately as 'unobstructed' in comparison with the earth plane, which is 'obstructed' by matter, for we exist in dimensions of space and time at variance with your own. To your senses matter is solid. To a spirit, matter is not solid. It is no obstruction to him; he can pass right through it. Even time as you know it on earth is not an obstruction to us because we are in no way dependent upon time—there is no day or night for us. If we wish to overcome distance, we think ourselves where we want to be and we are there, so distance is no obstruction to us either.

"Yet this first phase of life after death exists at exactly the same place that you are—the earth. We are not floating about up in the clouds somewhere; we are just where we always have been, and many who are unenlightened are still doing the same things they always have done. Usually our biggest worry for a while is that you people no longer see us, hear us, or feel our presence. Your senses are designed to keep you in touch with conditions in your realm, but not with ours. We have passed out of the world of matter into the world of spirit; and learning to accept it and live with it is complicated for those who are not prepared for it."

We are told by all communicants that spirits have bodies which are just as real and solid to them as their physical bodies were; but they are invisible to us because they are composed of substance which is vibrating at a much higher frequency. When airplane propellers are revved up to a high speed, you can look right through them. It's said to be similar to this with spirit bodies.

While we're on earth, this spirit body resides within the physical body, not only interpenetrating it but extending beyond it, where it can sometimes be seen as the aura. Many mediums can see auras. We don't have to depend for evidence of this on their assurance alone, however, or on James's or White's statements. There has been scientific evidence to prove it.

In 1968 a group of Russian doctors announced the discovery that all living things—plants, animals, and humans—not only have a physical body made of atoms and molecules, but also a counterpart body of energy. They called it "The Biological Plasma Body."

A hundred years before this Baron Von Reichenbach, the German chemist who discovered creosote, had also reported extensive research on some sort of energy or luminescence radiating from humans and plants and animals. He called it "odic force."

Dr. Walter J. Kilner published a book in London in 1920 reporting how he had discovered the same phenomenon—an aura of energy around the body constantly in motion. In 1908 at St. Thomas' Hospital in London he was doing some electrical experiments and chanced to use a viewing filter stained with dicyanine dye. Through it he saw hazy outlines around people which he identified as auras. He began to experiment and found that ill health, fatigue, and depression all affected this; and he soon learned to diagnose for his patients according to the colors and forms of their auras.

Today in Russia master electrician Semyon Davidovich Kirlian and his wife Valentina, a teacher and journalist, have discovered a process of running high-frequency electrical fields through living things that makes the aura visible. At varying frequencies, different details of bio-luminescence show up in the photographs they take, opening up a fantastic world of the unseen to those who perceive them.

Sheila Ostrander and Lynn Schroeder report that, despite all the materialistic scientists interested in the Kirlians' discoveries, "The philosophical implications were even more extraordinary. It seemed that living things had two bodies: the physical body everyone can see, and a secondary 'energy-body' the Kirlians saw in their high frequency photos. The energy body didn't seem to be merely a radiation of the physical body. The physical body appeared somehow *to mirror* what was happening in the energy body."

This is exactly what James had written for me, long before I knew anything about the Russian research, and, for that matter, long before the Kirlians published anything about their work. "Inside of every living person is a spiritual duplicate," James wrote. "Actually, the fact is that the material body is the *replica* of the spiritual, which formed the original pattern."

This spiritual body, as St. Paul called it, is known to others as the subtle or etheric body. White calls it the Beta body. It apparently remains neatly in place in most of us until our deaths, synchronized with the physical body so that no problems arise. Yet under some conditions, at times of crisis, trance, coma, epilepsy, or when one is under the influence of anesthetics, it may be spontaneously ejected from the body. Some persons even have the ability to cause their spiritual bodies to leave their physical bodies at will. When this occurs their consciousnesses may or may not accompany the spiritual body, so they may or may not be aware of what is occurring. There is a great amount of documented information about such events, which are called out-of-body experiences or astral projections. They will be discussed more fully later.

At death the spiritual body survives while the physical body perishes. A description of this is given by an alleged spirit in *The Way of Life* by Arthur Findlay: "I have a body which is a duplicate of what I had on earth, the same hands, legs, and feet, and they move the same as yours do. The etheric body I had on earth interpenetrated the physical body. The etheric is the real body and an exact duplicate of our earth body. At death we just emerge from our flesh covering and continue our life in the etheric world, functioning by means of the etheric body just as we functioned on earth in the physical body. . . ."

Because he looks and feels the same as he did in his physical body, the newly deceased is often unaware that any change has taken place. This confusion is compounded since he still finds himself in the same location, perhaps beside a bed in which there is a form which appears to be him . . . but which he is sure cannot be, because he feels so alive and well.

"There are always progressed entities who greet this new arrival in the spirit world and attempt to tell him the truth about his condition, if he will listen to them," James writes. "He is told that he has passed through the experience called death and that the power of his thought controls everything in the dimension where he now finds himself."

This man who has just died learns that the spirit body is affected entirely by mind power and so he will look as he thinks of himself as looking. At first, then, he will continue to appear exactly as he did when he died, no matter how miserable and decrepit he may have been. But as soon as he learns how to control his thoughts and begins his character development, he changes in appearance, for his improvement is reflected in his looks. Spirits who have begun their progression are beautiful, for they have learned to think of themselves as they were during the period of their greatest physical fitness and happiness on earth. Those who died with wickedness in their hearts were probably rather sinister looking, and they will remain that way until their thoughts about themselves change. This assuredly won't occur until the time comes when they have begun to improve their character.

How you look is comparable to how you act when you "go over." In order to get off to a good start, therefore, you should die aware of your need for self-improvement. If you do, then, according to my correspondent, "Life after death is so challenging and so marvelously engrossing that life on earth is nothing in comparison. I can truthfully say that when you come to this sphere you will find so much to interest and excite you that I cannot make it sound attractive enough. But you have to keep your mind open when you arrive in order to get started off properly and save yourself much wasted time, just as you have to keep your mind alert to new ideas and new opportunities on earth. The person with a closed mind, who will not allow any new concepts to enter his philosophy, will have an even duller time after death than he did on earth. He will have it, that is, until he wakes up and starts his progression. Advancement is inevitable. No consciousness which ever inhabited the body of a man on earth or any other inhabited planet is ever lost forever. All must ultimately reach the heights of achievement. The fact that they have to work to do it is what discourages some of them from starting, and what encourages others that it will be a challenge."

Nina was never one to argue about her beliefs, but she had accepted the idea of survival long ago and saw all that we were coming across in our reading as just an amplification of what she already knew in Christianity.

Veryl was as interested as I, though not inclined to argue with the material as much. But she and Nina were in sympathy with my efforts to assimilate it, for when we finished *The Unobstructed Universe* I kept on mulling it over and over. It presented a concept more inviting than any I'd encountered before and it wouldn't let me alone. It teased me and titillated my thinking, and soon I succumbed to the interest it aroused. I went to the library and got another book by White—*With Folded Wings*.

In that, as we read aloud together one Sunday afternoon, we came upon the statement that our loved ones who have passed on would like to communicate with us to reassure us there is no death and that they are often with us. White said if we will make the first move toward contact, they'll cooperate.

The idea of communication, the way he told it, would be plausible enough, if there really were spirits around. If, as he insisted, our friends were still hovering about, why shouldn't they want us to know it, to relieve our grieving for them if that were the case . . . to assuage their own egos, for that matter, for who would want to be totally ignored all the time? Also, when they became aware of one who was in terror of the gaping void of death, wouldn't they feel an intense desire to say, "Look, it isn't like that at all. I'm here still, you'll be here still, there's more to all this than meets the eye."

Just as a theory, I say, it sounded all right. But I didn't buy it. Still, the chance that it might be possible was enthralling to me. I stopped reading and went outside for a walk with Junior to consider whether or not, in all seriousness, I ought to try to reach my parents in an effort to prove to myself the truth or fallacy of all this.

There, on a crisp, sunny afternoon in March, as my dog and I ambled through a large field covered with dried grass and weeds, I was suddenly infused with a warm, loving awareness of Mother's presence. I could have reached out and patted her cheek—she was that close to me. She was as real and as *there* as she had been the last time I tucked her in for the night . . . or the many long ago times she'd given me my funny old teddy bear to hug and tucked *me* in for the night.

This was an incredible thing to me, coming just when it did, for I'd never had such a feeling before in all the six years since Mother's death. And life took on an immediate new dimension, which I knew it would never lose. It was a beautifully tender confirmation of the hope for survival; and no matter what happened to me in the future I would always cherish this experience and be eager if possible to recapture it.

I went back into the house with the decision that I wanted to try to communicate with Mother.

Chapter 11

THE NEXT MORNING after my sensational experience I awoke all sensible and material-minded again. When the memory of that feeling of Mother's presence began to warm me I stopped myself short with: "Let's be rational about this thing. It must have been a sensory illusion."

I knew the subconscious mind plays strange tricks. Heavens, I'd read enough about analysis at college. I'd had a go at deciphering

Freud, Jung, and Adler. I knew about self-suggestion and what it could do.

"But this wasn't something from inside. Mother was actually, overtly there. It couldn't be anything else but that."

According to psychologists, the subconscious mind is capable of producing many unusual experiences if one secretly desires them. Wasn't it more likely an unsuspected urge to escape back into the womb? Was I running once again to my mother for protection from the big bad world?

If this had started happening to me at almost any other time of my life that surely would have been the explanation. If it had occurred during my stay alone in the desert it would have been obvious that I was reaching to Mother for security. But now I had Nina, Margaret, and Trigg for constant companionship, a cozy home, an interesting job, an active social life; I was stable and settled enough in character that there were no big emotional problems of any sort confronting me, and I was even enjoying better physical health than ever before.

Well, if this were Mother, the smartest thing she'd done was to wait to try to get in touch with me until I was ready for it.

For days I went round and round with it this way. I'd start to glow with the remembrance of that moment of illumination; then I'd reject it and get on with washing my hair, or writing an ad for a "love of a lamp," or walking my dog, or whatever the project at hand might be. If I had let it go at that, soon the experience would have receded to just a pleasant memory of an unusual instant in my life and that would have been the end of it.

But that damned curiosity of mine wouldn't let it lay. So finally I told Veryl to borrow the Ouija and we'd have a go at it . . . and with that step I opened my own personal Pandora's box and let myself in for the most hazardous adventures of my life.

We were leery of using a toy for such an efficient enterprise as we proposed, but there wasn't any other way we knew to try communication. The Ouija is supposed to be the nearest thing to a telegraph-between-worlds, and we thought it was the only way for beginners to make contact. It's certainly a most unprepossessing instrument to use for a serious investigation, being a board which has the letters of the alphabet and numbers from one to ten on it and a little heart-shaped pointer (called a planchette) about the size of your hand with teensy short legs like Junior's. Two people put the board on their knees and one hand each on the pointer. Then, if you're lucky, it moves around on top of the board and indicates certain letters. If you're even luckier, they spell words that make sense and sometimes give really intelligent messages.

The only thing one can be sure of about a Ouija board is this: when *seriously* attempting to communicate, those who have their fingers on the pointer do not deliberately push the planchette around and direct it to the different letters. It moves by some force which does not come consciously from the people involved. Thus when sensible answers to questions are written, it is a very eerie business indeed.

Spirit communicators such as James and my mother advise me to warn people away from Ouijas and automatic writing until you have learned how to be fully protected. They say that innocent efforts at communication are as dangerous as playing with matches or hand grenades. They have me as Exhibit A of what not to do, for I experienced many of the worst problems of such involvement. Had I been forewarned by my reading that such efforts might cause one to run the risk of being mentally disturbed, I might have been more wary. That is why my story is now being made public—just in the effort to prevent others from getting into situations which might prove more damaging to them than they fortunately did to me.

Veryl and I, not knowing what a gamble it was, were determined to proceed; and since we had nothing else available, we used the Ouija to begin our great scientific safari. It was certainly the most unorthodox expedition in the history of research as Veryl and Susy, with board on knees and planchette under fingers, crossed over into the unknown and moved out into uncharted territory alone and unguided.

We sat there for about ten minutes, but nothing happened except a kink in my back. So I, without the fortitude of the intrepid explorer, said, "To hell with it," and went into my bedroom and lay down to recuperate.

Veryl, remaining with the board on her knees and her fingers idly resting on the pointer, suggested, "Call your mother. Maybe that will set the force in motion."

So I entreated, "Mother, if it's possible, please talk to us."

"Susy, come here quick!" cried my friend, for just as my words had been spoken she had felt a sudden surge through her arm and the planchette had jumped under her hand.

I hurried back and sat down again and as soon as my fingers touched it, the words were spelled: "It is Mother. I . . . love . . . you . . . I love you." Then in answer to our questions, with frequent incoherencies as if Mother were having difficulty making the apparatus work for her, it told her full name, my father's name, the date of her birthday. It was interesting, but there was no way to be sure it was Mother. I could have been feeding it unconsciously all the data reported. When we asked about Veryl's family, the answers were also correct; but she knew them. Although positive we weren't consciously pushing it, we were not a bit sure about anything else. Where that power and those words were coming from was a complete enigma.

To test the material, obviously we would have to ask questions to which neither of us knew the answers—but how could we then be sure the reply was right? We decided to ask the name of a neighbor's mother, and when told "Elsie" I ran over to check with him. He said, "No." Then we tried for half an hour, and a series of names was trotted out that would have entranced any good old-time Mormon husband. We received Josephine, Amanda, Sylvia, Kate, Martha, Adelaide, Genevieve, Brunhilda, Matilda . . . and each time our neighbor, who was sticking his head in the trailer window by now to see what was going on, snickered and shook his head. To this day we don't know what his mother's name was. He never enlightened us, and twitted us about it whenever we saw him after that, for he was sure we'd been taken in by our own subconscious minds. By then we were sure, too. It would have taken no end of argument to convince me my mother was having anything to do with the proceedings.

Yet if the chance that it were she was one in a trillion—let's not be small about this—even one in a quintillion, I was going to make every effort to learn the truth. If my mother—or anybody else, for that matter—was trying to prove to me there is no death, I'd never let her down in her endeavor.

A few nights later we tried again, without making any effort to test our source, but with a serious objective to our questioning, nonetheless. What we were actually doing was trying to salve our consciences. Since our last session we had read somewhere that spirits were able to know what was in people's minds, so we were feeling uneasy. If there was any possibility that I was going to be holding open house to my mother, I'd best do a bit of housecleaning first.

Our initial question after the pointer wrote "Betty Smith is here" was, "Do you know about the secret things that go on among earth people?"

The answer came, "We are so far above it that it doesn't matter." (The communicants have since explained that advanced spirits invariably have the good taste not to intrude into our most private thoughts or intimate moments unless they have been especially invited.) At that we gave sighs of relief. Then we asked, "Can you read our minds?"

"Yes."

Oh, dear. "Were you with me in Florida?" I asked timorously.

"Yes."

Blushing a little I said, "When people do things that you used to think were bad when you were on earth, do you now understand why they do them?"

"Yes."

"Am I forgiven?"

"Kiss."

I took that kindly. Up until the last remark I had been entirely suspicious that it was my own subconscious mind doing it. But that word "Kiss" sounded just like my mother, and not at all like me.

We didn't tire of this new amusement, and on the night of April 16th, Veryl, Nina, and I took turns playing with it. (Nina seemed to have become reconciled that we weren't taking our efforts seriously enough to endanger ourselves.)

After a few exchanges that purported to come from my mother, we began to receive messages from Nina's mother, whose first name had been Kizzie.

"Nina is not going to 'love' long," the Ouija wrote. "Nina won't love long."

Both Veryl and I immediately began talking at once. "What a

silly, garbled message that was," I said. "Of course Nina loves people and she always will." Fortunately Nina was so sleepy by then that she hadn't closely observed what was written and so she wasn't alarmed. We gave up the writing at once.

Next morning when Veryl and I met Margaret for coffee we told her about what had been received the night before.

"What could that message have meant?" I asked.

"It was saying that Nina is going to die," Veryl answered firmly. "I was sure it was trying to point to the 'i' for 'live' instead of 'love.' "

"That's what I was afraid of," I replied. "I actually tried to force it mentally to the 'o' because from the way the sentence was worded it seemed so obvious it was heading for the 'i.' "

"Funny," said Veryl. "I did the same thing."

"Nina has been so well, though, ever since we've been here in Salt Lake," I said. "Although she has high blood pressure, she hasn't been to a doctor once. I'm not as worried that Nina's mother was trying to prepare her for her fate as that it was my unconscious mind doing it. It looks to me as if I might have a secret death wish about Nina . . . but I couldn't have."

"Of course you haven't," Margaret reassured me.

"She's all the family I have left, and I love her. . . ."

"Why don't we try again tonight and get your mother to tell us the truth?" Veryl suggested. So I sneaked off that evening to Margaret's in order to have a session without Nina knowing it.

This time we received a lot of platitudes. "Be kind. Nina loves you. Nina loves Susy. Love is the most important thing of all." If this were Mother, we had her in a tight spot and she was trying to evade us tactfully; but I got bored with all that love stuff and said so.

The board quit us cold. We could get no action whatever from it, although we continued to press it for answers for about ten minutes. After that it began to move again. Deciding to avoid any leading questions and just play around like a bunch of kids, we asked silly things like "Who is Veryl going to marry?" or Margaret, or Susy. The answers were just as trivial as the questions, and we were told to marry any man whose name was thought of.

Finally I said, "This doesn't sound like you, Mother."

"It isn't Mother," was the reply.

"Who is it?"

"Kay Brown. I am going to marry Margaret."

"You mean you're a man named Kay?"

"Yes."

"Why are you here?"

"I am here by choice. About Saturday I am going to marry Margaret."

"Where did you die?"

"In this house." Margaret had an apartment in the basement of an old home.

"When?"

"1920."

"How old were you when you died?"

"Nineteen."

"Why do you stay here?"

"I want to marry Margaret. Marry me. Marry me."

We told him if he wouldn't talk sense to leave, and he docilely wrote, "Good night."

Of course we didn't have any hope that out of this foolishness we could possibly have a name or date that was correct; but a reporter tracks down sources, so I called the Bureau of Vital Statistics the next morning and asked if there was any record of a Kay or Kenneth Brown at that address who had died in 1920 or thereabouts. They found none.

However, a month later Margaret put an ad in the paper to sell a typewriter. One woman who called in answer said when she was given the address, "Why, I know that old house. I used to come over there often in my childhood to play in the big apple trees in the yard." These trees were still there, by the way. The woman added that some people named Brown had owned the house then and it had always been referred to as "the old Brown house."

Margaret at the moment didn't recall our conversation with Kay Brown and so didn't think to ask her caller about him; but when she remembered it later she telephoned me immediately to report that we had received something factual on the Ouija board, after all.

Asked if she was sure she had not known that the house was once called by that name, Margaret assured me she had never heard the name Brown associated with it at any time. She was a newcomer to the city and so were the present owners of the house. Nobody there knew anything about the name Brown in connection with the place.

But Kay Brown did . . . he died there. Or did he?

Chapter 12

"GET A PENCIL" was the instruction my Ouija board gave me one day after we'd been operating it at a loss for several weeks. This is the traditional invitation to do automatic writing. I asked how to go about receiving messages with a pencil, and the Ouija answered, "Go into a trance." Now how did one do that? I thought you had to be a natural-born medium to accomplish trance, or else be mesmerized by a gentleman with piercing black eyes and hocus-pocus hands.

Naturally I gave it a whirl, though. I went into my bedroom, closed the door and lay on the bed in the dark with a heavy black lead pencil in my hand and a large pad of paper under it.

"Go ahead, entrance me," I said. But nothing happened. I tried to make my mind a blank and stayed quiet, hoping for the best; but still nothing happened.

Nina kept calling to me, "Are you all right? Are you sure you're all right?" She was pacing the trailer floor—two steps north and then two steps south—nearly frantic for fear I'd strip my gears, knock myself out, swallow my tongue, or start having convulsions. But nothing horrendous happened as Nina feared. I couldn't go into a trance at all. Parenthetically, I have never yet learned to go at will into a decent trance. And it seems to be impossible to hypnotize me. I'm one of those obstinate persons who resists even when trying hardest to be accommodating.

So I just lay there patiently, hoping good intentions and complete relaxation were the next best substitute. And finally, after a long time, a message began to write itself on the paper. It was indeed the most peculiar feeling I'd ever experienced. The hand was just writing by itself without my conscious will being involved in any way. It wrote scragglingly across the page in runtogether words, "I am your Mother and I love you. There is lots to tell you but it is hard to do. Love to Nina. I'll write more next time. Betty."

I came out of the bedroom flying on my own personal pink and blue cloud. Imagine receiving a letter from your mother who'd been dead six years! It was hardly likely. It didn't make sense. But there it was in black and white written by hand on paper right before my eyes. It was tremendously exhilarating!

As time passed, this elation simmered down into debates with myself about what had really occurred; for with every new day came a new argument as to whether it actually had been Mother writing or my subconscious mind playing potsy with me. Nonetheless, I continued trying to maintain the correspondence thus established.

Each night after dinner I'd settle down with pencil and paper for a chat, and soon writing would come just as well with my eyes open sitting at the table in the trailer living-dining room. My communicant and I practiced and found that we wrote best when all the words were attached to each other as she had originally done it. But, oh, the problems of deciphering the script afterward, when typewritten copies were made of each evening's efforts.

Most of our first sessions were spent practicing for control, and we did Spencerian circles and up and down strokes, recalling only too vividly my childhood days when penmanship classes were so boringly endured.

Just the fact of sitting there accomplishing nothing more than circles, when I was so eager to receive evidence, was an indication to me that it wasn't initiated within my own mind; and when the messages did finally start they seemed of so little import that they just couldn't have come from me. My sublime subliminal surely would have produced more interesting palaver than, "Love is the most important thing. You must learn to love your fellow men."

Most of the time it was actual drudgery to sit and try to blank my mind so as to be receptive. After the thrill of receiving the first letter from Mother had subsided, it never again was an emotional experience for me. I felt no urge to write except the desire to be successful in this new endeavor. My stubbornness, as of yore, kept me at it . . . that and the bare possibility that it actually might be Mother.

I never experience, as some persons do who receive automatic writing, a sudden impulse to grab the pencil, or any other indication that the force, external or internal, is eager to write. Sometimes if the percipient or agent or medium, whichever you want to call him, is in a valid trance-like state, unknown foreign languages are received, or the script may come upside down or backwards. Even mirror writing, which is so reversed that it can only be read when held up to a glass, has come on many occasions. But none of this has ever happened to me because I have never been able to withdraw my own conscious awareness of what is going on. This, of course, made me almost sure it *was* all originating in the dark jungles of my nether mind. My own thoughts and beliefs sometimes were evident in the writing, for my mind was right there personally running things even when I was trying hardest to blank myself out of control. This, I learned from Stewart Edward White, is called "coloring."

A medium or psychic—a person who is more receptive or sensitive than others to impressions from the spirit world—is not a machine. No matter how withdrawn into trance he or she may be, there is still his or her own mind to contend with, to either a greater or lesser extent depending upon the amount of withdrawal and the psychic power available. So there is the possibility of the medium's own mental participation altering, in terms of his experience or understanding, the message coming through him. Coloring. It's as if the telegraph instrument kept trying to get into the act with an interpretation of its own of the dispatch transmitted over it.

Here was I, no medium at all, never anything but completely conscious when doing automatic writing. Naturally I intruded and no wonder so few evidential messages came.

After reading about this perplexity called coloring, I would frequently ask Mother if what she had just written had been colored. If it was mixed up, or not quite clear, she would usually say it had been. Then she would try again, and she managed to get it straight after a second or third attempt.

Frequently I consciously anticipated the next word to be written, but if it was not what Mother intended she crossed it out and persisted until she finally wrote what she wanted. She was just as insistent upon getting her thoughts through me without distortion as I was in unwittingly interfering, and we fought it out until our battles themselves were indication to me that there *must* be some outside force writing through me. If there was that much inner conflict, wouldn't it be evident to others that I was ready for the funny farm?

With the fight she was having with my coloring and my questioning and doubting, my communicant was undergoing a rough time, too. It's no wonder her messages were for the most part routine; but I was disappointed when our hour's work each evening was productive only of dissertations on such topics as "loving your fellow man" and "development of character" and "positive thinking." I could have written essays on them without going to all the trouble of automatic writing, so it was invariably boring to accomplish what seemed to be so little. Yet Mother gradually made her point, by dint of sheer repetition, that I personally must adopt the ethics she was insisting upon.

"Love is the most important thing and you need to love all the time," she wrote. "You must learn to think more kindly of others. You are much too critical. You need to love everyone, not only those to whom you are attached and who are kind to you. It takes real work to love everyone, but you can do it. And then everything will go smoothly and you will be happy all the time."

I began to make a special effort to try this as never before. When it was difficult, Mother gave me pep talks about it, bringing it up when it wasn't expected at all. For instance, when asked if she had any message for me one night, she answered:

"I want to tell you to love, love, love everyone all the time. You need to love more than you do. Love everyone every minute and your life will be a big success while you are on earth as well as afterwards. Heaven is the state of love."

Mother seemed to feel that compassion, understanding, and sympathy were fairly good counterparts for this love which is so difficult to attain; and I must go on record that she was right. Even the effort consistently to have compassion and understanding for others makes an immediate change in your life. This soon began to be evident in mine, and then I was glad she'd been so determined about it.

One thing Mother wrote which wasn't hard to accept was that at the time of her death when she had said, "I wish someone would tell me where I am," it was because she had suddenly seen Daddy and Aunt Ivy. And she'd said, "Don't leave me" to them.

I was told that since his death in 1933 my father had concentrated on his spiritual advancement. After he'd seen to it that Mother was properly oriented in her new existence and was keeping an eye on me, he went ahead with his progression.

I didn't have any idea then what Mother referred to when she used that term "progression." Later she explained it to me, and recently James has given it in greater detail.

"You survive death as a conscious entity," he started off, repeating himself for emphasis as is his usual custom. "In an unbelievably improved and exalted state you will live forever. The improvement is all up to you, and you accomplish it by your own efforts and at your own rate of speed. You survive as yourself, your own conscious self, not in any way altered or distorted.

"When you have gone through the experience called death you have not changed one iota from the person you were. You have left your physical body behind, but you continue to exist in a form which is just as real to you as the body you wore on earth."

When a person dies his relatives and friends who have preceded him are always there to greet him if there has been warmth between them. They give him such information as they have acquired, and it varies depending upon the condition each man was in when he died and whether or not he has learned anything new since. If these entities were unenlightened, they may not have become aware of much of anything new since their passing. If their lives were rich with spiritual significance, they undoubtedly have already learned a great deal more since death and are knowledgeable about their situation and their hopes for ultimate achievement.

"Much that ignorant spirits think they know about conditions in the hereafter is incorrect," James wrote. That explains why various ones can communicate such conflicting testimony through mediums, even those spirits who claim to be great and exalted Masters. The very fact that they make such claims should frequently be suspect. New arrivals in the first plane after death—the dimension usually known as the "etheric" plane—may sometimes receive wrong information and follow incorrect beliefs for a long time until finally the truth is brought to them by someone in whom they have confidence.

"You will not, of course, progress automatically after death just because you have been wealthy or successful in a worldly way on earth. You do not start upward until you have finally recognized that you must take certain steps to improve yourself. When you do, then your advancement starts immediately. You are on your way to the heights!

"If it could only be understood that life after death is as individual an undertaking as life is on earth. Nobody forces you to do anything. There are not even police around here to keep you in line if you should stray from accepted procedures. Only advice from wise spirits can guide you. If you accept it you will have success. If you do not, you will be unhappy until you finally do. Some people will not listen because they wish to attempt to live their lives without assistance, just as they did on earth. You all know those opinionated individuals whom nobody can tell anything. These may remain a long while in the dismal condition termed Hell. Yet again, in a relatively short time it may become apparent to some of them that they are getting nowhere and then they will begin to absorb some of the wise counsel and apply it. Then they will be in Heaven, which is truly a state of mind, just as its counterpart is.

"If you listen and start eagerly to seek a higher spiritual level it will be the most joyous undertaking imaginable. As you live each day for others, you will soon realize that you have to think very little about your own soul's development. It comes about almost automatically."

James assured me time and time again that every aspect of the work you undertake will be interesting and challenging. This is most reassuring. I was always suspicious of a Heaven in which there is no work. Since having responsibilities to meet and tasks that must be accomplished is essential to peace of mind, it is encouraging to learn that constructive effort which is not drudgery goes on after death.

"Nothing here need seem dull or routine," James writes, "for what you are doing can almost always be made pleasurable. When you have achieved the highest point of development one is capable of attaining in the etheric plane, you pass on to more advanced dimensions farther away from earth. Life on the higher spirit planes of existence becomes unbelievably happy at all times."

This explains where my father has gone. I didn't know at the time any more about it than just what Mother wrote then. Nearly a year later a letter was to be typed through my fingers from my father on one of his rare visits back to "Planet Earth."

Margaret Adams, who is an excellent sculptress, spent most of her time in Salt Lake City doing huge clay portraits. But she was curious about what I was up to and interested in hearing of it. Once, while writing automatically in her presence, I handed the pencil to her and it kept right on going, with an answer to a question for her.

"That's spooky!" she cried, giving the pencil back to me quickly. But after that she understood that I was not consciously pushing it myself when writing. It seemed to me that she watched my undertaking with more interest after that.

Because my efforts to receive evidential material were so unsuccessful, I tried to talk to Mother about conditions in her world, philosophical concepts, and other subjects of a nonpersonal nature. As it has turned out, the most interesting evidence for anything genuinely supernormal coming through me has been the precognition the writing has given from time to time. That, of course, is the most unaccountable kind of ESP because there is no normal way to explain knowledge of the future.

As time went on I was never to receive any one big piece of evidence, and yet the many small inexplicable incidents add up to something highly curious in the overall picture. For those who are already chomping at the bit waiting for exciting scientific proof to be revealed in this book—it will never come. However, the number of small incidents carefully observed and recorded adds up to something that may be found to be reassuring indications that I have actually been in touch with the surviving entities who purport to communicate. The delineation of their personalities, particularly Mother's, comes to have real significance as time goes on.

As my "Guardian Angel," she revealed her sweet, but bossy, self in many ways in our communications. When she told me she was playing this role in my life, I asked her, "How can we develop our own character if we are constantly guarded and guided by someone invisible?"

Mother replied that our Guardian Angels can give suggestions and warnings that may be extremely helpful to us on occasion; but they do not want to tell us what to do with our lives, for it is by making our own decisions that we grow. Mother tried to maintain this attitude, but she was human enough and *herself* enough not always to be able to do it. She sometimes still told me "what spoon to stir the gravy with." It was natural that she would do what she could to make life easier for me, however; and it was very pleasing to think that someone might be handy to make an occasional effort on my behalf.

Mother wrote that she enjoyed tremendously the fact that I was beginning to be conscious of her presence. She wanted to have a large part in my life, hoping that my awareness of her could be improved to the point that I would finally be convinced that she really was there and stop having doubts. For my part, I encouraged this, too, by trying to be receptive enough that she could give me something so evidential of her actual presence that she would convince me entirely, and, along with me, everyone else. She has never yet been able to do that with one big specific incident, but the accumulation of small things grew daily.

One of these was when we made a dress together.

Early in May I decided to see if Mother could help me sew, and she said she'd give it a whirl. If we had success this would be quite a feather in her etheric cap, for I have never been able to use the sewing machine comfortably or successfully in my life. Its sounds and movements make me nervous; I always do everything backwards and grumble and cuss and hate it. But Mother said if I would just remain passive and let her do the thinking, she might be able to help me.

Somebody should have been thinking when the material was purchased, for I came home with stripes that were designed to go horizontal and a pattern to make them vertical. When the pattern was spread out on the table, the instructions overwhelmed me, and I became agitated as usual. I could no more have relaxed and let Mother take over and cut out the dress than I could have roped a cow.

Within moments there was a knock at the door and Loraine, the young woman who lived in the trailer on our left, came in. She so seldom visited us that she was as surprised as we were that she'd just gotten a sudden notion to show us her new hairdo. Then she asked, "What are you doing?"

"Trying to cut out a dress, but I haven't the foggiest notion how to go about it."

"Let me help you," Loraine said. "I've made my own clothes since I was a child." She not only cut the dress out but explained what must be done. Then she brought over her own sewing machine so one wouldn't have to be rented.

After Loraine left, about eleven o'clock, I took pencil in hand to tell Mother what had happened. She was way ahead of me, replying that she hadn't been up to taking me in hand at this late date and teaching me how to cut out a pattern when she'd had such poor luck with that in bygone years.

"So," she wrote, "I put the idea into Loraine's mind to come over so that she could help you."

This had to be coincidence. I couldn't accept it as anything else, no matter what the pencil wrote. But how does one account for the fact that when my sewing started the next day I was almost an expert? I never seamed the wrong sides of the material together as invariably used to happen. I was able to work out problems of facings, buttonholes, plackets, zippers . . . things that previously had eluded me entirely. And I was as calm and happy as Mother would have been . . . as she always used to be at home when her old sewing machine was humming.

The dress came out fine; so I rushed right out and bought more material and made a skirt for Nina and another dress and a sunsuit for myself before the joint endeavor terminated.

This sewing experience persuaded Nina that Mother really was making her presence felt, and from then on she never had any doubts about our communication. It was slightly convincing to me, too, especially because I have never since been able to achieve that kind of rapport with Mother when sewing and so have reverted to my previous ineptitude.

Then I had high hopes that it would be possible to maintain such closeness all the time. I came to the conclusion that sewing was just the thing to while away spare hours, with Mother at the throttle doing the mental work while I, you might say, just lent a hand and a knee to the proceedings.

Chapter 13

MY ABSORPTION in the adventure of communicating was complete. Still, I worked at my job every day, competently enough, no doubt, and no one suspected that my main interest lay in the evening séances when I took pencil in hand and tried to prove to myself that there is no death.

While at first it had been more of a fun thing, it developed for a brief period in May into a very trying situation. This centered around the manuscript of the book about my Florida experiences which I had started while in the desert and completed later in Maryland. Although sensing that it was a feeble effort, I decided that perhaps it was worth sending to a publisher and had mailed it off in March. It could be expected to take as long as three months before an answer might come, either accepting or rejecting it, so I put it out of my mind most of the time.

One evening in late May when doing automatic writing I asked, "Mother, tell me what is going on with my book. Do they like it?" The reply was that the publisher adored it and would let me know it soon. While somewhat encouraged, I was too wary to accept this as convincing, and dropped the matter. But the communications wouldn't let it go. Even when I had no intention of asking about it, preferring, or at least thinking it more advisable to write about impersonal things, the subject would be brought up every night. The book would be published very soon, it was said. Word about it was coming within the next few weeks. I'd be flying to New York in early June.

A writer who sends out his first manuscript is, of course, more anxious and apprehensive about it than is a seasoned author who is used to acceptances and rejections. Still, I would normally have spent little time worrying about the reception of this manuscript. I was made unnecessarily concerned with it because of the constant talk about it, not completely able to convince myself that it might not be genuine supernormal information from my mother.

Finally one night, as another attempt to get an evidential message from Mother so that I could make sure I was genuinely in touch with her and that the information concerning my manuscript wasn't just coming as the result of my own desire, I tried a test that was provable, asking if Margaret had gotten a job she was applying for that day. The reply was Yes, that she was to go to work Monday. I was even told her salary. So I phoned her and said, "Congratulations on your new job."

"I didn't get it," she said. "It was filled before I got there."

I was intensely chagrined, almost agonized. My Mother couldn't have lied to me, so evidently my whole process of communication had just been a figment of my own fancy. I'd been making a fool of myself for many weeks.

"Either Mother has really been writing or I'm sick," I cried to Nina in despair.

"Honey, I know you've been writing to your mother at least part of the time," she consoled me. And then she offered an idea that had never occurred to me. "Maybe some other spirit writes sometimes and claims to be Betty."

"Do you really suppose it could be that?" I asked. "Wouldn't that be against the rules?"

Somewhat cheered, however, by that possibility, I took up the pencil again, this time making a point to ask for identification. When the pencil started moving of its own accord I asked, "Who is writing?"

"Your mother."

"What's your name?"

"Betty Smith."

"Your full name?"

"Elizabeth Maude Anderson Hardegen Smith."

"What was the name of our first dog?"

"Arapaho Mountain Lassie."

These data were correct, so I took a chance and went ahead with the writing, insisting on being told what was going on. Mother said the misinformation had been written by spirit intruders, who were sometimes able to exert more power than she and so could push her aside and gain control of my pencil. She said that she had tried constantly to warn me about them on the few occasions lately when she had been my communicant, but that until the awareness of their activity was in my mind she couldn't put it there. She cautioned me always to test with personal questions before accepting anything further as coming from her.

"Then I guess all this business about my book came from them," I said, and Mother agreed. She added, however, that a letter from the publisher was actually in the mail for me at that moment and that I would receive it the next day. When I asked her whether or not it would be favorable, she said my mind was so preoccupied with the subject that she would be unable to get the truth through to me. She warned me about ever trying to query her about anything I was too closely involved with because my own coloring would naturally change the message. This is true of all mediums, I have learned. They know better than to try always to depend on the personal information they receive.

Still, Mother had actually given me a specific date when I would hear from the publisher. This was the first time anything of such a definite nature had been received, so it put her on the spot. As I waited with jitters for the mail to come the next day I realized that my belief in the veracity of all my communication hinged on whether or not the letter would be forthcoming.

It was! The publisher didn't want my book; but I wasn't downhearted, because Mother had passed her first test, and that was cheering. It was just exasperating that those interloping ghouls had gotten me so stirred up over it.

Then I began to check back over all my automatic writing and to understand that much of the time I had been blaming my coloring or my unconscious mind for inconsistencies, they could actually have been caused by intruders. Apparently unenlightened spirits are delighted to interrupt any effort at communication, just for the pleasure of making their presence known to someone on earth. They wrote any kind of gibberish, for it didn't matter to them what was said. It is even possible that they might have been deliberately attempting to cause me confusion. Invisible pranksters can be very naughty if they wish. I was struck then with the realization that I'd been specter-hectored often during the past couple of months, and that this was the explanation of an incident during the first week of my writing which had worried me considerably.

On the fourth night, when those penmanship classes with Mother had just begun, all evening long I had been forced to do huge circles and vertical lines as tall as the entire page. The tiring motions were continued over and over as fast as the pencil would move until I was drooping from exhaustion. But I wouldn't stop because I thought Mother was giving me something disciplinary— like how to remain in contact when fatigued, or any other stupid reason a tired mind could come up with.

Finally came a half page of writing, but it sounded cold; there was no feeling of Mother's presence—actually the whole thing was almost repellent—yet the letter was signed Betty so it didn't occur to me then that it might be anyone else writing.

Nina said, "I know your mother wouldn't do a thing like that to you."

Still flagging with weariness, I replied, "Well, my subconscious surely wouldn't torture me like this, would it?" And as far as I knew then, that was the only alternative. Somehow, Kay Brown's innocent appealing to Margaret to marry him when we used the Ouija board in his house didn't in any way cause me to be suspicious when this strange manifestation began in connection with my own writing. I wasn't that confident of the actuality of Kay's existence. And I just didn't dream that letters to me signed "Betty" or "Mother" could ever be from anyone but my own parent. Nobody I knew would muscle in on a private correspondence, why should one assume a spirit person to be so uncouth?

What kind of a spirit would be? Perhaps the James communications can clarify for us just who these earthbound entities are who cause so much trouble.

"The thing that seems to be most surprising to the average person," James states, "is to learn that there is no abrupt change of personality or locality after death. You are exactly the same after you die as you were the moment before death. And you are in the same place. The area in which one finds himself after he has left the physical body is identical with the earth plane of existence. All one does at death is to shed his physical body. The same man, the same consciousness, the same awareness of self continue to exist, and he feels as though he is still in his physical body. Thus if he was a low type of person, an individual without any spiritual values, he is still that same kind of individual. Or, as my friend Reverend Archie Matson of Idyllwild, California, says, "If you were a weed on earth, you won't suddenly be a flower in Heaven."

James goes on:

"The expectation of an abrupt alteration into some amorphous spiritual state entirely different from anything they have ever known frequently makes people unable to understand what has happened to them when death occurs. For those who believe that when one dies he immediately soars into a Heaven of beauty and bliss, or is thrust into a Hell of fire and brimstone—depending upon his moral status—it is a shock instead to find himself right where he was and in what seems to be the identical situation."

For one who believes that death is the end of all existence, James says that it is an even greater shock to find himself still living while at the same time he can see his own body on the bed below him, or in a car at the scene of a fatal accident, or perhaps in the water beside an upturned boat. There are many incidences where such a person refuses to believe what has happened and decides that he is merely having a bad dream. It is possible for someone like this to be in a state of confusion for a long time until some spirit missionary finally makes him realize that he has actually passed from the physical life into the spiritual.

James has written something in clarification of this that to my knowledge has never been stated before. Yet it helps us understand much that has previously been written or given through mediums about conditions immediately after death. "There is no precipitate transition from living on earth to living in the next dimension," he said. "If an individual is prepared for this fact— that the adaptation to the life of spirit is a gradual one—he is better able to accept it when it happens to him. We have always thought that if we lived at all after death we would have to be entirely transformed immediately into something ethereal. We expect, if we expect anything at all, a change of conditions so vast as to put us into an altogether different state. When this does not occur, we are confused and find it difficult to accept. But I must make it clear that your transition is gradual for a very definite reason. Supreme Intelligence planned it that way as the most sensible and workable arrangement for man's progression."

You see, at your death you are the same You, and nobody else. You are the person you were, with the same characteristics, the identical attitudes, thoughts, memories, likes and dislikes, and habits. You have now left a physical body that is no longer of use to you, and you are going to have to learn how to get along without it. Therefore, James says, in order for you not to find this so overpoweringly confusing that you are unable to cope, you are permitted by the system to live in your spiritual body in such close proximity to earth that you can continue to feel at home in your new environment.

"It must be noted that you are on your own after death just as much as you are during your lifetime on earth. There are those who will make every effort to help you and to tell you the truth. You are informed by them that you are a spiritual being who will live forever and that you must now bend your efforts toward progressing to a state of perfection; you are given to understand, however, that you can make your progress at your own rate of speed and that you do not have to leave the earth environment until you are thoroughly ready.

"Until you listen to all this you will make mistakes, just as you do now. You do not arrive at the feet of St. Peter or anyone else who will judge you, direct you, and make everything all right for you. You have, instead, to choose your own paths and make your decisions just as you always did. You have the help of teachers and guides who can give you assistance if you will take it; but you are no more likely to listen to them after your death than you were to listen to advice on earth. If you were a warm, loving, open-minded person you will probably have relatives of a similar nature to greet you and you will heed them. But if you were the kind of an individual who never could be told anything, you will still be that kind of person. If you knew all the answers on earth, you will think you do in the next life, and will continue to act the same as you always did until you finally begin to realize that you are getting nowhere. Then out of pure boredom or misery you will pay attention to those who state the facts to you."

Such spirits are called "earthbound," being so attached to the physical aspects of life or to the sorrows or sensations to which they have been accustomed that they continue to cling to them. Drug addicts and alcoholics are particularly earthbound prone, remaining close to those like themselves on earth in a vicarious effort to continue getting their kicks.

"There is nothing that keeps all these unhappy souls in that disagreeable condition," my invisible associate wrote, "except their lack of a desire to improve themselves, or their inability to accept elucidating truths. It may take some of them, who have led dissolute or criminal lives, many hundreds of years before they face up to the fact that they must work on themselves in order to leave the unpleasantness in which they find themselves. When they do start to make an effort, it is very difficult for them because it is work on their character development and their thinking techniques, and they have little or no character and their thinking is about as negative as it is possible to be. If they had been aware of this in time and labored for improvement on earth, they would not now find themselves in such miserable circumstances."

Well, you wouldn't expect it to be as easy on those who had been rotten on earth as on those who had at least tried to live worthwhile existences. It was appalling to me to learn that these earthbound types are the ones who hang so closely around us and attempt to make their presence known whenever they find an opportunity. Someone working a Ouija board or doing automatic writing is someone opening his mental doors and crying out gaily to them, "Come in! Come in! Whoever you are!"

"Yes," agreed James, "they are particularly apt to intrude their presence on anyone who is attempting spirit communication of any sort. Some do it out of mischievousness, some out of genuine malevolence."

When I try to envision the type of spirit who would intrude himself upon those who cannot see him and attempt to disturb them mentally, or merely to josh them, I am naturally reminded of the nasty individual who spends his time calling people on the telephone and whispering filth into their ears before they can hang up. If he wasn't fortunate enough to be reclaimed into a decent person before his death, he would be just the type who would reject assistance from well-meaning spirits after he died and continue to ply his viciousness between planes of existence whenever he found the opportunity. Someone communicating with spirits would be fair game for him.

Even though my efforts at writing during that first spring in Salt Lake City were not dependable, I didn't then know the perils, and so I wasn't about to stop trying to talk with Mother. The way I looked at it was this: Suppose you lived in a police state and every time you tried to get news from other countries over your radio the goverment jammed the airwaves with static so that you got mostly garbled messages. Yet occasionally you received news so revealing about conditions on the other side of the boundary that you felt the urge to know more.

Suppose most people you told laughed at you and said, "Everyone knows there is nothing beyond," or, "It's illegal. You mustn't try to rend the veil." Would you give up? Or would you continue trying, hoping to clarify your reception until you had something of definite value and positive proof to offer your fellow men?

But I didn't want to escape from reality, either, over this experience with the unknown, whether it was caused by conflict with my own subconscious mind or spirit intruders. So, beginning to sense the very real dangers, I resolved to keep my feet on the ground ever firmer than before. I wrote very little after learning about earthbound spirits and, always wary, asked for identification. Discovering that any hesitancy about the name of someone from my past indicated a trespasser, I'd stop the discourses immediately. It didn't take the phonies long to realize that it was no fun any more working with a wise guy, and all but one of them went away.

This one usually identified himself. His name, he said, was Harvey, and he always got stuck trying to make the "H," repeating the initial stroke several times. He didn't care what he said, eager to write what he thought I wanted most to hear. He particularly liked to write "I love you," for being a man he presumed he could cajole me with that.

Harvey told me he was a carpenter who had died in Salt Lake City at the age of eighty. He said his last name was Boone, and, at first, he was so horribly agreeable that he was perfectly willing to be Dan'l's great-grandfather or any other Boone we suggested. In fact, he'd admit to being almost anyone—except the invisible rabbit named Harvey. That he vehemently denied.

Harvey stuck to me like a Rocky Mountain spotted tick from the very first; and whenever I picked up the pencil in the loose way that indicated willingness to palaver for a while, no matter where I was—even in a cocktail lounge once—almost immediately it started to write, "I'm your Harvey. I'm here. I love you." When asked for Mother he'd write, "I'm your mother" and if checks weren't made to be sure it was not she, he'd go on pretending. But he always flunked personal questions and revealed himself. He heard me testing Mother with family names and learned enough of them that he could answer correctly up to a point . . . until he gave himself away by the difficulty he had making his H: "What's your name?" "Betty Smith." "Your full name?" "Elizabeth Maude Anderson H H H H H H . . ."

At first I believed Harvey to be harmless, but Mother always told me not to write with him or he'd hurt me. I couldn't figure how he could hurt me, and anyway, sometimes I'd be talking to him without being aware of it. That is how he harmed me, of course, by keeping me from successful communication with more enlightened spirits. If he said Mother wasn't around—"Not here, Mother's not here," he'd write—I'd believe him. Even though Mother insisted she would stay with me, I thought she must have been called away for a while on important business. Because if she was there why did she let Harvey write? That business about him having more power than she did was pretty hard to take. Yet apparently it was true that when he flexed his mental muscles and exerted more strength than she could, her force wasn't enough to overcome his.

Once someone suggested that Harvey might be a malefactor, so I asked him, "Are you a malefactor?"

"I don't know what that is," he wrote in reply.

"Are you harmful to me?"

"I don't want to hurt you," he answered. "I just want to stay with you. I love you." And stay he did, although the love he expressed was very selfish. He was obviously there only because he could talk to me.

Harvey became the butt of all our small jokes around the trailer —the little invisible man who hid things we misplaced, or who bumped our heads, or who got too much salt in the potatoes. And Margaret even blamed him for the chicken she lost to me on the Kentucky Derby.

She had been a longtime Lexington resident, so naturally she said, "Let's put a bet on the Derby" when we turned on the television to watch it.

"Who's running?" I asked her, not having paid enough attention to the race even to know the names of the horses.

She ticked them off on her fingers, "Well, there's Nashua, he's the favorite, and Summer Tan, and Swaps. . . ."

"I'll take Swaps," I said, and we bet the chicken we were going to Kentucky fry for dinner on the outcome. Swaps won. Wish that chicken had been a mink coat.

Margaret said, "Harvey, that's no fair. You cheated, telling Susy."

So all right. Of course I don't think Harvey told me. But I never picked a winner before, at least not without studying such odds as who was the prettiest horse or which had the cutest jockey. And why does someone who has made a million wrong decisions suddenly start guessing right almost constantly when she begins dabbling with psychical phenomena? It was one of the first of the long string of more-than-coincidences that have occurred in my life since that April day when I first took the future in my hands and began my Heavenly harkening. And mathematics tells us that when coincidences start coming in quantity they lose all the accidental characteristics of coincidence.

Memorial Day, 1955, was warm and muggy and Trigg had come over to help me clean house. Nina said she felt slightly strange—not sick, just a bit peculiar—so I made her take it easy all day and she sat in the yard and read. Trigg and I worked hard at our housecleaning and by late afternoon the trailer was shining, as Margaret and a friend came by to take us all for a ride.

"Can't I watch TV instead?" the boy asked his mother, and Nina said, "I think I'll stay home with Trigg."

Without them, we took a ride for about an hour to the queer salty lake that gives the city its name. When we returned and pulled into the trailer court a red police ambulance was standing in front of the Gingerbread House. We saw Trigg outside and called to him, "What's the matter," and he replied simply, "Nina died."

Shortly after we left he had heard a small moan and turned around to see Nina laying her head back against the pillow behind her on the couch. He jumped over to her and felt her pulse, then dialed the operator and said, "Send a doctor or the police, someone's dying." Our little Nina was already gone then, her glasses on her nose and a *Time* magazine on her lap—she died quickly and easily as she would have wanted to go.

Mother wrote to me that night, identifying herself by numerous family names, and told me Nina had come gladly and had a happy reunion with her and with her mother and father. How could I grieve for her after that? At seventy-two she had just been marking time until she could join her relatives and friends on the other side. But she was my only tie with my childhood and all the family I had left, and I felt, oh, so lonely for her.

I couldn't help but be thankful, however, that everything seemed to have been arranged in the easiest possible manner for both Nina and me; and the experience didn't faze Trigg at all. Had Nina died when alone and I'd walked in on her afterwards, or had I been alone with her when it happened, it would have been terribly upsetting. As it was, resourceful Trigg seemed instinctively to know what to do. The city doctor and the police who came at his call told me they'd never seen a boy of twelve who was so calm and capable in an emergency.

And so the disturbing prophecy that we received from the Ouija board in April was fulfilled in May.

Nina didn't "love" long.

Chapter 14

AFTER NINA'S DEATH Margaret and I decided to go to California to seek our fortunes; I gave notice at the newspaper, and we were ready to leave by late June. During the month I had made room in the Gingerbread House for the Adamses and their quantity of possessions, and they moved in.

When my new trailermates arrived it quickly became evident that the reason Nina and I had gotten along so well together living in our mini-mansion was not any credit to me . . . it was because Nina was so tiny, so quiet, and so adaptable. Margaret spilled over with vitality and ideas. Trigg was interested, inventive, and hyperenergetic. Their parakeet frequently took part in our conversations, and whenever we talked to him Junior was jealous. All this buzzing activity in a twenty-two foot space and we're still friends; but . . . we haven't tried to live together since.

Before our trip, my little Chevrolet Bel Air was gone over thoroughly, and we thought it was in shape for the extra duties that would be required of it to pull the mobile home. A man from the trailer sales company helped us pack for the journey, and he taught Trigg to undo the sewer pipes and the electric wires and remove the jacks the trailer sat on. They all then had to be cleaned thoroughly and stashed inside when we were in transit . . . along with Trigg's bicycle!

It took us all day to pack, and it was late afternoon when we finally started out. I found driving with a trailer in tow rather enjoyable after all. It bounded along behind us with a kind of bubbly feeling.

"We can record this in our memoirs as a champagne trip," I said . . . with spectacular lack of foresight. Evening traffic going out of town proved to be no problem because everyone gave me a wide berth as I drove slowly at the right side of the main street. If they'd known what a novice was pulling the trailer, they'd probably have climbed telephone poles to get out of our way.

The next day we began to approach mountainous country. At the first deceptively rising grade through a lonely vista the car just inched its way to the top. There it panted and wheezed and steamed. Trigg investigated and said we'd have to add water . . . but did we have any? We finally found a supply in the tank of the trailer's toilet. At the next service station we filled up every pan we had . . . and we were to need them. We crawled up all the mountains along the way, sat half an hour or so at the top broiling ourselves in the searing summer sun as the radiator cooled off. Then we added water and proceeded.

Descending the mountains wasn't much easier. There is a funny swing and sway motion a trailer gets when going down hill on anything less than a super highway that can rock a car and cause it to go considerably faster than you had intended. It gives you an unpleasant feeling. Actually, a panicky feeling. I enjoy rock 'n' roll, but not when my bustle weighs two tons. So we learned to go down hills in low, too, as well as up them. Fortunately, we had no deadlines to meet in California.

Because I presumed all our problems with the car were merely the normal results of its pulling too heavy a load—besides the trailer, its trunk was filled with six of Margaret's massive sculptures—it didn't occur to us not to take the side trip across the desert to Zion Canyon. I had seen it once before and was so impressed with it that my friends just had to share my pleasure. So we headed our caravan off the main highway and into the wilderness. There's one stupendous mountain to shinny up on the way. The scenery down over the side was breathtaking and as we ooched upward I tried to peek at it whenever an eye could be released from the steeply climbing road and the rapidly elevating temperature gauge.

When we reached the magnificent canyon it was worth all the effort. We camped the trailer in the shady shelter of a grove of young aspens, then drove around all afternoon craning our necks to gape at the monumental rocks and cliffs. That night we sat out under the trees with moonlight peeking through the leaves and a man at a nearby trailer playing a banjo. It was not easy to tear ourselves away from that spot the next morning.

From St. George, Utah, there are eighty-three miles straight across uninhabited desert to Glendale, Nevada. There was nothing in Glendale but a service station and a restaurant, and little else but fifty miles of expanse between it and Las Vegas. As we pulled into the garage at Glendale at 8:30 P.M. Margaret, who was driving, commented, "This trailer gets harder and harder to pull." The attendant discovered why. It had just had a flat.

When we later stopped on a hill overlooking the lights of Vegas we walked a little way into the desert to be alone with the starry sky; and we probably each whispered a little word of thanksgiving that the Gingerbread House had had its flat just as we pulled into a garage instead of in that isolated wilderness or on top of one of those desolate pink Utah hills. I hoped Mother was listening, for I couldn't help but wonder if this was an example of how she would be my Guardian Angel as she had promised.

It's easy to begin to attribute every favorable act of Fortune to supernatural machinations. In order to maintain a basic equilibrium in my life these days, I have required myself to ignore countless incidents that could be added to the string of more than slightly unusual occurrences that keep happening to me all the time. So rest assured that the odd events I mention are among many others either forgotten, not recorded in time to be remembered completely, or discarded because taking note of so many would be tiresome reading.

In Las Vegas a mechanic discovered that the trouble with the car was a gasket that had to be replaced, and after that we rolled easily onward, the car pulling the trailer with no effort at all.

Drawing into the environs of Los Angeles, we found a trailer camp near the shore in Hermosa Beach. But our big success in California was slow materializing; Margaret wanted to attend her daughter's wedding in Kentucky; and in a bank box in Maryland lay some of Nina's bonds that would come in very handy for me almost any day now. So in a month we were off again, leaving the trailer to await us in California. Driving night and day through an extravagantly hot spell of weather we soon arrived wilted in Lexington. There Margaret, Trigg, and their bird got off, and I continued on to Oakland alone.

Shortly after I arrived there Margaret wrote that she couldn't return west with me because her mother was sick. I was sorry for my friend, and for her mother—and also just a tiny bit sorry for me, who had to face that trip back alone. Somehow my heart just wasn't in it this time. But the only home I now had was on wheels in California; and my only immediate prospect of making a living was a plan for a movie column which a Hollywood public relations man was working on for me. So what else was there to do?

I chose the Northern route, for its scenery was new to me; and Junior and I were soon enjoying the vastness of Central and Western United States. If my Guardian Angels were ever to be with me, there could be no doubt that they would be there when I was traveling alone, so the idea of their presence was accepted gratefully. And it must be admitted that my dog and my unseen convoy were all splendid traveling companions. If I suddenly decided to go this way, nobody gave me any argument about wanting to go that way. Well, actually, Junior, being a dachshund, a breed famous for their independence, was not always a seeing-eye-to-eye dog. But my invisible associates seemed to be in complete accord. There was not a peep out of them; yet they were there when we needed them.

Mt. Rushmore amazed me with its man-made monuments; then Yellowstone Park thrilled me with its scenic wonders. In late August, it also nearly froze me to death. After a couple of nights in those chinky log cabins I left there feeling like a strudel just pulled out of somebody's deep freeze.

The warmth of friendly greetings in Salt Lake City thawed me out, and I remained there for a few days to exchange pleasantries and to sign papers regarding Nina's will. Then I sped onward toward sunny California, eager now to rejoin my little Gingerbread House.

With the fantastic climate changes a thousand miles can effect, it was the heat that was unbearable as we drove through the desert toward San Bernardino, suffering because my car was not air conditioned. With windows all rolled down, I kept moving urgently toward the ocean and relief.

Junior had never been so uncomfortably hot in his life. He frantically ran from one side of the car to the other and leaped from the front to the back seat, trying to find nonexistent shade. I became as nervous as he, fearing he'd have a fit or jump out of the car, yet it wasn't possible to hold his busy body and drive too.

Finally I said aloud, "Nina, I know how you loved this little dog. I'm desperate about him right now. Won't you please see if you can quiet him for me?" He *instantly* curled up in the center of the back seat in a spot of brightest sunlight and went to sleep, never stirring until we arrived in Hermosa Beach.

The trailer was awaiting us undisturbed and I moved in, spending days transferring Margaret's belongings to storage. Then I unpacked the household possessions brought from Maryland, having all my own things about me for the first time in a year, exulting at being able to move around in the trailer without bumping into anybody. But loneliness quickly began to invade my little nest. I missed Nina's sweetness, and Margaret's sunniness, and Trigg's brightness.

If only I could get back into contact with Mother again, or if Nina would write to me—but nobody answered when the pencil was held lightly in an effort to communicate. Nobody important. Harvey was there sometimes. But just as often as not there was a complete blank of nothingness. Even though this was unpleasant, it was interesting—because if it had just been my subconscious mind involved, wouldn't it have written to me when I was lonely and particularly wanted it to?

Then on September 20th Mother popped in for a chat when I picked up the pencil, as casually as if she'd never been out of touch. Good as it was to hear from her, I fussed at her a little, telling her it was awfully hard for me to learn to believe in spirit communication when no spirits would ever communicate. She answered that I had been living such an active life that it was impossible for her to settle me down enough to get anything through my mind. But she assured me she was always on call whenever an emergency arose.

Then Mother suggested something that was to me quite strange. She told me to attend a Spiritualist Church, seeming to think she might be able to give me some evidence through a professional medium. Oddly enough, this had never occurred to me, partly because of being non-church-oriented and partly because at that time I had never thought of Spiritualism as anything but a fraudulent farce. (Of course, I know better now.) Still, if Mother said so, that was obviously the next step for me to take.

I picked a church at random out of the newspaper ads and attended the next Sunday, eagerly anticipating a message since she'd promised one. Of course, no one there knew me and no identifications were made.

After the service the minister gave a message to each member of the congregation. When it came my time for a reading she said to me, "Who is the old man with the gnarled fingers?"

"Oh, no, not Harvey! I don't want him!" I cried, incensed at his intervention.

The woman smiled. "Yes, he's nodding eagerly to think you recognize him."

That was all she had for me. Asked for news of my mother, her only contribution was a lady bringing me a rose, which could never have been Betty Smith who would more likely have brought me something practical like a roast beef sandwich.

At home later Harvey got the devil when he immediately answered the call of the pencil, smugly self-satisfied because he had produced verification of his reality.

"Why did the medium see you and not Mother?" I asked him.

He wrote, "Because I pushed in ahead of her."

"That's not fair," I cried. "You know how much I wanted a message from Mother."

My chagrin didn't faze him a bit. He was quite proud of himself, actually. Lonesome as I was in California, and eager as I was to have evidence of Mother's continued existence so as to be sure my current interests weren't all self-delusion, he had the nerve to brag about forcing his way in ahead of her into the minister's line of vision. I purely hated his guts.

"I don't care if she did see an old man with gnarled fingers like the eighty-year-old carpenter you say you were. I still think you're nothing but an invisible rabbit," I stormed at him. "Just stay out of my life . . . you jack rabbit!"

Chapter 15

║║║ COULDN'T BE SITTING AROUND all the time parting the curtain between the spheres. There was my fabulous career to get on with. I called to report back to the public relations man who was going to put my movie column into the big time, and learned that he'd taken a new job and disappeared without even leaving a forwarding address. I phoned the offices of the editors of the local papers, discovering their secretaries to be vigilantly protecting them from a columnist who wanted a personal interview instead of merely submitting written samples of her work. All the other contacts I attempted to make were as fruitless.

I never felt so thoroughly rejected. Sure, people had to be properly seasoned by Hollywood, but it didn't have to happen to me. I wasn't trying to break into the movies.

"So chin up," I chin-upped. "You'll never get anywhere sitting on your big fat chair out here in Hermosa Beach; get in closer to town where you can at least make a phone call without it costing fifteen cents."

Then I scooted around and found a trailer park in Santa Monica. It was much closer to the hub of activity and had a swimming pool! Arrangements were made to move the Gingerbread House there immediately.

As the owner of the Hermosa court was moving me out, there was a loud wham when the bottom of the trailer hit the street going down a steep hill. Then water began running out the end of my happy home. It was quickly revealed that the sewer pipe had rammed up inside and shattered the toilet bowl. The manager, who was covered by insurance, promised to have it replaced at once.

It took over two weeks for the new toilet to arrive, and there was no water all that time. I lived in the swishest trailer park in Santa Monica like a hobo in a culvert. The World Series came to my rescue, for I watched it every day on TV and time passed quickly. When the Dodgers won I gave a whoop and a holler that could be heard as far south as San Diego, and that somehow captivated my neighbors.

Clarence, the widower next door, kindly came to my rescue from then on when any maintenance problems needed solving. Various others invited me to play bridge. I swam in the pool every nice day, sunned in my miniscule yard . . . say, that was living! I couldn't arouse one jot of interest in trying to find a job. It seemed that I had an unconscious aversion to the prospect of the high-pressure Hollywood area as a place to sink a taproot.

Then I found a shelf of books about psychical research in the local library. Discussing the subject with no one, every night alone I pondered the possibilities, debated the doctrines, and marveled at the mysteries the books contained. It got a little morbid.

When mental activity becomes depressing, getting busy with my hands is always the solution. So I decided to paint my trailer.

There was certainly no encouragement from the men around, who all said they'd never undertake it themselves expecting to get anywhere near a professional-looking job. But my Gingerbread House was beginning to look more like a boxcar than a dream-boat. Somehow on the trip over from Salt Lake City a tree had gotten too close to it and its side was peeling. Anyway, its red color argued with my hair every time my head was stuck out the door. So I bought two quart cans of turquoise metal paint and jumped right in.

Observers were very helpful. Clarence thought a finer brush was necessary. Someone else said my paint was too thin. Another thought it was too thick.

"Gimme that brush," the assistant caretaker said, grabbing it out of my hand. Then he slathered on the paint in big strokes as if he were calcimining the side of a barn. It looked awful.

"You'll never get a good job on this," he said, handing the brush back and muttering to himself about women and how stupid they were. I set to work trying to repair the mess he'd made.

Finally a new neighbor was found who knew how to paint on

metal. He taught me how to put just the tiniest bit of pigment on the brush and work it in thoroughly until there wasn't a drop or a ripple before adding more. I did it his way, going very slowly and carefully, and then the job began to look nearly professional.

How proud I was finishing the first can of paint—a shade of turquoise like sunshine on the ocean off the coast of Florida. I told my kibitzers the paint in the second can wasn't right, but they all assured me it had to be identical because it was the same lot number. So I went ahead and used some of it—for touchups here and there. It dried an ugly gray-blue like the ocean in a rainstorm. I returned it to the dealer, waiting over a week with the trailer a two-tone tragedy while he negotiated with the factory.

One melancholy night during the time when the paint puzzle was most worrisome I had a vivid dream which must have been trying to tell me something. It was the first of several easily remembered technicolor dreams, seemingly directly instigated by Mother, that have since come to me during times when encouragement is particularly needed.

In the dream I was driving my car in West Texas and Mother was sitting beside me. There was a lot of water on the highway, and we were aware that there had been big storms in the area. Water was crowding the car, ominous cliffs closed in on us, and great dark clouds were overhead. I was frightened. Then Mother told me to move over and let her drive. As she took the wheel the cliffs immediately began to recede and the sun came out. Then the road ahead became a placid lake, the car turned into a boat, and we sailed right over the water.

I awoke at six A.M. and lay in bed thinking about an interpretation of the dream. Obviously it meant that I should put myself into Mother's hands so she could pilot me and then everything would be all right. I reached out as usual and turned on the bedside radio, and the news broadcaster was saying, "Last night a sudden storm hit West Texas and floods occurred in many areas."

I wasn't sure just what Mother had in mind but decided not to worry about the silly old paint . . . or a job either. Next day word came from the factory that it would be impossible to match my original shade but they would be kind enough to replace what I'd used so the trailer could be done over in the new color. I wasn't about to settle for having my home look like any rainy sea, so I got out my oil paints and mixed and matched and tinted and tested until the new batch was my original happy turquoise. Then three more coats were applied to finish the job.

Five coats of paint on the trailer and one on me; nearly a month of diligent application; and nothing to show for it but success. It looked as wonderful to me as the Blue Boy must have looked to Gainsborough as he stood back to gaze upon his finished masterpiece. It was admired, too, by my neighbors, who rallied 'round with words of praise. The man who'd been the most sure I couldn't do it came to take my picture beside my "Blue Boy" with his color camera, and got my biggest grin for his trouble.

It was just about that time that the library produced a book entitled *The Reach of the Mind* by Dr. J. B. Rhine, who conducted the Parapsychology Laboratory at Duke University. I'd heard and read about Dr. Rhine and his ESP work at Duke and believed him to be a pioneer in one of the most fascinating and far-reaching new fields of inquiry; but I had not somehow thought of him as being particularly interested in research about the survival of the human soul. I was correct, as I was later to learn. But Dr. Rhine stated in his closing chapter of *The Reach of the Mind* that ESP indicates that man does have a soul, which inevitably leads to the possibility that it might survive death. On page 217 he says, "Any sort of survival of any portion of the personality, for any length of time, holds such significance for human thinking and feeling as to dwarf almost all other scientific discovery by comparison." My sentiments exactly!

"Why, that's the place for me to go to learn more about this," I thought, eager for someone to explain things to me and teach me scientific procedures of research. So an immediate letter to Dr. Rhine informed him of my interest in attempting to prove survival and gave him a brief review of my background.

One of his assistants answered encouragingly and over a period of a month we exchanged correspondence which inspired me to plan definitely to go to Duke—not as a student but as a guest at the laboratory. Aware that the little bequest Nina had left me wouldn't last forever, or even for long, I hoped to show sufficient aptitude at the Parapsychology Lab to work into a grant or else to find some engaging data about which to write.

If the possibility of scientific proof of immortality was such a tremendous stimulus to me, it could also be to others. I didn't know enough about it yet to feel able to draw any conclusions, but my compulsion to learn more on the subject was so strong I was determined to take off for Duke immediately. This, of course, meant trundling my trailer clear across the country, but, there being no other way to get it there, I trundled it.

Chapter 16

"YOU JUST CAN'T DO IT ALONE, Susy," was the opinion of all my neighbors in Santa Monica. None of the women would have dreamed of attempting it, they said. Hands were thrown into the air in horror—all because I was planning to attempt to drive my car across the United States from California to North Carolina by myself with a trailer in tow.

One man was frank enough to say, "I wouldn't even try to pull a trailer that far alone myself, and I don't have the handicap you do."

My main handicap was lack of money, so I couldn't afford to hire a truck to pull it for me. "I'm like the rabbit who climbed the tree," I told them. "I'se 'bleeged to do it." And when you're obliged to do something, you just do it. Anyway, I didn't expect to be alone . . . I had my dog.

Anybody else? I wasn't sure. Nothing had been heard via pencil all fall. Even Harvey seemed to have deserted me. Then on the night of December 13th, just two days before my leaving for the East, Nina wrote when I took up the pencil to try to get some last minute encouragement for my trip. Her word was that she and Mother would be with me all the way and I wasn't to be afraid.

I was buoyed up for several days after Nina's letter and started my journey with confidence. It is just as well I did, for pulling a trailer alone is at best slightly nervewracking, and so is Los Angeles traffic. Put them both together and you have an excellent case for staying home and crawling under the bed.

I made it to Indio the first night and drew into a trailer court of sorts where there was no one to help me get installed. I had to back the Gingerbread House myself into the plot—something I'd never done before. Now, backing a trailer is no worse than hanging out the wash while balancing yourself on the clothesline in a stiff gale, but it's just as bad. The wheels all turn the opposite way from what you expect, you have a limited space to maneuver in, and like as not you get squeezed up against something in an area impossible to get out of. And then you have to get out.

Once when I managed to jam the back bumper of the car tightly against the gas tanks on the front of the trailer, there was a screeching as if the car had run over the six tails of six cats. But not finding any dead cats, or any dents or scratches on either car or trailer, I resumed operations, eventually landing my mobile home in a space sufficiently out of the way that it could remain there over night.

It was dark and sharply cold by then, and I sought refuge inside, tired out and freezing. Dinner by flashlight was a cold meatloaf sandwich accompanied by a fine, dry, distinguished California root beer, served lukewarm. And so to bed, with my clothes on for warmth. This was not quite the Beverly Hilton.

At six the next morning as I was leaving, my glance just happened to fall on a piece of bolt on the ground in front of the car. It was turquoise and undoubtedly off my trailer, but where? I finally discovered that the gas tanks were loose and realized that backing the night before had sheared off the bolt which secured them to the frame. If my eyes hadn't strayed onto the tiny object on the ground, my tanks might have bounced off in transit.

Not knowing where to have such damage repaired, I stopped at the first business establishment that was open along the highway— a lumber yard. There a boy put a new bolt on in five minutes and wouldn't charge me for it!

At Yuma, Tucson, and El Paso I stayed at legitimate trailer courts; but setting up each night and getting organized for living seemed too much effort when all I did was to sleep there anyway.

So at Ozona, a small West Texas town, came a better idea. Or, actually, it was thrust upon me because there was no trailer camp or park of any kind in the environs. So, finding a good movie, I just stopped alongside the curb around the corner from the theater and parked for the night there, enjoyed the picture, cleaned my teeth in the theater rest room, and then returned home to Junior, who'd retired early. This was so successful that I continued the procedure most of the rest of my travels, usually driving until dusk and then drawing up by a lighted service station. It was much less trouble and altogether less expensive.

The morning I left Ozona there was a heavy fog. The hazy driving didn't bother me particularly, since my unseen Girl Guides were probably out ahead blazing the trail. But as the sun glared forth about nine o'clock and we picked up some speed over the hills, persistent ideas started bombarding me to pull over to the side of the road and stop.

I said to myself, "Better get my sun glasses out of the glove compartment" and answered, "No, wait until the first roadside park." Because there is also a hand-brake to manipulate in order to slow the trailer, as well as the controls of the car to operate, it was too much effort just to pause alongside the road; and I couldn't reach the glove compartment without stopping. Then I thought, "Really should get out some eye drops and use them to wake up more." And decided again to wait until the next turnout. Right on top of this came the thought that maybe it would be wise to make sure the new bolt was still holding the gas tanks on safely. It all seemed silly, yet the impressions to stop were so insistent that I pulled over. As the trailer bumped to an unusually jerky halt I reflected on the dangers of pulling over onto roadside gravel, vowing never to do it again.

Going back to check on the gas tanks, just in case, I found that the connection which plugged the trailer brake into the car electric outlet had become unhitched and the socket was dragging on the ground! Its prongs were becoming so bent that another few feet of travel would probably have finished their usefulness. Had I tried to go down a steep hill or to stop suddenly without the brake functioning, the Gingerbread House, as well as the car and its occupants, would all have made a splash in the nearest ditch.

"Thank you, Mother and Nina," I said with the most fervent conviction yet exhibited. A few more incidents like this and I was going to be firmly dedicated to the principle of the Guardian Angel.

Pondering the necessity to stop a passing motorist to get him to straighten the heavy metal prongs of the plug for me, I thought, "No sir, if there's help in the big things, there's help in the small. There's nothing I can't do alone now—except possibly tango." And I opened the trailer, brought out a pair of pliers, applied several ergs of brute force, and fixed the plug myself.

When writing of this incident now, some years later, the correlation between my dream of Mother helping me with driving problems in West Texas comes to mind. Perhaps that was not only a reassuring dream but a precognitive one as well.

I spent the holidays in San Antonio, where friends eased me over Christmas with many warm invitations. I lingered another few weeks to refurbish my little isolation booth with new curtains and pillow covers and a good housecleaning, after which I returned courtesies with a series of small dinner parties. I wanted it known that mobile home living was no tramp existence—and there were numerous converts to my point of view.

Being eager to get to Durham, however, and begin my studies, on January 9th I started out again; and at 9:30 in the morning as we were loping along Loop 13 just outside of town, suddenly a car pulled out onto the road not twenty-five feet ahead of me.

I grabbed the trailer hand-brake and stepped on the car foot-brake, both so suddenly that everything went out of control at once.

"Help me, help me," I cried frantically as the trailer began to lash the car into a frenzy. The car lunged and jerked the trailer in return and the two were buckling back and forth as they bounded around the highway.

As the gyrations finally ended and we came to a stop facing in the opposite direction, I struggled for a moment with excitement, relief and gratitude that the entire kit and kaboodle wasn't over-turned, then began feeling the unperturbed Junior for broken bones.

Two men who had seen the accident rushed over to help, and they assured the police who popped up immediately that it had not been my fault. They pulled the trailer off the highway for me, changed the tire that had blown out on the car, and then refused anything but a handshake in return. A checkup inside the trailer revealed that everything was strewn about but nothing was broken; but when I finally drove off there was a clanking noise in its left wheel. Stops at a filling station and also at a trailer repair shop failed to diagnose it. It was suggested that it might be a burned out bearing and that I should drive along until I found a garage that had a mechanic on duty.

About five miles out the Austin Highway as I clanked along a truck honked at me and the driver pointed back, so I pulled over off the four-lane turnpike and found a flat on the trailer wheel in question.

Now comes the most unbelievable part of this story, and I offer it as evidence for nothing except good fellowship. A young man named John stopped to help and then gave me his entire day! He first rented an automatic jack from a nearby service station and took the wheel off, discovering that in the wreck the drum had almost become unriveted from the rim and that a rivet had since dropped down inside, ripping the tire.

John put Junior and me and the wheel into his car and took us back to San Antonio, where we spent all the rest of the day waiting while the wheel was welded, and buying a new tire. He even was able to get that for me wholesale!

He bought me a Coke. He bought me lunch. He never complained about losing his day's trip to Austin. And he told me his life's story in an accent so delightfully Texan that I was entertained all day. About five o'clock all our chores had been attended to and we returned to the trailer, where he put the wheel back on and started to say goodbye.

"John, it's impossible to thank you," I said. "I've never in my life seen anyone so generous with his time."

"Aw. . . ."

"It was way over and beyond the call of duty and good will."

"Well, just pass it on. Do a good turn for someone else," he said; and he pulled away, leaving me sitting alone on the highway in the dusk, my eyes damp with gratitude.

I almost didn't start out then. Reaction had been creeping up on me during the day and the temptation was strong to return to San Antonio, at least for the night. Yet like a pilot who has crashed, I must immediately become airborne again or my nerve might desert me entirely . . . so it was necessary to forge ahead into the deepening shadows. I drove to Austin that night.

Riding along I couldn't help but recall something Mary Elliott had said in Oakland when I was preparing for my last lonely cruise west.

"I just couldn't do it," she said. "I'd be scared to death."

"Well, do you think I'm not?" I asked her.

Chapter 17

Y FIRST IMPRESSION [of the Parapsychology Laboratory at Duke University was wonderful. I arrived in time for the morning coffee hour, when everyone was assembled in the library for their daily biscuit-dunk. All were most gracious during introductions, handsome Dr. J. B. Rhine himself being most prepossessing. As they discussed the morning mail over their coffee and cookies, I sat there all adazzle, overwhelmed that I, a nonentity, was being admitted into this imposing group of academicians.

"I'll never get over being thankful they invited me to come . . . to sit at their feet as a chela at a guru's," I thought. My eyes popped, too, at all the psychic literature on the library shelves, which I would be allowed to browse. And I did read constantly from those shelves my entire seven weeks in Durham.

But that sitting at feet . . . that pupil and teacher business, no. That wasn't achieved. I found no gurus in my particular areas of interest. Here were no fellow cleavers of the veil. Instead I found myself among scholars and scientists whose goal was to prove extrasensory perception scientifically, but whose intentions were not to get involved in anything that might spoil their other fine work by causing them to receive the label "ghost chasers." Since the need was still felt for more evaluations and classifications and analyses and repetitions of former ESP tests, this is how the laboratory people were spending their time then. They accepted me because they hoped I'd fit neatly into the groove and sit myself down with pencil and paper checking columns of precognition symbols.

I tried, really I did.

But with all those different schools I went to, about half my math had been missed, and simple things like decimals and percent have been ignored ever since, hoping they'll go away. So I didn't suddenly acquire an aptitude for critical ratios and standard deviations and frequency polygons; and sitting and checking figures is not my idea of brunch at the Plaza. Anyway, if one were going to master clerical work, it should be in order to hold a good paying job with fringe benefits in an office somewhere.

So actually, what I stirred up at Duke was a lot of complete indifference. I'd come clear across the country flying a trailer solo to learn from them, but nobody there would admit to knowing anything whatever about survival research. If I wouldn't check symbols then all they could do was lead me to the library and place material about the subject before my eager, trembling little mind, with the strict admonition to be sure to read only "critical" books—those which were entirely objective and gave no philosophy and carried no message.

I have come to be tremendously grateful to the Laboratory people for this introduction into strict objectivity, realizing that this is the best possible thing they could have done for me. Too many books in this field are pointless because their authors accept everything they see and experience at face value. Because of my lifetime of arguing with concepts, my professional skepticism, and the indoctrination in critical evaluation received during my time at the Parapsychology Laboratory, I have been able to maintain a more objective approach to my subject in all my writing. Of course, the publication of this autobiography, which tells of my ultimate conviction about communication with spirits, will end for all time any claim I may have to objectivity—in the minds of parapsychologists, at least.

Those critical volumes I read gave me an insight into the accepted way to evaluate phenomena objectively. One should always beware of errors of memory, observation, narration, and inference before accepting any allegedly supernormal experience as valid. I reconsidered my own events with this in mind. I was sure there were few errors of *memory* because of my point of writing down everything unusual the day it occurred—even incidents happening en route like the flat in front of the garage in the middle of the Nevada desert and my mental warning that caused me to discover that the trailer brake was unplugged.

I was fairly confident that my newspaper training helped me to make only slight, if any, errors in *observation* or *narration*, but what about the errors of *inference* proper researchers were so wary of? Would attributing my series of unusual events to spirit intervention be any less rational than ascribing them to coincidence, chance, Heavenly miracles, or a continued although repressed psychological dependence upon a dominating mother?

I learned that Dr. Rhine and his wife Dr. Louisa Rhine had expressed themselves firmly as convinced that there was not one iota of evidence that automatic writing ever came from anything other than the autonamist's subconscious mind. I was therefore faced with the fact that nothing I might say or think would be of any concern or value whatever to anyone at the Lab unless powerful evidence could be produced.

Determined to produce it, I tried to write automatically most evenings, but with very picayune results. Nonetheless, I pushed on in my naïve little effort, trying night after night to establish a smoothly functioning communication system with my Invisibles so that they could give me something so evidential it would *have* to prove survival to my Durham associates. I wasn't successful. Harvey invariably intruded at least once into every letter.

Willing at least to humor me, Dr. Karlis Osis devised a test whereby Mother could try to give me some answers; but I attempted it halfheartedly, sure that Harvey would bollix the whole thing up. Dr. Osis had twenty-five cards on which were pictures of five different colors of five different varieties of flowers. He laid out ten cards face down in his office one evening without looking at them himself. At home later I was to try to learn what they were.

When contact was finally established with her, Mother warned that tests of that sort were very difficult because of the trouble she had getting exact information through my mind; and, knowing on what shaky ground her offspring's convictions were again becoming, there among the scientists, she assured me that if we didn't get any results it did not prove we weren't really corresponding. The extreme difficulties of communication from both sides are disheartening, she said, but I must not give up if there was no success.

After that pep talk we tried picking posies. The first thing she wrote was "red rose" and immediately afterward, "No, that isn't right." Then she wrote "red iris."

"Who ever heard of a *red* iris," I cried, completely discouraged.

"That *is* right," Mother insisted; but obviously we weren't any more successful at this than at anything else. I stopped writing altogether.

The next morning Karlis greeted me in his fascinating Latvian accent, "Vell, vat deed you get?"

"Red iris, isn't that silly?" I told him, and he checked with his cards. The very first one he had laid out for me face down was a picture of an iris of a purplish rose color, and the label under it was "red iris." So the ESP testing team of Betty Smith and her daughter got one out of one, and that's our record. After that Harvey always interfered whenever the cards were laid out for us. And, incidentally, the way parapsychologists score their tests for psi, as they call psychic evidence, I didn't even get credit for that one hit. Two answers had come and only one was right, so it only scored fifty percent. The fact that the writing had denied one and approved the other was of no consequence to Karlis.

A lovable and brilliant technician named Esther Foster befriended me at the Laboratory, and she and I also tried a test together. In an effort to see whether or not Mother could look at something and communicate it to me by drawing, Esther planned to lay a picture which I had never seen on her desk before she left the office one evening. At home Mother was to use my hand to draw it.

But when she started writing that night Mother said Esther had forgotten to leave the picture on her desk.

"Not Esther," I insisted, "she's the most dependable person on earth."

Since we were planning to draw, Mother said she'd go ahead and try to make a picture anyway, just for the practice. Laboring for about an hour and a half, we both had as good a time as if she had been right there in her physical body and we were working on some project together.

It was a most curious and fanciful picture when completed, looking like a small ship with a huge parrot-like figurehead on the prow. And the technique was just what Mother would have used. She spent a long time blacking in each line and space, until I began to get fidgety and wish she'd be more sketchy about it as I would have been. But I had failed her on the flower tests and wasn't going to give up this time until she was finished.

Once the pencil went wild and scratched in a place Mother couldn't have wanted anything drawn because it would have disfigured the nearly completed picture. I laid the pencil on another sheet and, as suspected, there was Harvey trying to write. So I rested a few minutes. When the work was resumed later Mother was back and we went on drawing.

I said, "If you want me to erase the scratches Harvey made, move the pencil up and down." She immediately changed to a vertical motion, so Harvey's contribution was removed and we finished our work of art. It was signed "Betty Smith." On another piece of paper she wrote, "You and your Mother drew a picture together," seeming to feel as triumphant at the accomplishment as her daughter did.

Next morning when I walked into Esther's office, she gave a guilty start and cried, "Oh, Susy, I forgot to lay out the picture for you last night."

"I know. Mother told me," I responded, "but we drew one anyway . . . just for fun."

Now, sometimes I'd still talk with Harvey, but the next time Mother could exert more power than he, she'd insist that I must not ever write with him again. If I was so nutty that one part of me was madly urging me not to write to another part of me, I'd better go hire out for a pecan pie. Had a split personality finally caught up with me? I wondered. Was a crack-up inevitable?

In order to try to eliminate Harvey from the picture, Mother suggested we try the typewriter. She knew the keyboard, having used what she called the "hunt and peck" system for many years, so she assured me she could handle her end of the exchange if it was possible for me to get myself receptive enough.

I started sitting at the typewriter every evening trying to withdraw my mind from active participation. As always, it was difficult and nervewracking if kept up for very long, and unsuccessful in the end result. Finally one night Mother typed:

"It is important that you be in a trance-like state before we can write on the typewriter because it is too hard to write this way. It takes too much effort from me to do it when I have to fight your mind. I am just as eager as you are to write something to you that is my own thought not colored by what you want to have me say. But this takes so much effort on my part that it is hardly worth while."

That is the last time she wrote on the typewriter while we were in Durham. I begged her to keep on, but the results weren't commensurate with what she had to put out, and she refused.

With a little imagination, I could picture our cozy evenings "at home" in the Gingerbread House. Nina was sitting beside Junior, stroking him to keep him sleeping quietly so he wouldn't disturb my efforts to go into trance. No matter how much he barked at noisy neighboring children during an evening, he was always silent during typing sessions. Mother was standing back of me exerting all the mental force she could to make my fingers punch out the right words on the typewriter keys. And Harvey, tobacco juice dripping down his chin whiskers, was lounging on the lampshade, crowing in his delight at our failure to get satisfactory results.

"That'll learn these dang fools to stick to pencil writin' so I can play, too," is what he doubtless smirked to himself.

Well, if I couldn't communicate, books were still available, so I prowled the library all the more fervently, carrying home stacks of volumes every night. Since there was nothing else to do, I read constantly, trying to encompass everything possible about the subject—everything properly scientific, that is. Much of the reading was invariably morbid, even though it consisted only of case histories carefully attested to by numerous witnesses.

I sat cooped up alone in my little turquoise-colored ivory tower, huddling over the fire and reading about phantoms, hallucinations, apparitions. There was no one to talk with, and the principal ingredients of my life were rain and pain in the Carolina winter dampness. How miserable can you get?

Then one night while cleaning my teeth I glanced up at the skylight over my shower and there a ghostly face grimaced at me. Its wrinkled little visage looked so much like an old man's that it could be suspected Harvey had at last learned the art of materialization. Common sense said no, and daylight revealed that what appeared to be facial features were actually leaves and twigs dropped on the outside of the glass. But from then on my shower curtain was kept pulled at night so "he" couldn't leer at me. And it became evident to me that unless very careful, in my depressed existence I might let myself become overly emotional.

That did it. I ran for advice to Professor Hornell Hart of the Sociology Department at Duke, who had recently addressed the Laboratory people and admitted his belief in survival after death. Dr. Hart had had enough personal psychical experiences to make him aware that there is a great deal more to this subject than meets the eye of a merely dispassionate critical scientific observer.

When asked for help, Dr. Hart gave it to me freely. It was he who put all the conclusions I'd half heartedly reached into a usable philosophy adaptable for my needs, starting me on the road to adjusting myself to my peculiar situation. He did not think I was misguided, and suggested I was obviously receptive to assistance from the spirit world. He asserted that it should be put to use not just as a phenomenon with which to try to convince unbelievers, but as such an inspirational thing that my life would radiate my inner peace.

I'd had all the ingredients for contentment, but instead of using them I'd been fighting them and arguing with them and trying to prove them to the satisfaction of others instead of myself. But when I started trying Dr. Hart's suggestions, all the little pieces of the puzzle fell into place creating a beautiful, jubilant happiness that glowed within me for quite a while.

Dr. Hart recommended that instead of trying for more active physical communication I make an effort to achieve silent, passive awareness of Mother's presence. Via pencil later she agreed: "Try to be receptive. Try to attain true relaxation and elevation of your mind. You are closer when you reach out to me."

So I made a conscious effort at projecting, an expanding and surging mentally, and there was a wonderful feeling of intimacy with Mother, and also with Nina (who seems to have remained only a few days after Dr. Hart got me straightened out and then left to work on her own development by staying with another friend who needed help).

I learned to feel close to Mother by being mentally aware instead of by trying active communication. This was much more successful, for there were not so many frustrations. She had told me I had only to be receptive and all the love and aid a Guardian Angel could give would be available, and now I was finally willing to accept it wholeheartedly. Even though I yet argued and rationalized and quibbled with the evidence and knew I always would, still. . . .

I had peace at last, and it seemed that it might be possible to retain it.

Chapter 18

AFTER THE SQUEEZE they had gotten me into, it seemed better to leave those psychic books alone for a while; and, anyway, I was becoming so rainsoaked in Durham I was in danger of breaking out any day with mushrooms, so it appeared wise to start right away for somewhere else. I had begun to feel that there might be something worth writing about, after all, in my experiences; and Bill Hanemann, in Daytona Beach, who used to write those high-powered editorials for *Shopping with Susy*, might be able to help me whip it into readability with his invaluable suggestions. So within a couple of days after my talk with Dr. Hart, I hitched up and started for Florida.

Never having hauled a trailer in the rain, I drove slowly and carefully south, riding in a constant downpour for two days. But soon the car took the bit in its teeth and started speeding with eagerness to get to warmth and sunshine again; and the first faint whiffs of Florida smelled like Arpege to us as we flitted across the fragrant, flowering state.

It was in a palm-shaded trailer park in Holly Hill, on the river just above Daytona, that we settled down. There Junior and I began adjusting our shape into a design for peaceful living after all our recent traveling and travail. Time was passed visiting with old friends, reading, listening to concertos on my record player, hiking with my dog on the beach, playing bridge, basking in the sunshine attended by caroling mockingbirds . . . and somehow existence had never seemed lovelier.

Impressed by my serenity, friends were eager to learn what precious substance I had mined in the West.

"Whatever happened to you?" they said, and "Where did you get that spark?" So I told them.

The more I talked about it, the more it was revealed that many could go me two or three better—phenomena-wise. Until one begins to speak freely of psychic experiences, he just isn't aware that so many people have them. They may have a precognitive dream that came true or a simple telepathic episode, or they may see ghosts as a matter of habit—the point is that they rarely mention it for fear of being misunderstood. But when they discover someone they are sure won't laugh at them, they are eager to discuss the strange things that happen to them.

Yet the majority of those who hadn't had any personal encounters themselves found the subject engaging, also. They wanted something of what I'd gotten out of it. There were very few blank walls when ordinary unscientific people were told about my psychical research.

I asked about local mediums, eager to attend any sessions available. There was always the chance that professional sensitives might be able to give me more authentic evidence of survival than anything achievable alone. I have made it a habit ever since to case mediums in each new community I visit, taking careful shorthand notes of everything they tell me. A glance over my records reveals that much of what has been received is hit or miss; but some of it is quite exceptional.

My first Florida experience with a medium was with Mrs. Springstead in Daytona Beach. She was small, plump and pretty, and her specialty was psychometry. Psychometry is the faculty of divining knowledge about an object, or about a person connected with it, by holding that object. One possible explanation of why it works is the idea that everything has a force field around it and this force field retains impressions.

A basket was passed around and members of the audience were asked to place personal belongings in it; then Mrs. Springstead took rings or watches or billfolds at random from the basket and gave messages to their owners, who were unidentified until she asked them to claim the object at the end of her reading.

I went in as a stranger and did not say anything to anyone except "How do you do." But when Mrs. Springstead picked my ring out of the basket she said that its owner had excellent spirit influences around her. Then she told me my mother was informing her that we had communication via automatic writing.

"You have a wonderful mother who says that you talk to her frequently," she said, "but she just wishes you could hear her answer you. She's eager to make you see her, and she hopes to show herself to you some day."

(Later, at home, I said, "Mother, if you ever do find yourself able to become visible, *please* don't do it unless some skeptical person is with me who can see you too . . . or I'll go completely *mad* trying to tell people what happened without a witness to verify it!")

Mrs. Springstead then said, "You make your living in your own home," which seemed to me fairly accurate, since I had once again determined to become a professional writer. Then she asked, "Does Texas mean anything to you?" Not waiting for an answer she continued, "I'm told that San Antone, Texas, is closely associated with you."

"It's the city where I was raised," I replied. Then she said my work would be successful with Mother's assistance. That was all she gave me, but it was enough.

I knew one thing for sure from it, anyway. She had not been reading my mind . . . for nowhere even in my most elemental depths could she have dredged up the pronunciation "An*tone*." No self-respecting former resident of San Anto*nio* would tolerate San Antone for one minute.

The next Sunday found me at a different church, where I received only the brief message that an older man with a beard was with me. I thought, "That damned Harvey again." But she went on to say that the man looked like me from the nose up. She added, "He's related to you. You have a picture of him at home." The only picture at home of an older male relative with a beard was of my great-grandfather. I guess you could say there is a family resemblance, especially in the wave of his hair that was just like Mother's. But I tossed this off with the thought, "Who knows the resourcefulness of that Harvey. Now he's claiming to look like me."

Disappointed with my message, I didn't slip any money into the basket which was passed around for a "love offering." I didn't have that much affection for another medium's seeing Harvey. And then to proclaim a resemblance! That was getting to be just a bit too much!

I returned to the Gingerbread House and took pencil in hand for my evening attempt at a chat with Mother. (Yes, it was still a regular custom I hadn't been able to give up despite Dr. Hart's advice.) Harvey started writing as usual and said, "Your mother is not here." I asked if it were he the medium had seen, fully expecting the same smug affirmative he'd given me last fall in Los Angeles, but this time he said, "No."

"Who was it then?"

"Your great-grandfather."

"That's hard to believe."

"But," he wrote, "it's true." Then I insisted again that he let Mother write. He pestered a few minutes longer, however, and then the pencil very forcibly wrote, "Anderson."

I doubted if either Harvey or Mother or my subconscious mind would have thought of Grandpa Anderson by just his last name that way. I asked, "Who is writing?"

The answer came: "I'm your mother's grandfather."

"Was it you the medium saw tonight?"

"It was."

"Can you identify yourself further?"

"I'm Robert Ingram Anderson."

"Where did you live?"

"Oakland, Maryland."

"Is there anything special you want to talk to me about?"

"It is anything of which there is a question."

Just then Harvey pushed in with his silly "I love you Harvey" and other ineptitudes. After several attempts to dislodge him, in that battle of wills it was apparently necessary to wage with him, Grandpa wrote again: "It is Anderson now."

"Is it really you?"

"I'm really Grandpa."

"When will we ever get rid of Harvey?"

"Only when we are able to teach him, but he is a primitive person."

"What can I do about him?"

"You must not ever let him write to you. When he starts you must cease writing at once. It is the only way it will be conquered."

"Are you sure this is the only way?"

"Yes, it is true."

After that Harvey took over and I couldn't get Grandpa again. I thought it had been noticeable how differently he had expressed himself from the way Mother wrote. She always spoke as simply as possible, but his style was stilted and he used words like "cease," "primitive," "conquered." And he identified himself as "your mother's grandfather" instead of as my great-grandfather as I thought of him.

Naturally I wondered if the medium had just mentioned a man with a family resemblance because everyone has such in the spirit world and then my subconscious mind (that poor old catchall which had been catching all the blame for so long) had come up with the right answer in producing Grandpa by automatic writing. Role-playing by the subconscious mind is said by some critics to be the explanation for all the different characters produced by any medium. Somehow this didn't sound too convincing to me in the light of everything else that had happened—although as an isolated incident, that certainly would have been the interpretation to accept.

Then this other possibility occurred to me—that perhaps my great-grandfather might often have been visiting this descendant he'd never met in the flesh, but couldn't make himself known and wasn't able to write to her until she became aware of his presence from some outside source. Does that make sense, too? Since that time several psychics have given me the name Robert; and in 1965 in Seattle, Washington, medium Keith Milton Rhinehart told me definitely that a grandfather named Robert was my guide who stays with me. Keith gave me some personal information purporting to come from this Robert which nobody was likely to have known by normal means. This made me feel more secure about my earlier experience when Robert Ingram Anderson allegedly communicated by automatic writing.

I decided to return to this medium who had produced a relative over fifty-four years buried to see if she could help me to remove Harvey. She gave me an afternoon appointment at which I immediately explained my problems with my rude intruder. When she asked me to write to him, he eagerly participated as soon as I picked up the pencil, glad to be the center of attention. Then the medium announced that she could see Harvey. She gave him a little lecture and threatened to sic her Indian spirit guides on him if he didn't behave and let me write without interference.

The idea that American Indians are so frequently used as guides seems far-fetched to many people. But because they were so close to nature while on earth, deceased Indians are supposed to have more etheric power, or something; and, actually, in the days before the White Man came with his corruptions all great braves were mystics, commonly inducing trance and visions by prayer, fasting, and lonely vigil. Whether we understand it or not, many psychics claim to have Indians, primarily as bodyguards to keep spirit intruders away.

This medium told me that she could hear Harvey's answer to her threat. "What can they do to hurt me?" he asked with his usual flippancy. "They can't kill me."

She thought they could run him off, though, and so she invoked their aid. I went home reasonably reassured. I didn't try any writing for a whole week after that, confident the venerable braves had done their good deed, but reluctant to attempt to find out. When my pencil was picked up again in the loose way that indicated my willingness to palaver, Harvey was still there, boasting, "I'm not afraid of Indians." When assured that because of his meanness I would have to give up automatic writing altogether, he wrote, "You won't stop."

"Yes, I will."

"No, you won't."

I said, "Harvey, you're bad. You'll have a terrible time always if you don't learn to behave better."

He replied, "You'll come over and all will be well."

"Why, you don't think for one moment I'll have anything to do with you after I die?"

"You'll have to."

"I'm forced to give up writing because of you," I said regretfully.

"Not true," he wrote.

"For the last time before I stop altogether, will you let Mother write to me?"

"No."

So even unleashing the Indians on him didn't remove Harvey. Well, I didn't doubt either their bravery or their power, if there really had been any Indians there at all. Maybe there just weren't enough of them to take on a tough old bird like Harvey. There's always the chance that he might have been an Indian fighter himself back in the early days of the Wild West and knew a few tricks of his own. So I just gave up with Harvey, planning to try to cope with him some other time when maybe a more formidable tribe could be assembled to send after his scalp.

Or . . . if it were only possible to get word to his wife that he was here chasing this redhead. . . .

Chapter 19

||| HAD AN INTERESTING, if unpleasant, experience with psychic healing shortly after my arrival in Holly Hill. I was laundering my clothes with totally unfamiliar trailer court equipment which had a wringer that worked electrically but had to be hand fed—so I fed it my hand. Didn't actually mean to, but the manager of the park said something to me just as I was putting a small towel through the wringer. As I looked up to answer him my left hand followed the towel right on through.

I yelled and bounced around, trying to find the gadget that released the wringer. The manager finally got himself in motion and punched the right button, allowing me to retain a hand which it was doubtful would ever be of any further value to me. Inspection revealed no broken bones or lacerations, but the thumb and first two fingers began to inflate before my eyes, and they throbbed painfully.

I attempted to continue working, although approaching the wringer again unnerved me; so the manager volunteered to put the rest of my clothes through for me, feeling considerably like a hero about the entire incident.

I immediately applied the positive thinking, denial of damage, and request for aid from a higher source that were supposed to be of help in such an instance—and apparently they worked. The next day there was hardly a twinge of pain from the hand, and I didn't miss an hour at the typewriter because of it. It was my second experience of this sort. Once while we were in Salt Lake City, when frying tacos I had put my hand down into a big pot to drop a tortilla into the hot grease and a bubble burst and scalded my palm. It quickly became scarlet in color and hurt inordinately.

Margaret Adams, who was very big for Christian Science in those days, had paid absolutely no attention to me whatever, until my moaning finally caught her notice.

"Does it really hurt?" she asked, and received emphatic assurance that it did. So she "worked" for me for a few minutes. In those days I didn't believe in faith healing of any kind. I had no notion that how she thought about my hand could help me, but something did very suddenly. The agony left immediately, the scald never blistered, and there was not even any red in the hand by the following day.

After these two experiences I learned to use healing of such minor wounds as a matter of course. If I have any kind of a superficial burn now I tell it to go away, that it absolutely will not be tolerated, while at the same time running cold water over it. The combination of the cold water and denying that they can give me any trouble has removed several painful burns for me. For those who immediately surmise that it is the cold water and not the proper mental attitude, here is an instance that occurred in Miami some years later.

I spilled a mug of hot coffee in my lap. Immediately undressing, I discovered that my abdomen and thighs were scarlet, and they were agonizingly painful. Just then there was a ring of the doorbell and clothing had to be put back over the burn because it was some men to caulk the windows of the apartment, leaking after a recent hurricane. So they went into the bedroom to work and I stood around in the living room and suffered quietly.

Finally I remembered my special trick and firmly announced that enough was just exactly enough of such foolishness.

"I won't have this a moment longer," I stated, really meaning it. "This stinging has got to stop this very instant!"

Do you know, it did? That exact minute! There was one bean-sized blister resulting from this burn, but nothing ever hurt again.

I was attending a bridge luncheon at the Coral Gables Country Club one day when my partner arrived in misery. She said, "I'm afraid I won't be able to concentrate on the cards today. I just burned my thumb so badly that it's giving me fits."

"Come with me," I said dramatically. "It can be cured." I took her into the ladies' room and ran cold water over her hand for a while. Then I held the sore thumb in my own hand and talked to it, telling it we didn't want to hear any more from it. Certainly my technique would never be approved by Christian Science . . . or any other kind of faith healing, probably; but I just do my best with the little I know about such things. And quite often it works.

We went back to our luncheon, then played cards for several hours. A time or two I remembered the sore thumb, but didn't mention it, not wanting to call my partner's attention to it. Just as we were preparing to leave, she gave a start, then said, "Do you know, this is the first time I've thought of that burn all afternoon! It hasn't hurt me once!"

You see, it can be done on occasion. I have even used this system on arthritis discomfort, with it working sometimes and not others. Unfortunately I do not yet have the ability psychically to overcome any major illnesses or pain. Or if so, I don't know it and haven't been able to practice it on myself.

An interesting healing occurred during a business trip to New

York City in the spring of 1970—in fact, it was the occasion when I made the contract with Macmillan for this book. During my two months there I attended several meditation classes led by Hilda Charlton, a delightful and talented group leader. I walked in late to my first meeting, unknown to almost everyone there. At the time I had been overexerting physically as one does in New York, walking much too much, and my right knee was paining me so that it was doubtful if I would be able to sit through the evening without a lot of squirming, at least.

A chair was placed for me between two women who were strangers to me, and I sat down quietly so as not to disturb the program already in progress.

After the hour of interesting discussion and meditation was over, the woman on my right turned to me and asked, "Did you have pain in your right knee when you came in?"

"Yes."

"How is it now?"

I turned my attention to my knee, then, for the first time, and realized that it had not hurt once during the entire meeting. Looking at her in surprise that she should have known anything about it, "It's fine," I said.

"I took the pain from you," she told me, and was gratefully thanked.

I saw this same lady the following Monday at another meeting and she asked me how I was feeling. I told her that my knee had behaved itself beautifully ever since she took the pain away.

"I still have it," she said. I suggested that she let it go, for it really did not seem fair for her to have my pain, no matter in what supernormal manner she had acquired it. She must have done so, for not long afterward it returned to its rightful, if reluctant, owner.

Chapter 20

THE INTEREST of my Daytona friends in the stories I had to tell about my efforts to start a communication system with my mother inspired me to decide to get to work on my written account of it. So I started steadily telling it all to my typewriter.

One day it talked back.

At a loss for words as I pecked away at the very erudite treatise the Preface was becoming, I slumped in my chair to relax, letting my fingers lie lightly on the typewriter keys.

"I wish I knew what I'm talking about," I said aloud. Then my hands began to type slowly, seemingly of their own volition. What they wrote was as different from what I wanted to say as popcorn is from peanut butter.

I didn't quite like my typewriter making light of my dignified ideas this way. My book was supposed to have significance, yet here it was being told not to take itself so seriously. Don't push your conclusions at your reader, my typewriter intimated. Splash him with drops from your font of inspiration and let him brush them off or absorb them as he wishes.

After the initial surprise at being given an argument by this mechanical busybody at my fingertips, it suddenly dawned on me that Mother had found the way to communicate again. We hadn't tried automatic writing by pencil since Harvey lowered the boom, but had been well satisfied with mental communion. Mother had actually been sharing many of my daily experiences. Whenever I tried to pound a nail or sew a placket or cook an unfamiliar dish I inwardly asked her advice and assistance, and then went ahead with the task confidently and successfully. Mother was the type to wish to help with the chores, and she liked being allowed to take part in my life. In attempting to have a mental communion with her, as Dr. Hart had suggested, I was enjoying myself immensely.

Now she was voluble once again—apparently I was relaxed enough that she could get through to me on the typewriter—and she was indicating her interest in working on the book with me. I was delighted, and took the occasion to ask her to answer many questions that had been occurring to me. One was this Guardian Angel business.

"I really am your guardian," she wrote. "I protect you. If you will keep yourself receptive to the thoughts I send you, success can be yours, for together we can build for you a life of happiness and accomplishment."

"But, Mother, don't you have anything more important to do than hang around with me?"

"You are the most important thing in the world to me," she answered. "But anyway, this is my work as well as my pleasure. As part of our development we must stay with someone to help him, and naturally I chose you."

Before he progresses from the etheric plane, each spirit remains for his own advancement for some time with earth persons to whom he is attracted by affection or mutual interests or his own needs. James went into a good bit about this later, explaining how a spirit goes about giving assistance and how he develops character because of it.

He led into it by saying that in the spirit world an individual has no physical body with which to contend. I liked that word "contend" for that seems to be what I always have been doing with this corporeal calamity in which I reside.

"Most of your time on earth is spent taking care of your bodies," James points out, "for they must be housed, clothed, fed, and kept clean before anything else is done." Then you have to waste half your life sleeping in order to "recharge your batteries," and eating, exercising, dressing and undressing, cooking, sewing, cleaning or providing the income in order to buy everything that you and your family need.

"In my world nothing so mundane is necessary," James says. "If I wish to spend time thinking about earthly activities, I may do so; but I do not *have* to. I can rest if I wish, but I never really get tired. I could eat if I cared to, but it is not necessary. Nothing *must* be done which takes me from my efforts to improve my mind and character."

I was delighted when both Mother and James stated that there are many pleasures in the next world, for I've missed a great many of them here. I have always loved to dance and have done little of it in recent years; so I'm going to dance most of the first year after I die . . . and that's a promise. James explains how you can do things like that and also still have time to be somebody's Guardian Angel.

"I may spend my days working with those of you on earth whom I am attempting to help; but, not having to sleep, I may then spend my nights in gay carousal if I so desire. An enlightened spirit would want nothing so frivolous—but I could if I wished, for what I design and execute with my mind is an actual reality to me. Instead, I spend my time in many other of the various pastimes which are available to me—such as concerts, lectures from some of the greatest men who ever lived, and entertainments of all kinds which are more rewarding than any of the most wonderful offered on earth." But, Mr. James, you will save a waltz for me, won't you?

"When a man dies," my mentor goes on, "his first exciting discovery, after his reunion with his loved ones, is that all his memories are intact and available to him. If he wishes to remember any moment of his life, it is there in all detail. You may have fun with this for a while, recalling persons and places you haven't thought of in a long time. You soon become aware that this can cause you real anguish, however, as you allow yourself to relive some of your most traumatic experiences. So you stop the self-torture. When you begin your progression, it will be necessary for you to make a systematic survey of your life, going into all your memories carefully to learn where you made mistakes and to recall all the occasions where you did less than your best in a situation. Many unhappy events will have to be reviewed in detail so that you can learn what to do to make amends for them. You are now in a position to see the reasons for many of the errors you made in early life. Some of them can be rectified by thinking them through from a constructive point of view and understanding all the situations involved. Others may have been so unfortunate that more will have to be done in order to correct them. Yet each incident of your life will have to be gone over with the object of making amends for anything necessary. In many cases you may, even at this late date, be able to alter the situation by your proper thinking and corrective actions.

"As an example of how you go about remaking yourself, let us suppose that in reviewing your life you discover that you had a great many prejudices of a very deep-seated nature. You may have taken adequate care of your family and died thinking that in general you were a relatively decent sort of chap. Proper reconnaissance of your life now, however, reveals that there was one entire area in which you had a complete blank spot: you had racial prejudice. Therefore, no matter how tolerant you believed yourself to have been in other areas, you actually have a tremendous amount to learn. When it was impossible for you to think of a Negro as anything but an inferior person, you yourself were inferior. Or if you, as a black man, berated your white brothers in toto for the injustices perpetrated by specific individuals, you were equally guilty of racial prejudice. You actually hated mankind, loving only those who were like yourself, and so truly loving no man.

"Now that you have faced the fact that you went through life with a distorted image of the truth, you will have to decide how to correct this. You will discuss it with those of your associates who are more advanced than you; and you go to a teacher and listen to some of his lectures on this problem and how to cope with it. You will be told that until you can feel equally at home with anyone who is black or white or yellow or red you will not have learned brotherly love."

James says that if you were a white man with this problem of learning compassion, you will probably now decide that the best form of growth for you is to go to live in the terrestrial home of an underprivileged Negro. This will not be easy for you at first, when you may have constant revulsion at what you consider to be a debased way of life. Much of your effort in the beginning will have to be spent just in keeping yourself from leaving your appointed task. But after a while you will find yourself becoming interested in the daily lives of the family with whom you are making your home.

"From your vantage point of invisibility, you will be able to observe everything that happens in this family's life, and you will be aware of what each member is thinking. Soon you will begin to know what it means to be a black man in a predominantly white civilization. Then you will become sympathetic and will want to help these people. How will you do this? Your thoughts are all you have to work with, and so anything you attempt to do will be difficult for you.

"Let us say, for instance, that you learn by secretly visiting around in the town that a racist extremist is planning to plant a bomb under the house of the Negro family with whom you live. What will you do? Warn them, naturally, but how? Once in a great while a spirit finds conditions such that he is able to make himself seen or heard. Certainly if this family saw a ghost they would run out of the house quickly enough. Even if they *heard* an audible warning from you they would very likely heed it. But making a physical manifestation from the spirit world takes a great deal of effort. If you haven't the power to make yourself appear in a ghostly form or cause yourself to be heard, perhaps you can arouse in the most psychic member of the family a vision, or a dream that will give him the warning. If none of these measures is effective, you will then attempt to impress the family's thoughts with the danger they are in. You might find someone receptive enough that you can get through to him, and he will then think he has a hunch to look under the porch, where he finds the bomb, or to vacate the house in time to escape the explosion.

"Yet again, in the short time you have, you may get nowhere. You may repeat your admonitions endlessly, giving them all the force and thought power within you, without achieving noticeable results. The only thing to do then is to stick your fingers in your ears and wait for the blast. I am quite sure that by the time the bomb has exploded and you are trying somehow to help the bleeding children, your aversion to black men will have changed altogether. You will probably then have to work on your character to keep from blindly hating the whites who have perpetrated this crime."

James says you're seldom likely to come up against a situation quite as drastic as a bomb scare; but other events will be nearly as impressive to you.

"If you have stayed with this family any length of time you will undoubtedly have become fond of the children. It is not possible to look into the mind of a child and not learn to love him. Now, what if you should begin to realize that the ten-year-old boy of this family is exposed to the danger of becoming a juvenile delinquent? You certainly would make every possible effort to guide him in a different direction—and your thoughts are your only contact with him, remember. You can beam him constructive ideas constantly, encouraging him to stay in school and study his lessons and refuse to try drugs. You may be able to guide his thinking toward going to Sunday School and associating with playmates who are less inclined to lead him astray. But you will undoubtedly tend to become desperate about the child on occasion—as hopeless as the mother or father who are aware of the importance of his acquiring a sense of values which will not be corrupted, yet do not know how to encourage and protect him adequately.

"Yes, it will not be easy to try to aid this family, with only your thoughts to use; but as you come to understand the problems of these people you will be learning to love your fellow men. By the time you have lived a lifetime with them, watching the boy grow to manhood—perhaps becoming a good citizen largely because of the influence of your positive thoughts for him—you will have a genuine knowledge of what it means to walk in the shoes of a Negro. Will it then be possible for you to feel superior to any race? How can a man reject another by the color of his skin when he knows deeply all the problems which beset the heart of one of such pigmentation?"

Now, perhaps in evaluating your life you discover that you were especially intolerant of those who had different habits from yours, particularly if they had them to excess. It is necessary, says my communicant, for you to overcome your intolerance, even of evildoers. That surprised me, yet I realize he is right that you have every reason to hate the crime but not the criminal. Intolerance is bigotry. A bigot may declare his dislike of a vice, but he will seldom make any effort to assist those who have such weaknesses, because he thinks himself superior to them. (All us bigots will have to get over this.) Perhaps whenever you encountered a drunkard during your life you scorned him, instead of pitying him. Now you must learn to love him! How will you do it? You will go and live with the alcoholic and attempt to help him!

"Perhaps there was such an afflicted person in your acquaintance," wrote my invisible associate. "Instead of ever realizing that he was sick, you reviled and scorned him and spoke of him disparagingly to his neighbors and friends. You even once suggested to his wife that she should leave him rather than put up with such disgrace. Now, after your death, you realize that you must learn to have compassion for such a man as this, to the point of understanding him and his problems, and so you choose him to assist as the object of your personal campaign for self-improvement.

"In this man's home, reading his mind, you begin to understand the terrible humiliation he undergoes each time he comes out of one of his drinking episodes. You observe what an intolerable hardship it is on him to realize what he has done to his family and to know that he cannot make amends for it. You hear the impossible arguments he has within himself before he succumbs once again to his desire for drink. Can you now judge him?

"When you also become aware that there are a number of earthbound entities around this man with the alcohol problem, inciting him to drink and making his resistance twice as ineffective, you will be even more eager to help him rid himself of his difficulties. Talking to these spirits who hang around him, attempting to convince them that their existence will always be sordid if they stay so close to earth's unhappiest people, you will occasionally be able to give them new ideas which may cause them to start their progression and leave the poor alcoholic. If you can do this for him, your time with him will have been well spent for everyone concerned. As for your own reaction—you will now understand fully the problems of a drinker, and you will have grown a great deal in wisdom."

A few more efforts of this sort on your part will turn you into a truly compassionate spirit, says James, and then you can work on other aspects of your character in which you recognize weaknesses. It won't be any less difficult to accomplish these goals than to encompass the lessons of tolerance you have just been learning. None of the work on your character is easy, but it will all have to be done before you can progress into further planes of existence. It certainly would seem to be simpler to be aware on earth that you must gain from each experience, for you would then have a head start "over there" afterward.

Still, and I love James for these reassurances he always gives us, "Once you have put your foot on the ladder of upward progression, nothing can stop you. You will be so entranced with the adventures you are having, and so interested to see the results, that you will greet happily each new opportunity which presents itself."

Chapter 21

IN SOME of her initial typewritten messages Mother spoke of the fact that Guardian Angel relationships could be very pleasant, particularly if those on earth could know of their assistant's presence and acknowledge it. If it is someone you were very close to, you frequently can feel his proximity even if you have not tried to develop your psychic sensitivity as I have done; and when you think you have a feeling of his presence, be happy about it. But don't, for goodness sake, sit down with pencil or typewriter and try to exchange opinions with him on current events or politics, or even philosophy. Be forewarned by the gruesome involvements soon to be related here.

"Even if you can't achieve actual response from him, you can talk to your spirit companions," Mother wrote.

"No, ma'am," I objected. "I am not about to recommend that people go around mumbling in their beards."

"I didn't mean that," she answered. "You can speak to him mentally. When he knows you recognize his presence it is bliss for him, because the greatest hardship of death is never being able to make your loved ones aware that you are still with them."

"That's different," I said.

As we continued with our communication on this and other subjects, I was to begin having an accumulation of small bits of evidence that were peculiar, to say the least.

One night Mother told me she wanted me to read *Our Unseen Guest* by Darby and Joan in order to get some new idea which she didn't seem to be able to implant at the moment. It didn't occur to me that it might not be in any of the local libraries, for although I hadn't visited them since my interest in the subject began, it is a standard work on many psychic shelves.

So, "I wonder which library has it?" I mused.

My fingers were quiet on the keys for nearly five minutes and I was puzzled. Try as I might, it wasn't possible to get any response. Then Mother typed, "It isn't in either of the public libraries."

"So that's where you've been. I missed you," I said. "Well, it's probably at the Book Nook." The typewriter was quiet a few moments more as she went there to investigate, returning to deny that also.

Being skeptical that this well-known book wasn't to be found locally, I called all three libraries the next morning to check; and it was true, they didn't have it. I later borrowed it from a friend and read it for Mother.

Bill Hanemann, who was presiding over my writing in the capacity of chief consultant on grammar, rhetoric, and, "Susy, for Christ's sake why can't you *ever* learn the difference between 'lie' and 'lay'?" was finding his mordant Hollywood-conditioned mind occasionally disturbed by some of the things with which he was being confronted.

One day he was twitting me as usual about my etheric enthusiasms.

"If you're going to believe all this twaddle I'd like some personal evidence," he said. "Maybe it's catching after all."

"So all right. I'll ask Mother to tell us what you're thinking this very minute." I put my fingers on the machine; but nothing happened. Bill and I discussed the fact that, anyway, even if we got what had been on his mind it wouldn't necessarily be evidence of survival, just testimony for the existence of telepathy. But supernormal one way or another, to say the least. Still nothing happened. Then the typewriter wrote, "Yes, I know what he was thinking but I'm not able to tell you now. Wait until you're not trying so hard."

Bill, of course, thought this was a cop out.

Two nights later, after my fingers had been beating the keys for several hours receiving information about her world from Mother, I said, "Reception's as good now as it ever is, see if you can tell me what Bill was thinking the other day when we put you on the spot."

"A picture of you," she typed.

"What picture?" I asked, my mind busily trying to remember some photograph Bill might have seen. Naturally my thoughts got in the way of her reply.

Finally Mother sighed—I know very well that she sighed—and wrote, "You won't let me say what I want to. Just tell Bill he was thinking about a picture of you and let it go at that."

So the next time my severest critic dropped by I said, "Were you thinking of a picture of me the other day?" He gave me a startled stare. In fact, it was several minutes before he regained his composure sufficiently to tell me that just at the time I had said, "I'll get Mother to tell me what you're thinking" a ray of sunshine had come through the slats of the Venetian blind and had hit my hair in such a way that he had wondered if it would be possible to catch it with a color film. He was a photography buff and enchanted by unusual effects.

After Bill considered my message a few minutes he began to back out of it, as those who are trying to be strictly objective almost always do. (As I myself have done so often.) Maybe his lips had unknowingly whispered the words "picture of Susy" without either of us hearing him and my subconscious mind had picked it up. Maybe I had unconsciously lip read it. We go very far afield when we try to account for some of these incidents by reaching for explanations that do not involve the supernormal. Maybe, he finally concluded, there is such a thing as *delayed* telepathy.

"Or maybe I just happen to have an unusually bright typewriter," I said with just the slightest touch of sarcasm.

No use arguing with him about it, though. Why *should* he believe I was corresponding with a mother who'd been dead seven years? But for Bill the trouble was that he was never able to find any other explanation for the incident that made any more sense than the survival hypothesis. He decided the safest thing to do was to ignore it.

Soon there was another interesting exchange of this nature. My friend Irene Kellogg was in a hurry for a picture of a dove of peace which she needed as a model for a float the Pilot Club was entering in a forthcoming parade. But she couldn't find one, and her committee was ready to start decorating. She bewailed her problem over the phone.

"Maybe there's something here," I suggested. "I'll ask Mother." I went back to my typewriter and Mother wrote that we had exactly what Irene needed if she could just tell me where it was. Then, since I was sure the only place we could have such a picture was in a magazine or book, several highly colored answers came giving pages and issues, which revealed instead the faces of foreign diplomats or advertisements for cars or recipes for elaborately gooey cakes.

Just then a neighbor dropped in and when told I was trying to get a message from my mother she wanted to make use of my talented typewriter for her own needs.

"Ask my husband if I should sell my trailer," she said, so I wasted valuable time from my dove hunt trying for a reply which would amaze and convert Mrs. Thripp.

Mother wouldn't cooperate at all with this delay. My fingers wrote nothing while I was trying to receive word for my neighbor; but finally an abrupt "Get dove for Irene" was typed. I continued talking to my guest, however, while allowing my fingers to lie idly on the keys. After a few minutes, while we waited but got nothing, the typewriter wrote, rather crossly, it seemed to me, "You are not doing this right. Ask Mrs. Thripp to come back later."

When the lady left and I was back to giving Mother my full attention, the answer came quickly: "My autograph book." I hunted this out of a carton in the back of the car where it had been stored since the year before, and in it were two big doves with olive branches in their beaks—the sort of sugar-coated-looking pictures that used to be on Valentines. They were exactly what Irene needed. After we'd seen the parade a few days later we agreed that Irene's dove was the best thing in it; and Irene told everyone Susy's mother was responsible.

Yes, I had seen those doves in Mother's album from time to time during my life, possibly even when packing it in the carton before leaving Oakland the previous August. I can't say positively that my subconscious was not recalling that they were there, so this isn't offered as possible proof of communication. Yet to me it is of value because of the way it illustrates how Mother maintained her own persevering character, even interrupting me when she felt it necessary to do so.

She was always so consistently herself in her communications, expressing her own personality, having her own normal reactions to things. They are seldom like mine, but invariably like hers. If I tried to give her credit for powers she didn't have, she corrected me. She made no claim to be Superman, although with my lack of knowledge about conditions in her sphere I was often tempted to expect her to act like him. What is even more convincing, she refuses to accept credit for every act of friendly fortune in my life, which I'm quite likely now to attribute to my Guardian Angel.

One night I had a pot roast in the pressure cooker. Instructions were to cook it for half an hour, but within twenty minutes such a savory smell was assailing me that I was afraid the meat would burn. So I asked Mother, "Is my roast done yet?"

There was a brief pause then she typed, "Not quite."

"How much longer will it take?"

She completely surprised me with her reply: "I don't know. I never used a pressure cooker." And it was true, as I counted up the years on my fingers, for Mother had died before we got ours.

About this story of my life and times which was trying to get itself down on paper, she had ideas of her own. She didn't hesitate to revise, repair, or reject where she felt necessary. We often argued about pet phrases of mine which seemed to her awkward or not in good taste, and she usually won out eventually. She also admitted when she was wrong, and once after having typed an entire paragraph she said later, "I know I gave that to you but it's no good. Take it out."

As I first wrote about my fascinating communications and the exciting implications, I had a missionary's zeal, being tempted to feel an obligation to spread the word to the world. Impressed as I am with the magnitude of this concept, that reaction was almost inevitable. Mother talked me out of it, however. She said I must stick to my own simple style of writing and just tell my story as it occurred. So that is what this book tries to do. It won't impress any of those who are looking to be impressed either by big words, authoritarian statements, or esoteric mysticism. But perhaps others will be entertained, and, hopefully, given something new to think about.

Mother helped me every day as I wrote, and then she said she thought conditions were good enough that she could start dictating a special chapter of her own to explain about immortality. So we put the reminiscences aside and wrote at a rapid clip about her world. I sat there hour after hour trying to make my mind a blank as she wrote through me, yet still aware of every word that was written. She claimed that this actually was beneficial, even if more difficult for us both, because then if the information was received incorrectly she could tell me so and make the necessary changes.

"No, that's not right, fix it," was her most frequent interruption as day after day and night after night we polished each sentence and each paragraph until she was satisfied with it.

Some of what she wrote I had already read in more complicated language in the books of Stewart Edward White and others who have tried to depict life in the next world. Of the rest, I have since seen much that is almost identical in other books about survival. But there is also a certain amount of amplification and explanation here that to my knowledge has not been published anywhere before. The reason is that whenever Mother made a statement not thoroughly understandable I questioned her until it had been clarified. This has been continued with the more involved material furnished by the entity called James after his advent early in 1957.

Mother and James both seem to want to put pressure on no one to accept what they state to be the truth about the survival of the human soul. They say they don't care one way or another what people believe about conditions after death. We will find out the truth of that soon enough. They have only one goal, but this they emphasize strongly: "Our object is to convince the world of nothing except *the need for continual conscious spiritual and personal growth.*"

It appears that all the troubles encountered in the hereafter would be mitigated a thousandfold if people only understood while still on earth that we must ever be aware of the need to realize our own greatest potential. Those who die so unenlightened that they become earthbound are hazards, and the time must come when they are eliminated. This can only be done by not allowing them to die in such a low state.

Mother, in what I have always referred to as "her chapter," gave a summary of all the vast amount of material James was later to elaborate on. At the time "Mother's Chapter" was written, there were assuredly various invisible ones who were working to get the information into my head and through my fingertips. It does not surprise me that the writing style of all the alleged communicants sounds similar no matter who is purporting to write, and also that it sounds somewhat like my style when I try to write with dignity. It must be remembered that it has all been filtered through my mind, no matter how much I have tried to keep my thoughts from coloring it. It must also be realized that I do not *know* all this information . . . how could it possibly have been unconsciously *instigated* by me?

The communicants have since stated that the reason they can give philosophy through me is because I had no firmly held preconceived notions about any philosophical or religious concepts. This, they explained, was what made me especially useful to them as a channel who would not distort their material by my own opinions.

The fact that I am awake and somewhat alert when the typing is going on is said by the communicants to be an advantage, because I can then be critical about the wording of the information received and ask about anything which does not seem to make sense to me or which is confused or unclear. They do not object to my querying them, for it is my own reception I am questioning, not the validity of their information.

I have also been told that the reason the team of Betty Smith and her daughter were used as the means of such communication was because our characters are in some ways so much alike, particularly in our stubborn desire and determination to do what we attempt as well as possible and stick to it until we accomplish our goals.

The following chapter is the one called "Mother's Chapter."

Chapter 22

"THE CONSCIOUS SPIRIT of each individual born on earth eventually achieves unity with God," my mother wrote. "I do not mean the anthropomorphic (like a man) God of earth conception, for that is limiting to a force which cannot be limited, which is inconceivable in its infinity. God instead is the state of highest awareness, power most superlative, illimitable love, infinite consciousness.

"When each conscious spirit attains his highest development he is incorporated into this great ultimate which is God. Yet he still retains his individual personality and identity. This can be understood when one thinks of the ocean which is increased by every molecule of water which enters and becomes one with it; and yet upon analysis each molecule is found to maintain its own individuality.

"The same Natural Laws which systematically bring the flowers into bloom and the trees into leaf and which cause the planets to move in their orbits also cause each consciousness from the first instant of its inception in an earth body inevitably to continue its movement forward until it finally achieves the ultimate, although the free will of each individual controls the length of time his progress will take.

"Usually, when a man dies, a spirit who has his interest at heart welcomes him and explains to him that he has passed through the experience called death but that actually he is still alive, and that he has maintained his conscious individuality without its being in any way changed. He is told that he now finds himself in the etheric plane, which is coexistent with the earth plane, but in a different dimension. He is informed that although he has shed his earth body he has still retained its etheric counterpart of identical appearance, but of another substance; that his conscious spirit will always continue to live, passing through numerous planes of existence, his advancement depending upon his own efforts.

"It is made clear to the new arrival that he will have assistance constantly along the way, but that no one can force him to choose the right path, the decision being entirely up to him.

"He is told that all his talents must be used and that the capabilities he was born with for love, forgiveness, compassion, reasonableness, mercy, tenderness, sincerity, generosity, kindness, courage, patience, justice, tolerance, unselfishness, and all other character-building virtues must be increased to their highest degree before he may proceed out of the etheric plane. He cannot leave the etheric, no matter how long a time it takes, until this is accomplished by his own conscious effort.

"Now the kind of man who was aware of his personal responsibility for his spiritual growth and who recognized his obligation to love his fellow men will experience in the etheric constant forward progress, and as his character improves so do the surroundings in which he finds himself. There is great, unimaginably great, beauty here," Mother wrote, "but it can be seen only by those who have achieved awareness of it. It will be possible for this enlightened spirit to live in an unbelievably sublime world, to hear and appreciate splendid music, to spend his time occupied by enjoyable tasks among friendly companions, including many he loved most while on earth. The spirit who goes upward indeed lives in Paradise.

"But if his nature was mean and weak, he will exist in sordid, dismal surroundings which will become increasingly more dreary until he sees the error of his thinking, for each spirit makes with his thoughts the conditions in which he lives.

"It is possible to go through an entire earth life without developing any of one's capabilities or facing up to the need to do so. Heredity and environment play a large part in one's natural inclination toward or against such self-improvement, but no man is accountable for more than he is potentially capable of achieving. However, anyone who makes an effort to learn to love his fellow men and to gain wisdom has a more successful life on earth and is further advanced when he reaches the next plane. It is an eventual necessity in world progress that more and more people be reared with awareness of the importance of character development. It is much easier to build it on earth than after death and a great deal of time and misery later will be saved if you have begun your progression before you die.

"Sometimes it takes many hundreds of years before some especially closed-minded spirits can be made to understand the need to start their own personal strivings, and often its urgency almost never can be learned. Even persons of intelligence, if their minds have been corrupted by hatred, may be blindly unwilling to accept the fact that their own endeavors and nothing else will get them out of the low spiritual state they are in.

"The average person during his life on earth is so preoccupied with making a living and with raising his family and with trying to accumulate material benefits that he spends almost no time on conscious efforts to improve himself. Although he doubtless leads a life of some service, whatever discipline he acquires is purely coincidental, for he does not take advantage of the fact that the problems he has to face are challenges which present him with the opportunity to strengthen his character. He manages to increase some of his good qualities to some extent; he steps forward and he backslides; he does something really fine and then something futile or inept. When he dies this man already has some quantitative development. It is not difficult for him to be convinced that his future progress in the spirit world is up to him.

"If he accepts this fact and begins to work on himself, informed spirits will give him as much time and instruction as he needs along the way. An entirely new understanding is necessary, for everything is instigated and accomplished in this plane by thought power. Even movement from one place to another is done by thinking of where you wish to be, and with sufficient concentration you suddenly find yourself there. All character building is consciously motivated, and you must decide upon the course of action which will enable you to improve each of your capabilities, and then act upon your decisions.

"Usually your first step is to stay close to someone on earth who requires assistance in the very virtues which you need to improve. The only way you can help this person is with your thoughts, but if they are positive enough and strongly enough held, you can frequently give him substantial assistance with many of his problems.

"It is much easier to guard your speech and your actions on earth than to try in the spirit world to correct harm that you may have done. It is also less difficult to follow the Golden Rule than to make retribution, for if you have done anyone an injury during your life, then when your progression starts after death you will feel obligated to remain with that person to help him until recompense is made.

"Of course, assistance may be given to loved ones, and most spirits become companions or Guardian Angels to those on earth they care for, impressing their minds with advantageous thoughts whenever possible.

"Unfortunately, sometimes those who die are in such a state of degradation and ignorance of moral values that they will not pay attention to those who explain to them what has occurred and give them advice about their future. Without previous knowledge of what to expect after death, they may not even be aware that they have died and so think what they are experiencing is a bad dream. But if they will listen to the informed spirits who make it their practice to rescue these newcomers and tell them the truth, their future success is assured without too great a delay.

"Frequently, however, men and women who die in an unenlightened state will not accept what is told them. Thinking they are already in Heaven or Hell, depending upon what they had conceived to be their prospects, they will consider no other possibility, and remain in the same ignorant condition making no effort to improve. These are the people it is most urgent to reach with the truth before they die.

"No other thing that man can do to man is as bad as murder, which liberates a soul who is probably totally unprepared to progress. Capital punishment is just as wrong, because it allows to enter the spirit world one with hate and revenge in his heart. You do not destroy an enemy by killing him, you merely unleash him in another and invisible form. One who murders must spend so much time in the next plane undoing the wrong he has done that there is nothing but hell for him for seeming eons of time. To kill a person is the worst thing ever done by any man, and to kill yourself is just as bad.

"It is necessary to learn to love one's fellow men before it is possible to progress, for without love little growth can be attained in any other capability. And despite the mental discipline it demands, this necessary trait should be developed as highly as possible before one dies.

"I am not advocating a thing impossible to do. Jesus did it as an example for all. In fact, many have lived only for others and their lives have been exemplifications for the world to follow. Actually, those who have revered humanity have been the most successful of all men. St. Paul, Moses, St. Francis of Assisi, Siddhartha Gautama (Buddha), Florence Nightingale, Jane Addams, William and Evangeline Booth, Abraham Lincoln, Clara Barton, Mahatma Mohandas Gandhi, and Albert Schweitzer are only a few of the many who have devoted themselves to helping mankind.

"The lives of these men and women illustrate that it is possible for happiness to be found in selflessness. But the entreaties of all religions that men learn to love their brothers have never been embraced by the world as a whole. They've been rejected because people thought they were meant for others rather than for themselves. They've been overlooked because life seemed complete enough without them. They have not been followed because it appeared too difficult.

"There is no quick or easy way to learn good will toward humanity, but the first step is taken when one begins to see the need of it. Since all are enduring the same struggles and learning the same lessons and trying for the same goals, it should not be difficult to attain a feeling of kinship and compassion for others. To think kindly of men will be easier when it is realized that each must eventually become aware of the necessity to progress. For if you know and a man who injures you does not, then you can pity him for his lack of understanding of the monumental task ahead of him. Instead of hating him, forgive him because of his ignorance, think to yourself, 'God bless him,' and then forget the grievance.

"The way to learn to improve yourself is this: Know first that thoughts are actual things and then you can realize that every negative thought that enters your mind must be denied and a positive thought substituted for it so that the power which the negative thought exerts may be cancelled by a positive power immediately put into action.

"It is laborious to do this when it is first attempted, but it will grow easier with practice until finally the reaction of denial to any negative thought will become almost instinctive. And then the substitution of a positive thought will also become a matter of habit. Soon you will notice evidence of the progress you have made and the improvement in your life because of it. When friends begin to ask what it is that has brought that glow of happiness to you so constantly, you will suddenly realize that a constructive force is revealing itself continuously in your life. And you will know such peace as you previously would not have believed possible.

"Those who call you ingenuous if you try to live by the Golden Rule will have a much more difficult time than you do in the etheric. They are the ones who are really naïve because their minds are closed to the real delights of life. Only when one begins to master himself, instead of deceiving himself by believing his mediocre existence to be satisfactory, may he know what real joy is. For there is such pleasure in each contact, such harmony of mind, that all friction disappears.

"Love of mankind could be learned easily if it were taught to children so they would be raised with it always in their hearts. Too many adults don't implant in their children the importance of tolerance. They train them by precept to hate and belittle others instead of insisting that it is necessary to have brotherly love for everyone no matter how misguided or how ignorant or how different in race or color or habits. If it were learned in childhood then it would not be so difficult for the adult to practice as a part of his constant thinking.

"Actually it is unfair to raise children who do not know about the necessity to attain wisdom. It is a disservice to them to allow them to grow up without inner harmony or awareness of the significance of achieving it, and if they discover after death that their entire lives on earth have been practically wasted because so little character was built, it is hard for them not to feel that their parents were neglectful, no matter how indulgent they seemed to be. It is too late then to learn these lessons by life's experience, and there is nothing to do except to start in the etheric with whatever slight amount of spiritual development one has and build upon that.

"Each baby comes into the world as a consciousness (or soul or ego or spirit) wearing a body as it would a coat. It lives on earth for one purpose—to establish its identity and then use life's experiences to acquire wisdom, build character, and attain individual stature. When the body is discarded at death the consciousness continues in spirit dimensions until perfection is achieved.

"Advanced personalities may remain in the etheric plane for as long as they wish in order to help others. This may be done by conducting classes for those who desire to learn, by doing what might be likened to social work among unenlightened spirits, by helping to raise those who died in childhood, or perhaps by making efforts to contact earth people for the purpose of giving them information about conditions beyond the grave.

"Or this discarnate intelligence who has attained his advancement may go immediately to the next plane beyond, where he refines himself until a condition is reached in which he never for even an instant allows a thought to cross his mind which is not loving, compassionate, and peaceful. He will continue his joyous journey after that from plane to plane until he reaches, after unimaginable spiritual development, the ultimate plane of existence, which is perfection, and God.

"So it is true that consciousness is in a state of evolution, and that it eventually achieves union with the highest. But one can leave the etheric only after an advanced stage of development has been achieved, so the importance of knowing the necessity to mature your character on earth cannot be overestimated. Otherwise, hundreds of years may be wasted as an ignorant soul flounders in a morass of despair or hatred, or an opinionated spirit hangs onto his old beliefs.

"So I must repeat once again," Mother wrote, "it is essential to progress as much as possible before you die. You do have free will and you must give more than lip service to your philosophy or religion, acting on its precepts in an attempt to improve yourself as much as possible. Unless you have a good start on earth, your advancement will be impeded after death . . . until you finally become aware of the magnificent destiny which awaits you."

Chapter 23

WHEN WE WERE PUTTING the finishing touches on Mother's Chapter, we began to have an influx of intruders who ultimately caused us no end of trouble. There began to be weeks when Mother's power to write was so counteracted that she was unable to send more than an occasional brief message; and my hands were actually pulled from the typewriter whenever they were laid loosely on the keys hoping for contact. When I wrote for myself under my own steam there were no problems; but my relaxed hands were never allowed to remain on the keys.

Harvey had made it quite clear to me that mischief-makers could be obnoxious. Yet, still, it was difficult to believe that they could be the cause of physical manifestations. I tried to find every possible normal excuse for this; to this modern woman anything was preferable to believing in evil spirits—even when her type-writer was acting possessed.

It was disconcerting and, yes, frightening, to feel my fingers raised from the keys by a force I could not fathom. When I believed it was my mother communicating, I did not mind having my hands moved without my conscious effort. But this was alto-gether different. It seemed abnormal, and even chilling, as though something diabolical were taking hold of me, when my hands were pulled away from the keys against my will.

Mother, with her understanding of ultimates, was not alarmed; and her refusal to worry, when she could get in a word to reassure me, calmed me somewhat . . . until the next time my efforts to write were rejected.

Soon the intruders began to dash off little messages to me—although they seemed to do it unwillingly—which revealed them to be human, at least, even though it did not explain why they were there. This writing began as a cold "Yes" which typed itself when I sat down to contact Mother. It was repelling to find this on my paper instead of Mother's cheery, "Good morning, Susy, dear" or "Let's go, honey."

If I persisted, trying to learn more about what was going on, the intruders might give out with, "You are not to write with your mother." Then they'd stop and nothing more would be written and my hands would be removed. An occasional "guard" would add a few words more. One was quite garrulous:

I will not tell you anything. They forbid me to talk to you. This is wrong. I mean wrong for me to be typing. It is wrong for you to make any contact with me. You are not to do so. I do not wish to type with you. It is I who pull your fingers from the keys because I am not allowed to let you write to anyone. It is definitely prohibited. I must not write to you.

When asked who made such rules, they did not say. One was quite vehement in his assertions, however. He wrote:

It is no use trying. You won't ever again be allowed to talk to anyone with a typewriter or pencil so there's no use trying.

Once for a day or two the guard was either foreign or an ignoramus. He expressed himself thus: "This not mother. This man want you not write book."

Mother, when she could get a word in, insisted the guards were just misguided spirits of men who needed help to learn the truth about their condition. She always got back to that. I must never think there were actual "evil spirits" or "devils" causing the harm —they were only unenlightened invisible people.

When I began to realize that, I set to work to reform them, and had good results. I began to read Mother's Chapter aloud to them, and they listened. It clarified things for them they hadn't understood before. The first evidence of this occurred one night when the long-suffering Smith-Corona typed:

"Mother is not here. It is not Mother."

"Who is writing?" I asked.

"It is not anyone you know. It is someone who is not supposed to be a friend, but I must talk to you. Why is progression so important? I wish I might discuss it further with you."

I immediately began reading aloud, and the next day the typewriter had a new guard, for overnight the previous one had started his upward journey. I could tell it was somebody new because the same old routine was started, fingers pulled off keys, and then finally words typed, "No, you can't write." After a day or two, this one also began to ask questions.

Frankly, I was much inclined to doubt the genuineness of the conversions made this way. It seemed too easy. I found it hard to believe that a few words from me could make such a quick change in anyone. When Mother got the chance to explain it she said: "The truth is that because they can see you in a physical body and hear actual words come from your mouth addressed to them, they will listen to you. They hear nothing from you they have not already heard countless times since their deaths from the spirit helpers, but they pay attention because it comes from the familiar earth surroundings instead of the new and strange. The moment a spirit understands his situation and expresses a desire to advance, his progression starts."

As our conversions became more frequent, the interruptions lessened, and soon the Smiths were having their good old type-written chats again. Then I unburdened to Bill Hanemann the problem of the interference we'd had. While it was at its worst, I did not dare talk about it for fear he'd misunderstand, but when it was behind me it didn't matter.

At first Bill peered at me for symptoms of hysteria. Satisfied that I had myself under reasonable control, he then began insisting that Mother be questioned to find out just what the hell was going on in a universe where malevolent characters were allowed to run around undisciplined, pulling people's fingers off keys.

Mother's attempt to explain stressed her point that each individual must learn to discipline himself.

"You should not forget," she reminded us, "that everyone arrives here in the same mental state in which he lived, for no one's mind is any different immediately after death than it was the moment before. If he was a delinquent or a man with a bitter or a corrupt nature, that is what he remains. It is the opinionated person whose mind is closed to new ideas who has the hardest time. He resists all new concepts, rejecting everything he doesn't understand. On earth no one could tell him anything; in this plane no one can tell him anything either."

Mother said that an unenlightened newcomer in the spirit world is in more or less of a fog which continues until his perception is cleared by the development of his understanding. He sees only what he concentrates on, and that is most likely to be the place where he died and the people or type of people with whom he had passed most of his time. He may spend many years wandering around in his own personal miasma trying to stay as closely as possible to the earth life he previously knew. To be told that by his own thinking he makes the conditions in which he exists, means nothing to him and he becomes inured to conversation about it.

"I can't see why he wouldn't listen and give it a try," I commented.

"Some do. More don't. It's exactly as you yourself wear mental earplugs against the exhortations of the radio to buy this and buy that," Mother answered.

"Well, if there is an audience, no matter how invisible, I'll lecture every day."

"I'm glad," Mother told me. "I hope you always will try to get the truth to them. There are so many who must be taught, and, as I said, they will listen to you. Since there's no way to discipline these earthbound spirits who are troublesome, it's only possible to aid them by converting them one at a time to their need to improve themselves. And no matter how deep their degradation, some day someone will get through to each of them with the truth. It is inevitable."

"But pulling fingers off typewriter keys seems like awfully silly work for spooks who could be using their time and talents to haunt houses." I still couldn't see why they bothered with me.

Mother said it was because I was dabbling into their sphere of action. Anyone who tries to communicate is to some extent putting himself at their mercy. That's why she doesn't recommend using the Ouija board for purposes of contact with the spirit world. There are too many risks involved.

"Everyone who dies rebellious is a potential source of mischief," she wrote. "If they knew all that I've been telling you before they died, there wouldn't be as many unhappy souls in the hereafter with nothing better to do than play pranks or make trouble."

"If we hadn't personally put up with Harvey and these other juvenile delinquents I'd think you were out of your ever-lovin' mind," I said. "Real live dead people invisibly wafting about in the air heckling us communicators . . . honestly!"

"You don't hear me arguing," Mother replied. "I'd never have believed it myself until I got here."

I had more proof that she was right very shortly. And this is how. Once late in the spring after Harvey had been in limbo for several months because he had never learned to type, I was sitting outdoors in the sun proofreading copy. I needed a comment from mother about something she had written the night before, and so picked up my pencil and held it for her to write.

What was produced instead was, "I love you, Harvey."

I shrieked, "Oh, no! Not Harvey still!" It had been so long since he had troubled me that I presumed he'd gone away. When

Captain Merton M. Smith

Elizabeth H. (Betty) Smith

On my third birthday

Our San Antonio home

The Oakland house in winter

Susy in college

Susy in the Democrat office, Oakland, Maryland

H. William (Bill) Hanemann

Susy and Junior in Daytona Beach

*Colonel Harlan Sanders, Margaret Sanders Adams,
and Trigg Adams*

asked why he continued hanging around even when he couldn't talk to me any more, he wrote that he'd been learning a lot. When he'd had to stop pestering me because he couldn't type he was furious. Then, while incommunicado, he began listening to what Mother and I were discussing about progression and all that. He heard so much about the opportunities for advancement for a young spirit willing to travel that he became interested. Now he was almost bursting to tell me of his eagerness to start his progression.

Mother and the other spirit helpers around gave him the answers to his questions—things they'd tried to tell him before when he was so contrary he wouldn't listen—and now he responded eagerly. He apologized for all the trouble he'd caused me, stayed around a few days longer, and then suddenly he disappeared . . . never to return.

Remember when Grandpa Anderson told me several months earlier that the only way to get rid of Harvey was to cease writing to him and to teach him? Thus the little moral to Harvey's story seems to be that Mother and her grandfather knew what they were talking about when they wrote: "The only way to eliminate evil is to convert it to good."

Chapter 24

ROM TIME TO TIME Mother continued briefing me about this life and the next. "Natural Laws govern everything on earth and in each plane of existence," she wrote. "Every person lives his life within these laws, and only when they are observed is he successful. There is never an instance when Natural Laws are set aside or broken to help either a person on earth or a spirit on any other plane. If it seems that there is, it is only because of your limited understanding of these laws. What seem to be miracles are only the operation of lesser-known laws."

It makes life intelligible and purposeful to know that we live in a planned universe where system predominates. We so often tend to attribute things to blind chance. But, no, Mother told me, according to plan each man lives his life on earth to learn from his experiences and from his daily contacts with other people, and then he continues in the etheric to gain more knowledge until he has advanced enough that he may progress to other planes. This design is the same for each man and woman who lives, there being no individual arrangements, no special privileges, and no divine dispensations for anyone.

"Hard luck can be endured with more fortitude when one realizes the instruction he can get from the unfortunate situation," Mother said, adding that then the same lesson won't have to be mastered in some more difficult manner later.

"There is no person who escapes any of life's lessons, and if it seems that a benevolent providence protects some and not others, that is only a misconception, for character is at no time achieved without toil. If one's life has been so effortless on earth that he has acquired no wisdom, then it will be necessarily more difficult for him on the next plane."

"All this sounds to me like Cause and Effect," I commented.

"It is, exactly. The effect doesn't always occur to the one who caused it to happen, but it is still a result of the act. And one who makes a careless mistake or does a malicious deed on earth must rectify it to the best of his ability or else he will have to make recompense in the etheric."

I was startled. "You mean there's an accountant who keeps records of each person's life?"

"No, there is no one whose duty it is to keep tab on each man. He does it himself. All his memories are available to him after death; and when a spirit begins to progress it is his own decision what he shall make requital for and how he will go about it. If each man on earth knew that his own progress is dependent upon himself alone, he would be more eager to begin his forward growth before he dies."

"You and your reactionary theories," I said. "Cause and Effect

. . . Evil Spirits . . . Free Will . . . Self Discipline. The behaviorists would be after your head."

"I can't help it. These terms are all valid. Just because concepts are old is no reason to reject them. But then, just because a belief has been prevalent for a long time is no reason to accept it, either. Man has had many glimpses of the truth in the past and he'll have many more before he ever gets the whole picture. But eventually every child will be raised knowing how to think properly to bring out his finest capabilities."

"That'll be the day," I said skeptically, musing about Human Nature, another of the old saws she was apparently overlooking.

"Yes, I'm an idealist," Mother wrote. "We all are here where I am. But we have the advantage of knowing the overall long range plan or scheme of the universe. It is good, believe me, it is *good*."

We had a visitor shortly thereafter who told us from his own experience about the various dimensions of existence. One night Mother paused in her typing, and at that moment I had a sudden feeling of my father's presence that was overpoweringly strong. Then Mother typed, "Your Dad's here."

I got all goosebumpy and said, "Put him on, quick." And then he typed with me. After greetings, he identified himself with personal information such as his middle name—a great secret because he disliked it—and then went on that night and the next day to write several pages to me. I was so elated I could hardly keep my fingers going, yet eagerly let him type in order to learn what he wanted to tell me. The most encouraging part of it was his bragging on me:

I'll never know how you have managed to develop into such a sweet person all alone in the world for so long as you have been. Your Mother has been gone seven years. During that time you have been alone most of the time trying to make your way in the world . . . and with a handicap, too. But out of it has come this lovely, lovely person.

At this point I came right out and stated that this was obviously wishful thinking on my part; that my subconscious mind was certainly feeding me what I most wanted to hear.

There is no subconscious mind involved here, it is your own father who comes back to earth from another plane of existence and finds a daughter of whom he can be very proud.

Dad explained that he had worked extremely hard on his progression during the nearly twenty-five years since he left us and that after Mother joined him he had been ready to advance, and so he went on ahead to the next plane. He tried to make me aware that he lives in a condition of serenity in which he always thinks thoughts of love and never is negative about anything . . . and yet life isn't dull for him. This last was in answer to the question I knew Bill Hanemann would inevitably put when told about this. Dad said he is surrounded by fascinating people who are always busy doing interesting and enjoyable things. It sounded to me as if he had already achieved Paradise, but he said he has a tremendously long way to go yet to reach the heights.

To me the most curious circumstance about my father's visit was that Mother could not see him. She knew he was there because he talked with her and she felt his presence even more strongly than I did. But she on her plane lower than his was unable to see him just as I was unable to see her. They explained this by the analogy of the electric fan, which is used by many writers to show why those on earth cannot see those in the spirit world. When a fan is stopped or going slowly all the blades can be seen. When it is turned to a high speed we know the blades are still there but they are moving so fast we can't see them—we can see right through the fan to the other side.

The spirit body, with its different consistency, is like a force field which is moving at a frequency so much higher than ours that we cannot see it, just as we can't see the blades of the fan when they are moving fast. This vibration increases as the spirit progresses from plane to plane, so each level cannot see the ones who have gone on ahead unless they go through some special processes of slowing themselves down. Evidently Dad didn't do that.

He was only able to communicate with me twice, but he was around for several days, and he has returned a few times since then. When he left he said for us to be sure that he is always sending his loving and helpful thoughts to us, and that he will come whenever he is needed.

I was very soon to need all the kind and constructive thoughts he could muster.

Chapter 25

WHEN I OFFER the assurance that this chapter does not report a hysterical interlude, I hope it is believable. If because of publishing this experience I can keep even a few persons who hear voices they can't account for out of institutions and help them into a sane realization of how to cope with their situations, my torment won't have been suffered in vain. Unfortunately, too many people are getting into similar situations because of their ignorance of the dangers of attempting spirit communication.

Because my unseemly adventures were what might be considered mental, there is the possibility that a critic would be sure it was a psychotic episode. I must declare, however, that during the entire time these disturbances were going on I felt exactly as sane and sensible as at this moment—if anyone can ever be sure he is entirely sane and sensible. My mental state would have been similar on any ordinary day of my life under any normal circumstances if at the same time I was bedevilled by a plague of mosquitoes, or if there was an incessant ringing of my telephone. It was irritating and tiring, and it even became frightening; but my own consciousness was uninvolved at all times.

I now know in various cities all over the world people of education and reasonableness—the type who might get together for a study group of any kind—who are developing their psychic abilities. They have discovered that in one way or another they have some type of psychic sensitivity, and they sit together at regular intervals to improve it. They feel an obligation to become as proficient as possible—just as one would who discovered he had an aptitude for music or art. Some of these persons have a talent for telepathy—they can give accurate reports of what others are thinking at certain times. Some are clairvoyant and see pictures or lights and colors that the rest of the group are unable to see. Some, clairaudient, actually hear voices that are inaudible to others. And some are aware of words spoken independently within their minds—clairsentience. For those who develop these gifts under guidance everything proceeds satisfactorily, because they are all perfectly normal types of mediumship by which evidential information is frequently produced.

My problem was that I got into a clairsentient phase without knowing anything about it. It came on too suddenly without proper preparation. At the time I was acquainted with no one who had ever been through anything similar so that he could give me advice; and I had no idea what to do to overcome it. It was, quite frankly, the most unnerving experience of my life.

Just after I awoke on the morning of June 2nd, singing in my mind were the words, "Happy birthday to you, happy birthday to you." It seemed very chummy of me to sing to myself, but it had not been consciously instigated. I wondered why, if my subconscious was doing it, it wasn't singing my usual version—"Happy birthday to *me*." As the song progressed it was obvious to me that Mother was the one serenading. I thanked her and went on about my business, unaware what an unusual thing had actually occurred. It certainly was not then evident to me that this was my first indication that a new psychic talent had developed.

The next evidence of it was revealed by my Aunt Ivy, who had been in the spirit world two years longer than Mother and had gone over with a long head start. When on earth she had been the most Christlike human I had ever known, devoting her life totally to helping others. Now, in her invisible form, she had called on us several times during that spring in Daytona Beach. The first time she came my fingers were in position on the keys when suddenly I felt luminous, as though a bright shine was pervading me, and I thought of Aunt Ivy. Then Mother typed, "My sister is here."

Aunt Ivy didn't try to type with me—she never was one for

mechanical things—but Mother relayed on the typewriter a few exchanges from her, and this kind of social confab went on after that whenever she dropped by.

On June 6th Mother typed that Aunt Ivy was there and that she wanted to try to communicate with me in my own mind. Always agreeable—beyond the point of questioning anything they might undertake; what could startle me now?—I tried to blank my mind in preparation for whatever might happen next. Then, spoken distinctly within my head were the words, "Aunt Ivy is talking to you, Susy Ethel." It was surprising after all, because she had never combined my two names before—nor had anyone else. Apparently this was her way of proving it was she and not my own mind, which had tossed out "Ethel" long before.

I sang out happily that I could hear her, and she went on: "I was sure you were ready to try to communicate with us in this manner. I am beaming these words into your mind telepathically and you understand them."

As she slowly and distinctly impressed each thought upon me, it came to me exactly as though words were being spoken inside my head but not being instigated by me. My own ego or consciousness was intact, remaining quietly by in a different spot in my head listening to what Aunt Ivy was saying. Also, the conversation was not anything I would have been in the least likely to bring up. She talked mostly about her own son and daughter, with whom I have lost touch, and her eagerness to have them learn the truth about survival.

Then other words came, interrupting Aunt Ivy. "Let me try it, let me try it" . . . and there was Mother, eager to test this new mode of communication. She and I had a good time playing with it after that for nearly a week. My day began with "Good morning, Mother" spoken aloud and her reply in my mind. We continued this way all through the day, even to her, "I'd iron the sleeves first if I were you" and "Don't put that egg there, you'll knock it off."

Yes, she bossed me just as she always had all my life, but now it didn't bother me. I'd proved able to live without her guidance, so now was able to take it in the spirit it was intended without getting my back up.

It was all great fun at first, but then something different happened. Everybody tried to get into the act. Other entities who heard us talking learned Mother's technique and took over. The Baddies muscled in on our new diversion and spoiled it as they did everything else. For three entire days and nights I was heckled constantly by mental conversation from outsiders who had no right to intrude. Then for the rest of that year they bothered me on occasion until I learned how to close my mind to them entirely —even though it also meant closing out those who had a legitimate right to talk to me.

"Can you become insane on just one subject and still be normal in every other way?" I wondered. I had not lost touch with reality, but my demons began to try to make me think so. The invisible hoods who heard me wonder about it to myself answered with, "Yes, you're going crazy, you're definitely losing your mind. We'll drive you crazy." This went on inside my head all day long.

At first I panicked. "If I haven't already cracked up, I certainly will if this keeps up. Positive thoughts! Mother's good old standby . . . try them." So I'd give myself a fight talk: "You're not a sissy, Susy. You've overcome all the other things that have come up in your life and you'll lick this."

Then the intruders took up that refrain: "Susy's a sissy, Susy's a sissy." They interspersed that with their, "You're going crazy; we're driving you crazy."

The first night they almost got me. I called for help from everybody I knew in the spirit world: Mother, Dad, Aunt Ivy, Nina, wherever she was, Grandpa Anderson, even Uncle Charlie! Trying to sleep and being unable to have a moment's peace because of the constantly reiterated, "You're going crazy. You're a sissy and you're going crazy," I got out of bed time after time to read, having discovered that the only way to shut them out was to keep my mind so occupied with something else that I couldn't pay attention to them. But whenever drowsiness would overcome me and I'd retire again, the refrain would resume. I don't know why it didn't occur to me then to try to convert them, as I had done with the typewriter guards; but this, somehow, was so different and so much more appalling that it hardly seemed as if it could be coming from anything human. I was just too involved at first to even think of reading Mother's Chapter to them.

It did occur to me that praying might be a good idea. I still wasn't sure about any kind of a God who might be interested in paying personal attention to me, but I was now willing to try to find out. So, standing up in the middle of the floor of the trailer I dared the unknown to harm me, saying firmly, "I have help greater than any of you and I know how to reach it." Then I hurled out into the great expanse of spirit, clear to this new concept of God Mother had presented to me (but which I was not yet aware was *within* me as well), a powerful prayer for assistance.

In just a few moments a gentle voice spoke to me . . . inside my mind, of course, like all the others. But he sounded kindly.

"Your rescuer has arrived," he said. "I have come from a far plane to take care of you. You will have no more trouble." He was convincing, and he stopped the others from talking.

"Thank you, God," I said, relaxing in the peace that ensued, slipping back into bed as if into my new friend's sheltering arms.

"There now, rest," he said, "you're safe now. Just relax." And I projected my thoughts toward him, reaching, yearning for his reassurance.

"Come to me, come to me, Susy," he lulled me. "I can protect you."

This was so great that I rested, soothed, comfortable for the first time all day long.

"Come to me," he went on, slowly and softly, "leave your body . . . slip right out of your body and come to me."

A cold, hard lump dropped to the pit of my stomach and I started up quickly to complete alertness . . . and terror. His suggestions reminded me of everything I had read about the dangers of out-of-body experiences. Sometimes, it is said, one's consciousness might leave his body and be unable to return because a spirit entity jumped in and possessed it while it was unoccupied. His idea was against all Mother's teachings and I realized it in time to reject him.

"You're not trying to help me! You're evil!" I shouted, leaping out of bed as if to run away from him.

How he laughed! "I almost had you," he gloated. "One more minute and you'd have come soaring right out to me . . . then you'd never have been able to get back into your body."

"Go away!" I was shaking all over by then. "You can't harm me. I have protection, lots of it. Leave me alone! Mother, Dad, help me, please!"

"Oh, I'll get you, never fear. I'll either kill you or drive you insane. You'll never publish that book."

I went outside and walked up and down the road, afraid to go back into the trailer until the sky began to hint that the safety of daylight was approaching. Then sleep finally came.

My antagonist was there the next morning as soon as I awakened, trying to kill me as he had promised. He was sending some kind of electric shocks through my body constantly. These were something entirely different from any evidence of nervousness or tension, although naturally I suspected that at first. Completely debilitating and shattering, they weakened my whole system.

On top of that he was talking to me in the dirtiest words he could say. All that day spoken into my mind were four-letter words which I personally never used. This was before the era when one had become used to them because of encountering them in almost anything he read, and they were revolting to me. My discomfiture only made the entity continue it all the more. I had a whole day of this, with only one slight advantage—if you can call it that—by evening my body was so weak and exhausted by the attack on my bowels that I dropped right off to sleep.

I did not know it then, having never read about such things, but this profanity deal is standard operating procedure for the malevolent communicator. As far as the physical shocks are concerned, I have never heard of that particular treatment being given to anyone else; but much other unpleasantness occurs, frequently involving sexual urges. Fortunately I was spared that.

The third morning my invisible enemy started with the same routine, apparently determined either to kill me with his etheric shocks or else bore me to death with filth; but that day I found the way to finish him off. On one particular occasion he tried to use a vulgar phrase that I didn't know, and he couldn't get it into my mind. Realizing what he was trying to do and how he was innocently being blocked, I laughed . . . then taunted him about it. He retaliated by sending more bolts of his enervating lightning through my system, while repeating viciously, "I'm going to kill you. I'll *kill* you!" I almost thought he was succeeding.

I'd finally discovered his secret weakness, however. He could be made fun of. If I couldn't lick him, I'd join him and rib him to distraction.

"All right, Sam, you son of a bitch," I said. "I've been around, too, you know. Just because I don't use dirty words is no sign I don't know at least some of them." Then I said a few choice epithets to show him. After that whenever he spoke profanity in my mind I matched him aloud with some of my own. And I addressed him as Sam every time.

Then it wasn't a fight any more. My intruder degenerated from an infamous fiend of magnitude coming from outer space to do me great harm into a petulant invisible derelict who didn't like being referred to snidely as Sam and didn't want to be laughed at. He particularly could not understand my mirth. He began to talk to me about it.

"How can you laugh at me?" he asked. "Why don't you hate me? I'm really trying to kill you." He wanted me to hate him because violent emotion challenged him. My lack of rancor toward him after all his meanness was incomprehensible to him.

"I can see into your mind," he said, "and I don't see hatred for anyone. It isn't just me alone. You really don't hate anybody. I don't understand you." This was extremely encouraging. I was glad to know the results of my year's efforts at self-improvement were so obvious.

"My mother insists on the importance of loving my fellow man," I explained. "You probably have to be considered in that category, however weird you are." I told him it wasn't actually possible to love anyone as misguided as he, but compassion was the next best thing, and that I had . . . and sympathy for him because he was so ignorant of his true situation. This cued me straight to Mother's Chapter and he seemed to go along willingly, apparently listening as I read it aloud.

When I was through he said, "So that's why some of these goofy guys around me are always insisting they can see people and lights and hear all kinds of music that I can't." Then he thanked me and left me alone for the rest of the day. The next morning he was apparently gone, but unfortunately there were new voices to contend with, calling in my mind, "Can you hear me? Can you hear me? I'm going to kill you or drive you crazy."

"Oh, no, you're not," I said immediately. "I'm going to convert you instead." Short work was made of each new entity; but it was still a darned nuisance. I couldn't get any work done for reading that chapter aloud all the time. I didn't appreciate the idea that my mind was open and vulnerable to the likes of them, anyway. Even if they had become removable, I didn't feel up to handling a new batch of trouble like that every day. It had to be learned how to keep them out in the first place.

My own guides hadn't actually seemed to be much help. Where else could I turn? To a Spiritualist minister, obviously. So I returned to the medium who had tried to help me rid myself of Harvey—even though her Indians hadn't known as much about spirit psychology as Grandpa had. She told me a sure cure for my problems. She said to dip my hands and arms into water up to the elbows and instead of drying them to fling the water from them. At the same time I would fling away all evil spirits, she said.

I was even desperate enough to try that, with no results, unfortunately. The entities who were intruding themselves on my thoughts just laughed at me . . . until I read them Mother's Chapter.

This medium also said that if the water-flinging by any chance didn't do the trick, to stand barefoot outside on the ground with my back against a tree, for trees have great life-force and I could absorb power from the earth through my feet. It seemed only the slightest degree more sensible than flinging water from my elbows, but I gave it a trial, too. In fact, several nights during the summer when I couldn't sleep because of being tormented by unseen talkers, I'd slip outside in my nightie and robe and bare feet and lean against the rough hide of the big palm tree out front and ask it to share its strength with me (but not its palmetto bugs). Getting outside, away from the increasing oppressiveness of the boxlike trailer, was good, for at least I was cooled off by the freshness of the night air if nothing else.

Bill Hanemann was finally burdened with my problem because I had to talk to someone about the voices. He *knew* the oft-prophesied hysteria had finally arrived, even though his prying scrutiny could reveal no traces of it in the rest of my thinking or reactions. He insisted I give up all efforts at communication immediately.

Dr. Hornell Hart, appealed to at Duke, advised the same thing.

Of course, my parents had been implored for help constantly all during this time. "Get me some Indians!" I'd demanded. Everyone who believed in spirits believed that Indians had more power to protect you from the boogies than anyone else. So, "Get me some Indians," I pleaded, "a whole tribe, big and brawny with etheric power. Send for help, Mother, for God's sake. Get me some Indians!"

Do you know what Mother said in return, the few times she could write anything to me because of the interference? She agreed with Hornell and Bill that my best bet was to stop any efforts at communication until this thing blew over!

I told Bill I was exactly like a man treading water in the middle of the ocean. It was easy enough for everyone to shout advice to him to get back to the shore. But how could he do it? The only raft they threw him was a warning to ignore the water! It was enough for them to talk. I was the one breasting the bounding billows, still treading water with all my might. Every time my mind lay idle for a second someone was communicating with *me*. I wasn't the one communicating. I was being communicated at. Stop treading water, they said. Rush back to shore, they said. Don't talk to *them*, they said. Ha!

Or, to use another metaphor, let go of the tail of the lion who's chewing on your big toe.

It was reassuring eventually to learn that my father and Aunt Ivy had been there rendering aid. Apparently, however, they weren't doing anything except talking to the interlopers and rounding up other bands of spirit missionaries to talk to them. This supplemented the daily "sermons" I gave to those who pestered me. And gradually these villains, too, began to be less obnoxious and to become aware of themselves as something better than pests. So the vocal persecution eventually let up just as the pulling-fingers-off-keys had eased. But I seldom dared to take a chance to instigate any communication.

I did not stop working on my book even though it was obviously unwise to appeal to Mother for help on it. My life was so involved with it that there was nothing else in the world I wanted to do but keep at it.

It was the hottest summer imaginable, in an uninsulated trailer in steamy Florida. I sat under an electric fan every minute, wore the skimpiest costumes legal, and perspired constantly. I had to make a conscious effort at all times to keep my mind closed against the voices. Whenever they'd bother me I'd start singing a song, paying careful attention to my articulation of each word, or read a detective story or some other book that would grip my interest at once . . . when I wasn't reading Mother's Chapter aloud. I had to keep my mind occupied constantly, for let my thoughts lie idle for the merest instant and in rushed the clatter.

Altogether I can't remember a more difficult time, for I had to remain on constant red alert. Yet for some strange reason it isn't recalled as an unhappy period. I knew that our mental processes are so terribly complicated that we haven't started to understand them . . . that there are as many miles of unexplored territory in the human cortex as in Brazil . . . that there was just as like as not the possibility of my entire experience with voices being subjective . . . that hallucinations always seem real to the person who has them. But I had my friends to attest that except for this slight tendency to hear voices inside my head I was in just as good shape as anybody. Aside from the fact that I certainly didn't want to become mentally disturbed, I hoped for another reason that my intruders were of an external source. If they were actually what they purported to be, then they gave just that much more proof that what I was coming to believe about the survival of the human spirit was really true.

That, somehow, uplifted my soul and sent it soaring.

Chapter 26

▌N EARLY OCTOBER, for the first time since my return to Daytona, I called Minnie's Beauty Shop for an appointment to get my tousled topknot professionally groomed. It was surprising to have such a strong compulsion to tell my old friend Minnie about my interest in psychical research; but as soon as I sat down in her chair a recital of my current interests began. (As you become more and more sensitive you seem to know instinctively to whom you can safely talk about this subject.) Then, all the while she was doing my hair, Minnie was besting my stories, for she had personally seen apparitions of her grandmother and her father-in-law. I had nothing to offer in any way as sensational as that.

I told her of my need to develop my incipient mediumship to the point where controls and guides would always be there who knew how to protect me. My beautician then had a suggestion for me. Another customer of hers—Emmaline Gerts, we'll call her —was a nonprofessional medium who had said she would like to have someone attend development classes with her. It is through such sittings that one's psychic abilities grow, so this might fill my need exactly. Minnie felt confident of the integrity of this woman, whom she had known for years; so I called her on returning home and made an appointment for that Saturday night.

On my arrival, tall, heavy-set Mrs. Gerts immediately took me to the basement of her upper-middle class home where she had a séance room, with dark curtains over all the windows so that it was possible to black it out completely. She put me in a chair across a table from her and then turned out all the lights. There we sat in a pool of ink.

The dark had never done anything particularly reassuring to me (although since then I've learned rather to enjoy sitting with development groups in darkened rooms); and being in it alone with this sizeable seer was disconcerting. I didn't know for sure what mediums did when you were alone with them in the dark. It was doubtful that she personally might be interested, say, in swinging a chair at me, but who knew what notions would occur to some entity who might possess her?

Just then she set up a loud snorting and sputtering, and a noisy etheric character named Dr. Sommers started shouting at the top of her lungs. But his message was friendly even if his audio control left something to be desired. He gave a little dissertation of welcome, assuring me of his active interest in my welfare.

The medium, who had remained conscious while her vocal apparatus was borrowed by Dr. Sommers, thanked him for coming and then began describing lights which she could see all around me. She said they were the emanations of benevolent spirits.

"They're *very* welcome," I said, in my eagerness indicating for the first time the possibility of any urgent need on my part. Mrs. Gerts had been told nothing about me by either Minnie or me except my desire to sit for development.

"Hey, there, you with the yellow light," Mrs. Gerts vigorously addressed the blackness around her. "Who are you? What's your name? Shine up your star there, boy. Speak up. Oh, Yellow Fox, is it? Are you her guide? Speak louder so I can hear you. What? What?"

Then she relayed the information that Yellow Fox was an Indian who was now mine, all mine. During the evening she also discovered the brilliantly glowing light of a young Indian girl who was going to stay with me. She would be my control when I developed my mediumship.

Now we were getting somewhere. The acquisition of a sufficient number of feathered chums might let me get back into active contact with Mother again.

"Wonder if they're Comanches or Iroquois or Sioux," I mused while sitting there quietly in the dark. "A gal named Susy really should have a Sioux Indian as her . . . ."

"Who's that?" roared Mrs. Gerts, and I jumped two feet, seven inches into the air. She described then a beautiful violet light beside me.

"How wonderful for you," she said, seeming almost envious. "You have a great teacher here, an Oriental gentleman." She told me his name was something like Solas—I'm not broadcasting the true names given me for my guides, it is not considered good taste. "He and the Indians have been with you for the past month. They will stay. Your family on the other side has been instrumental in securing this group of spirits to protect you."

"He's welcome," I greeted him, quite set up at the magnitude of my new coterie. "They all are."

"Solas is bearded and wears a strange type of turban," Mrs. Gerts added. "I can't exactly place it . . . I think it's Persian or Turkish or something like that. Yes, he tells me it is Persian."

We sat a while longer in the dark but nothing new developed and then I went home, not as encouraged as one might think. Parapsychologists would have scoffed at all this Indian powwow, and hence so must I, for she really hadn't given me anything evidential . . . that couldn't have come from her imagination. So I was much inclined to dismiss her and the three spirit strangers she'd introduced me to, feeling that another door had been closed in my face.

All the next day I took stock of myself, rather dispiritedly. Without Mother to answer questions for me nothing more could be done on the enlightening aspects of my book, and I'd brought the narrative portion of it up to date. I was in a state of doldrums, not knowing what to do with myself. Maybe I needed to get into something creative with my hands again . . . but what? The trailer didn't need painting. What other big project could one start? Well, it would soon be getting along toward Christmas, maybe I could make my greeting cards. Let's see, what kind of gimmick would assure them to be indigenously Floridian? Sea shells, of course; shell poinsettias glued on my cards. Why, come to think of it, they gave courses in jewelry-making at some of the shell shops . . . I could even learn to make my own Christmas presents.

So there I was, all enthusiastic again, with a project ahead of me.

Early Monday morning I trekked across town to a shop where

this Florida specialty, jewelry intricately designed from dyed shells, is manufactured and sold. I joined a class and sat for several hours awkwardly manipulating tiny pikakas and gars with tweezers into acceptable flower-like shapes.

Once, leaning back for a rest, I let my eyes wander around the room, and noticed an Aquarian Bible among some books on a shelf. I mentioned it because it is read by many metaphysicians and learned that Lois, the instructor and owner of the shop, was a newly ordained minister in the Spiritualist Church. After the lesson I waited to talk to her, asking her if she had a circle which sat regularly for development.

"Sit by yourself," Lois said in her abrupt manner. "You can develop mediumship that way. I did."

"I'm afraid to," I told her. "I have intruders who try to talk to me much of the time. What I need is protection."

This woman intimated that I was a softy to want any more spirit guides and protectors than were already with me.

"But I don't have any!"

"You do, too. You have two Indians and a Master from the East right here with you now. What more do you need?"

"Really?" I was alerted quickly. "Tell me more."

Lois peered somewhere back of my left ear, as if sizing up this contingent she saw there. "One of the Indians is a big brave and the other is a young girl—I'd say in her middle teens. The older man, the Master, wears an Oriental turban of some kind. He has a beard."

I was delighted at this independent confirmation of what Mrs. Gerts had told me. Having already learned that a medium could take whatever you revealed and make something of it, I had said nothing personal to either of them and deliberately had not spoken to Lois of what Mrs. Gerts had produced. Frankly, I had not taken it seriously enough to bother repeating it.

These women had not given me anything routine, either. An Indian brave and a young Indian girl and an Oriental gentleman are not necessarily the usual familiars of one developing psychic sensitivity. It could as easily have been three braves and five squaws or Mommy and Daddy or Aunt Violet and Uncle Harry or any other combination.

The mediums, not knowing each other and living in opposite ends of town, could not have gotten together and made up the story to tell me. Lois had not even known I was coming until her opening door revealed my countenance. On knowing them better I came to realize that both women were scornful of subterfuge, strictly lone wolves, attending to their own business. Yet both had given me identical information in almost identical language.

Unless telepathy is so highly involved that the second medium read from my mind thoughts the first one had implanted and which I had rejected and was not at the moment recalling, then something highly interesting had been presented to me. And there is no evidence of any sort that telepathy does work in such a convoluted fashion.

For the first time I began really to take Indians seriously. I went back to Mrs. Gerts after that and sat regularly with her for development every Saturday night for twelve weeks. During that time nothing ever happened of an evidential nature; but my group of spirit associates was enlarged and my contact with them strengthened.

Those who form my protective band were said to be doing this Good Samaritan stint as part of their own spiritual progression. Throughout our relationship since then, each has always played his own individual role, and, although I have never been able to learn much about him personally, has always seemed to stay in character. I am sure they have done what they could to protect me; but it took much more cooperation on my part than I at first realized. I don't think they were then aware, either, that bodily defense would be needed as well as mental. But on December 4th they were suddenly alerted to twenty-four hour sentry duty.

That day, tripping over a small dog who came to play with Junior and got himself tangled in my feet, I threw myself to keep from stepping on him. I landed solidly on the ground with my arm against a brick bordering the flower bed and broke my right wrist in two places.

I hardly dare to claim specifically that rascally influence up-ended me, or that they caused any of the other accidents that began to happen to me consistently for a period of time; but I'd lived for many years before without breaking anything more important than an occasional dish or a daily breakfast egg. I even managed to slide through ten winters on the icy hills of western Maryland and successfully evade a spill. Now I was finally brought to earth by a sunkissed Florida puppy, and from then on for over six months accidents kept happening to me almost constantly.

My guides, napping until the moment my wrist went craaa-aaaack, went into immediate action, and after its initial intensity the pain was always bearable; and I was calm. So calm, in fact, that nobody would believe me. I had a terrible time convincing any of my neighbors that my arm was broken so that someone would take me to the doctor.

After I finally got to the hospital, though, and returned with my arm in a cast, Irene, Nan, Rena, and Bill and Helen Hanemann were mobilized. All kinds of wonderful service was available from then on.

It wasn't too unpleasant, actually, living alone with a broken wing, except that Junior didn't understand. He demanded his customary attention, including his usual number of walks around the block every day even though I hadn't promenaded without my stick for fifteen years and found it exhausting. Cooking wasn't a problem at first because Irene showed up the next day with a huge pot of stew so I wouldn't have to think about what to eat for a week. There was such a great quantity of it that I've rarely thought about eating stew since.

I did feel mistreated a few days later when I tripped while trying to negotiate the step into the trailer and gashed and bruised my shin on the sharp metal doorsill. This time I gave a whale of a wail, afraid my leg was broken, too, and that would have been almost too much.

But everything came out all right eventually. The arm was out of the cast in ten weeks, numb for over six months because of using the cane too soon, and then entirely well and that was the end of that episode.

Except for one little thing. Several weeks after the cast was removed I accompanied a friend to a crowded Sunday afternoon session at nearby Cassadaga Spiritualist Camp, where a visiting medium from New York was to give messages. The question I wrote on my slip of paper (called a billet), which was put with all the others into a basket, was merely, "A message, please." I signed the initials "S.S." on the outside of the folded sheet.

Later the basket was placed in front of the medium and she began to give readings. Eventually she picked up my billet and called out my initials across the large auditorium. When they were acknowledged, she asked, "Have you recently tripped over anything?"

"Yes," I answered.

"What was it?" she asked. "I'm just curious."

"A puppy."

As the audience laughed in sympathy, she added, "Well, I just wondered, for the message I get for you is this: 'Your tripping days are over. You will be taken care of.' "

A nice sentiment. I only wish it had been true.

Chapter 27

THE MUSE BECOMING ACTIVE again, a broken arm couldn't keep me from work, so right after the first of the year I was back at the typewriter, left-handed at first but not for long. Fingers in a cast are supposed to be exercised, so I exercised them. I had to be positive my facts of etheric enlightenment were correct before daring to send my book to a publisher, so it seemed imperative to get my communication system reactivated. The talkers in my mind had stopped bothering me because I had kept myself closed to them for so long, and I made certain not to attempt any oral concourse with Mother again. But there seemed no reason we couldn't get together at the typewriter, and we did.

Very soon, though, Mother turned me over to a new scribe, who she said would help me with the philosophy because he would have more power to get through to me and he knew so much more than she did. My new communicant identified himself as James Anderson. When asked personal data about himself so that I could try to check if he was a real individual or some figment of my subconscious, he told me a few vague facts but nothing identifiable. He said he had died early in this century, that he had lived in Massachusetts, and that he'd had children. Nothing more exact could be learned from him.

As time went on I came to suspect that "James Anderson" was a pseudonym for some well-known person who was still active trying to send enlightening data to the world; but for a long time no indication was given as to who it was. It will be told in its proper sequence how his ostensible identification came about. Certainly if he had originally come to me as that individual he would have been rejected at once, for I was quite wary of imposters by then and would never have believed the truth.

After Mother had me well-established writing with someone else she could depend on, she apparently went off on a much needed vacation, or to take a post-graduate course in something educational. It is difficult to be sure just what she was up to, but she did not answer the typewriter for some time. And of course I never attempted to talk to her mentally. My mind had to be kept completely closed against reception at all times or the intruders might have moved in again.

Mr. Anderson and I worked on the manuscript most of the winter. He is the one now referred to as James; but at first I was more formal with him. The initial thing he said he especially wanted to write about was the danger of Ouija boards and automatic writing. Even though I had personally gone through much pandemonium because of my own efforts at communication, no warnings about such pitfalls were yet in the book. I was very wary of writing about negative experiences because I was sure readers would find them difficult to understand. James said warnings were so important, however, that they must go in.

What he wrote was that it is not even wise to play with the Ouija as a game, because you might begin to take it seriously. He maintained that uncritical acceptance of messages received on it is definitely perilous, for the spirit who claims to be the one you wish to contact may actually be an ill-natured invisible interloper trying to make trouble or mischief. He described the menace of the unseen rather entertainingly.

"It's as hazardous," he wrote, "as advertising in the newspaper for an honorably-intentioned mate."

I agreed with him perfectly from my own experience with Harvey. When this was mentioned, it was revealed that James did not know anything about Harvey, for his name hadn't been mentioned around there for some time. He had been briefed about my talkers, but neither Mother nor I had thought to mention Harvey to him.

While realizing that Harvey had been quite a problem to me, James said he was not nearly as dangerous as the hairy monsters some people make connection with.

"It wouldn't be so bad," he wrote, "if the trespasser could immediately be identified as such, as he would be if you were able to see him, for then all communication could be stopped before he gained too strong a hold. But he's invisible, so who can stick a label on him? Many persons accept as truth what they are told by mischiefmakers, thus making a pen-pal of a type of spirit in whose company they wouldn't want to be caught dead."

I wished I'd had such warnings in advance. The mess I'd gotten myself into had come because each step had been taken alone without advice. Very little has been written about earthbound entities—there was no mention of them whatever in the type of critical books I read, of course. Perhaps authors who have had difficult experiences of this kind are reluctant to make themselves look silly by admitting to them. But somebody has to do it.

Today, after having published some fifteen books on ESP, I receive many letters from readers who recognize me as one who can sympathize and possibly help them with the problems they have gotten into by their efforts to communicate. My experience with readers was recently reinforced by an article in FATE magazine, May, 1970, entitled "Spirit 'Possession' Fact or Fallacy?" by my friend and fellow author on psychic subjects, Harold Sherman.

He writes: "Almost every mail brings tragic evidence that a percentage of those who make a parlor game of Ouija board experiments and automatic writing have 'opened mental and psychic doors' so that 'tramp spirits,' masquerading as loved ones or high spiritual beings, can enter and take over. Once establishing residence in consciousness, such beings cling parasitically and tenaciously resist efforts to dislodge them. . . ."

Harold quotes a reader who says, "It seems incredible that I could be in the grip of this evil influence which won't let me alone day or night."

Another wrote him, "It started when I thought I had made contact with a loved one or highly developed spirit. The messages seemed authentic and inspirational in nature and won my complete confidence. I did everything to make my mind receptive and to surrender to these spiritual influences. Gradually I began to hear voices inside my head and I could sense things without having to write them down. Then, after a trusted spirit had gained control of my consciousness and I let him direct me to do and say things, his character suddenly changed. His 'talk' became vulgar, suggestive, and obscene. I was commanded to say and do unsavory things, to submit to sexual stimulation, to renounce my friends and loved ones, even urged to commit suicide so I could be with the 'possessor,' or to kill those who were opposing my 'changed attitude and conduct.' "

Harold, a great psychic himself, says, and my own letters confirm it, that this pattern is repeated time and again in outpourings from men and women relieved to feel that at last they have found someone who can understand the psychic dilemma in which they are trapped, a dilemma doctors, psychiatrists, ministers and even worried relatives and friends in the main refuse to accept.

It is not only kookies and dimwits who attempt communication, especially not today with the current upsurge in ESP interest. A great many nice folk, and particularly many young people, are doing it, and those who get into trouble need help. As Harold Sherman says: "If you accept the fact that under certain conditions, mind can communicate with mind, and if you accept the likelihood of an existence after death, then you probably would accept the possibility that the mind of a discarnate entity still could influence the mind of a living individual."

Whether we like the idea or not, there apparently are unpleasant entities hanging around just waiting for an opportunity to make their presence known in any way possible. Aside from their ability on occasion to impress unhappily receptive minds with negative thoughts, we are mainly at their mercy only when we attempt to communicate, or open our minds to receptivity, without knowing how to protect ourselves. For this reason it must be insisted that beginners must never sit alone to do automatic writing or to use the Ouija board until they have learned the proper safeguards. Those who assure us they are protected by their innocence, their good thoughts, or their love of Jesus are naïve and they might as well admit it, but they probably won't until they've gotten into a peck of trouble.

If you still feel a strong urge to try to communicate even after my warnings, then find a development class in your community and sit with it until you are sure you know exactly what to do. You will probably discover that a medium in your town holds such meetings regularly. Even a medium who is not particularly competent to give evidential messages may be a good group leader. If you don't find compatible persons this way, write to me care of the Survival Research Foundation, Box 50446, Tucson, Ariz. 85703. By then I should have available a roster of development circles in all parts of the country where you can improve your psychic abilities under competent leadership.

What you are doing when you attempt to communicate is what has been called "invoking the spirits." It is utterly fallacious that in an effort to consort with those you love in the spirit world you are causing them to return unwillingly from some far place at your bidding. That is not the problem at all. Those who love us are probably with us much of the time, making every effort to help us. They are there of their own volition, and by doing what they can to aid us they are performing acts for their own self-advancement. They want to be with us and will be whether or not we are aware of their presence.

It is true that one who mourns inordinately and continually cries out to a loved person who has died holds him in the bondage of his grief, causing him much unhappiness and anxiety. This should be avoided, and would be were you to realize that your separation is only temporary and you will one day be "rejoined in the hereafter." But an ordinary effort to make ourselves aware of the continuing presence of those who have gone on is perfectly legitimate and to be desired. It is in trying actually to communicate that you are likely to come a cropper because of the uninvited entities who may arrive at your call. If you take what they write as factual and accept them seriously as who they purport to be, they may cause you much confusion. They may even take you over and move in on you, overshadowing your own mind completely.

Mother evidenced herself later that spring, refreshed enough that she could relieve James Anderson of his duties as correspondent. We polished up her chapter some more and then went over one or two incidents in her childhood. Then one day I said, "Is there anything you particularly want me to add that I haven't said yet?"

"Yes," Mother typed. "I want you to give some words of warning about the danger of taking the Ouija board too seriously."

"But, Mother, James and I did that while you were gone," I said, somewhat startled. I read her what we had added during the winter.

"It's all right now," she wrote, surprised and pleased.

I thought there was a certain amount of evidential value to all this. James, when he started writing, had not known about Harvey and how he had originally attached himself to me because of the Ouija board. Dad had been aware of very little that had occurred to me personally during his absence. Now Mother did not know what had been written while she was away. You get the feeling from this that they are truly the ordinary persons, advanced to the status of spirits, that they claim to be, and not superhuman entities of any kind.

If we are going to explain all these characters with their personal eccentricities as coming from my own subconscious mind, we would once again have to resort to the split-personality theory. And I have been told by a competent psychiatrist friend that whatever I am, I'm not schizophrenic.

Chapter 28

WHEN MY INVISIBLE WRITING pool put their final O.K. on the manuscript as being the best we were able to do at that time, I started thinking about what publisher in New York to send it to. But my typewriter wrote that I was going to take it to New York myself. Mother said she knew positively that I would soon move there to live, so there was no use arguing about it.

The idea had no appeal whatever. I'd always fought shy of tackling the biggest city alone, and now it was out of the question because there was very little money left. Reluctantly, however, because she insisted, I began to make plans to put the Gingerbread House up for sale, thinking to do my packing during the summer and leave for New York by fall. When my typewriter said instead that I'd be leaving for the North within a month, there seemed no possible way to comply. Such a big step should take much more preparation than that.

Junior proved Mother right. He hadn't been lively for some time and I'd teased him about getting old, not suspecting that he might be sick. But suddenly his hind legs began to stiffen and he screamed with pain whenever his back was touched, so I rushed him to a vet. He had a slipped disc in his spine and his condition worsened fast. Shots of cortisone relieved his pain only temporarily, and the prognosis was ultimate paralysis, or else an operation which only possibly might be successful.

I discovered that in Alabama, just off the route to New York, was the best veterinary college and hospital in the South, where spinal fusion operations were performed frequently on dachshunds (whose long bodies are especially prone to this disability). So I packed the car in a rush, left the trailer with an agent to sell, and started north well within the time prophesied.

We caught the head surgeon at the Small Animal Clinic just two days before he left for his summer vacation, and Junior underwent surgery early the next morning. It was Memorial Day exactly two years after Nina died, and so doubly difficult for me as I paced the floor of a motel room. The thing I was most afraid of was that Junior might be meant to be taken away from me. It would be complicated to try to work in New York with a dog who hadn't been trained to stay alone. He would probably present many problems there, so I tried to adjust my thinking to the possibility that it might be necessary for me to give him up. But with all my stiff-upper-lipmanship I couldn't accept the thought of losing my dear little companion of the past seven years and prayed that he could stay with me.

Junior had a rough time, was even in an oxygen tent for a while; but he was so sure New York was for him that he pulled through in order not to miss the big adventure with me. The second day after his operation I made a bed in the front seat of the car, the doctor showed me how to handle the tightly bandaged little dog, and off we started. We visited my friends Billie and Bob Feagans at their estate outside Lynchburg, Virginia, for ten days while Junior recuperated, and then we hit the road again.

Now, besides Junior's sudden damage and subsequent repair, here follows a list of undisastrous misadventures that happened to us within a few brief weeks . . . and if you didn't know me pretty well by now you'd be sure I was lying:

The morning we left Lynchburg a service station attendant looked at the Chevrolet's bulging cargo and put extra air in the back tires to support the load. When the heat of the road and my fifty to sixty mile-per-hour cruising speed made them expand, there were two blowouts of two back tires within two hours. In both instances when the sharp report sounded and the car became suddenly unmanageable I was able to hang onto the wheel, pull over to the side of the road, flag down a passerby for assistance, go buy the necessary replacements, and proceed on my way with a minimum of aggravation. But I gave my group of invisible back-seat drivers "what-for," nonetheless, for letting it happen.

"If you can keep me from wrecking after a blowout, why can't you tell me in the first place not to let the guy put too much air in my tires?" I demanded. But got no answer any more intelligent than the old bit about the "difficulty of getting new ideas into your mind."

I spent the night with Audrey and Joe Soukup in Baltimore, took a shower in their tub, put all my weight on the built-in soap dish handle to support myself when turning around, the soap dish pulled loose from the wall, and I crashed to the bottom of the tub. Results, one slightly sore muscle and a half-inch cut on my leg. Nothing more.

The next day we skimmed along the Jersey Turnpike and those well-marked throughways which skirt New York on the north and arrived in Stamford, Connecticut, to visit Bart and Jean Fonda, who used to work for *Shopping with Susy*. We stayed there a week until I found an apartment in a brand new building in New York City and moved in.

Junior's bandages had been removed, revealing a skinned hide where he'd been shaved from his neck to his tail, and a beautifully healing scar. He handled himself carefully and was convalescing much better than anyone but me had expected, with complete use of his back legs once again. But I still lifted him up and down from things and had been warned never again to allow him to traverse flights of steps under his own steam.

So the second morning at Jean's he decided to leave our bedroom before me and start downstairs. I saw him on the top step and shouted, "Wait, you can't do that!" This startled him, he lost his balance, and fell down the entire flight of fourteen steps. Frantic, I stood at the top and shrieked, "Oh, God, help! Save him, save him!" It was less than two weeks since his operation, and it didn't seem possible he wouldn't be killed.

Instead, he slid and scrambled and skidded on the highly waxed stairs, never once rolled over on his back, landed on his feet at the bottom, and looked up at me with a rather discouraged expression as if to say, "There must be a better way to do it." Then he walked out into the kitchen and hit Jean for some breakfast.

Just a few more of these and I'll be through. The second week in my new apartment in New York City, in the dark I fell flat on my face through the open door of the bathroom. Didn't hit the tub, didn't hit the washbasin, didn't even so much as skin my knee.

I fell off a bus a few days later. Missed the top step and picked myself up off the sidewalk, stunned and shaken, but not cracked, chipped or bent, quite able to walk the three weary blocks home. Then, shortly afterward, I tripped on the metal strip across the entrance of an old-fashioned elevator and stretched my length on the floor. The only thing hurt then was a finger.

Each time something like this occurred I mentally thanked my invisible associates for their very kind assistance in keeping me from being badly damaged, and also gave them the devil for not assuring that these accidents did not happen in the first place.

"This sort of thing becomes wearing in time," I ranted at them. "I need me all in one piece."

They informed me mentally that they could protect me in advance, if I would only cooperate by the proper thinking, and eventually they were able to get their technique into my mind so that I would know how to do it.

Even with all the experiences with Harvey and Sam and the others, the theory of malicious spirit influence was very difficult to take. I just didn't want to get into the habit of ascribing blown tires, slipped discs, horizontal descents from busses, fanny flops in bathtubs, or, for that matter, even ingrown toenails or spilt ink, to discarnate delinquents. I knew such beliefs were for people who stick feathers and cow dung in their hair, shake rattles, and wear masks. They could hardly be accepted without indicating atavism. I didn't want to return in my thinking to the dark jungles of my origin.

But, by George, there had been too much mischance in a brief period of time to be attributable to chance alone. Then had I suddenly just happened to become accident prone? Well, just as suddenly, when doing what my associates told me to do for protection, I became un-accident prone, and the curtain rang down on my comedy of errors. I settled down in my New York apartment, took Junior for walks and watched him adjust to big city living with no problems at all, and days began to pass in the normal unexciting way that days are supposed to pass.

What my guides told me to do actually sounds so innocent that it is difficult for me to describe it here and expect to be taken seriously. Yet at the time I was forced by my need to accept the simple rules; and I found that they worked so successfully that I have continued to use them most of the time since then.

I was told to mentally wrap myself in protection at all times. I was supposed by then to be aware of the power of my thoughts, and so it should not be too difficult, the guides said, for me to use my mind to keep any intruding entities from getting near enough to harm me. The ways to protect yourself are varied, but they all amount to the same thing. You mentally enclose yourself in something that acts as a barrier to the intruders. It does not really matter what you cover yourself with. It is the power of your belief in its ability to help you that protects you. It was suggested that I visualize a white light and see myself wrapping it around me as if encircling myself in swaddling clothes. Not one spot must escape my protective efforts. Then, if the belief were strong enough, it would present an impassable wall through which the entities who attempted to harm me could not force an entrance. I must also keep constantly in mind the thought that "Nothing can come near me or in any way influence me that does not come from God in love and peace."

Of course, as one goes on living, he will have occasional misfortunes from time to time as may naturally occur. This has nothing to do with such a series of accidents as befell me because of the apparent exertion of those invisible miscreants who were trying to do me in. But, whatever the explanation, and whether you believe in all this or not, when I learned to wrap myself in protection, the multi-manifestations of mischance stopped and they have not resumed.

Although discovering this entirely on my own, I have since learned that forming this protective encasing of yourself is standard procedure among those persons who believe in the existence of spirits and have learned how to cope with the malicious ones. It is most frequently described as "enveloping yourself in the white Christ light," although some people think of hardening their auras around them until they become like eggshells that are impenetrable. There are various ways of doing it, but all depend on a firm belief in their success.

One more of the things that I came upon alone without any previous knowledge about it and then discovered that others everywhere else in the world also do the same thing is the idea of spirit missionary work. When I learned to convert Harvey and the other villains, I didn't know it had ever been done by anyone else. Shortly after my arrival in New York, I met a pleasant little woman named Harriett M. Shelton. Mrs. Shelton, who has since died, was the author of a book called *Abraham Lincoln Returns.* She told me that she sat regularly every day and did work to help the spirits. Entities who wished to be of service spoke through her when she was in a trance-like state and what she said was tape-recorded. Then she played the tapes frequently in order that misguided entities who were nearby could hear them.

I told Mrs. Shelton my similar experiences reading Mother's Chapter in order to give such information to these unfortunates. She said that she also happened onto this technique of giving assistance alone and without knowing anyone else did such a thing; but when she went to England she learned that the Spiritualist Churches there had missionary groups that met regularly for the purpose of passing on exactly this kind of information to those unseen entities who needed help. I have since participated in rescue circles in various areas of the country where lost or unenlightened spirits are allowed to possess the medium. Then members of the group attempt to impress them with the fact that they really are dead and need to understand where they are and how to adjust to their new situations.

Whether or not parapsychologists will ever add up such numerous small coincidences as these of mine into anything resembling evidence for survival, I doubt. But to me it was reassuring, at least, to learn that these processes I happened onto alone and unassisted are actually used by those who accept a belief in spirit survival as a way of life. It was another of the small consolations of which I was to need plenty as my New York existence began.

BOOK MARK.

Chapter 29

NEW YORKERS DID NOT RUSH forth to greet me. There were no ticker-tape parades; in fact those many millions of people hardly seemed aware that Susy had arrived in their midst. I moved into a brand new apartment building on East 76th Street with a rent of $143 per month, on a two year lease. I was sure my book would sell quickly and there would be no question of being able to keep up the payments. I was determined to approach all new problems with positive thinking, so didn't let myself consider any alternative.

I was lonely, though. So with my Texas informality I began talking to people in the elevators and the lobby and in general acting as if the building were a small town. Soon I was taking jello and hot soup to those who were sick, and dog and cat sitting for various ones who wanted an evening out or a week's vacation. I have since learned that this is not quite the way one behaves in New York, but it produced many nice contacts at the time.

Publishers to whom my manuscript about my life and early experiences with communication was sent were less than enthusiastic. If there hadn't been a certain amount of encouragement from mediums, I might have folded my tent very quickly and disappeared from the great metropolis.

Locating good sensitives was not easy, however. The scientific organizations in the field, The American Society for Psychical Research (which I joined along with its counterpart, the British Society) and the Parapsychology Foundation would not recommend any psychics in the area. It is not the custom for objective groups to take a stand on the ability or integrity of mediums. They are quite right, because one person may get a good reading and another may be terribly disappointed. One does indeed learn that recommendations are seldom wise.

Persons like petite, dramatic Lucile Kahn, to whom Hornell Hart had given me letters of introduction, were more free with their suggestions; and Miss Gertrude Tubby was most helpful. Tubby, as she was called, was a lively old maid in her eighties who lived in nearby New Jersey. She had been secretary to Dr. James Hyslop of Columbia University when he was the president of the A.S.P.R. many years before, and she was a scientifically-oriented believer. She knew enough to approach everything psychic from a critical point of view, yet she thought there was so much evidence for survival that it was stupid of researchers not to accept it. Being such a rugged individualist, Tubby was quite outspoken about it. For years she conducted development classes in her home in Upper Montclair, and I was pleased to be invited. Had it not been such a long bus ride I would have attended regularly, instead of only twice.

Members of Miss Tubby's group had progressed well in their mediumship, for she was especially successful as a leader or teacher. Psychic Mary Tallmadge, who now leads her own development groups in Northern New Jersey, was one of her pupils.

When strangers visit a class of this type, members usually attempt to get messages for them. On my first visit Nancy Craw received automatic writing for me that was heartening. It started off: "There has been great suffering here, but from it has developed a very beautiful, deep, joyous soul. She is exuberant, buoyant, sparkling over with happy enthusiasm. We need so many more like her." This was pleasant enough to gratify me; but there was more yet. "There is love of music and of dancing here—all forms. I get no husband. Much of her family is on the other side. Her father is a lovely person. She is a daughter very much beloved. The initial M." (Merton, of course.) "She is a writer, too. She will be a mighty force. Her development at this time is alone. I do not see any understanding companionship here which might help her—no husband. She can write and also lecture. . . ."

Naturally, after this I returned home from the meeting quite set up. There was just enough factual data in the message to make me hope that the kind words might also be true. At this time I had never lectured in my life and would have been scared to death to attempt it, but would willingly have made the effort if anyone had asked me. Lecturing has since come to be a very big part of my life's experience.

I rode home on the bus from that New Jersey meeting with a most attractive young woman who had also been a guest—Lex Tice, who always captures everyone with her Virginia charm, her enthusiasm, and her pixie face framed by very short, prematurely gray hair. She has remained one of my good friends every since, and her moral support during my difficult first years in New York was important to me. She even came to see me once during that first autumn when things were particularly drastic and handed me $100, saying, "I felt you might need this to tide you over." That is a rare kind of friend.

The first professional medium I visited in New York was cultured, gracious Caroline Randolph Chapman, who has since retired. After her initial recounting of the complete history of her life—a tedious habit of hers—I took down in shorthand everything she said to me, and much of it was significant. Although she rather rambled on and said a few things that were not particularly pertinent, most of what she said was factual, and her precognition came true.

I went to Mrs. Chapman anonymously, a complete stranger who made it a point to say little more than "Yes" and "No," to nod and smile, but to reveal nothing about herself. Good mediums want you to be cooperative, but if you begin to give them personal information they invariably say, "Don't tell me. Let me get it myself." They have a pride of accomplishment that they don't want you to spoil with too many hints. Most people have the wrong idea about mediums, thinking that a visit to one is always a matter of being pumped for information which is then handed back to you. This is not the practice of the greats in this field, of whom Mrs. Chapman is undoubtedly one. It does occur with some mediocre mediums, who ask questions and encourage you to talk, then return to you what you have given them. The only thing Mrs. Chapman gleaned from my conversation was that I was from the South, and she admitted that my accent had given that away.

After her preliminaries, the first thing she said to me when my message started was, "You will never become unbalanced. If

you'd been going to do that, it would have happened before now."
I thought about my past year coping with entities who talked in
my mind and pushed me around and was somewhat inclined to
agree with her. She went on, "You have read a great deal on this
subject. You are quite literary and very artistic, have an eagle eye,
an analytical and critical mind. You see a lot of flaws in other
people. Your spiritual work is helping you to remodel yourself."
Yes, Mother had been working on that ever since my days in Salt
Lake City.

"What you do must be done well or not at all," Mrs. Chapman
went on. "You love a home. You have to have a home of your
own even if it is only a 2 x 4." My recently abandoned Gingerbread House was witness to that. "Dogs and cats like you. You
are developing and will be a medium. Remember my words, you
will uplift the fallen. You will enlighten them and give them help."

This was all very fine, but enough of the small talk, I thought.
Let's get down to something evidential. She did, then, saying,
"There is a grandmother here on your mother's side. You never
saw her." This was correct. She then gave me three specific
names, Anna, Jane, and Charles—who were all mother's relatives. She added, "There is something about your name that is a
little different. There has been a change in your name." (Ethel to
Susy.)

"Have you been married once?" she asked. "I see a broken ring
over your head. You had a wonderful mother. You were always
very close to her, more like sisters. She had an abundance of
beautiful hair at one time." My greatest disappointment in
Mother had been when she cut that gorgeous long auburn mane
and began to wear it short.

"Are you doing any writing at all?" the medium asked. I was
not, at the moment, so hesitated. She pushed on with it. "Are you
a writer, do you do literary work? There is something you are
writing or have written that is going to be published. It is only the
beginning of your writing. Mother has helped you a bit on your
book."

After a few comments about my wonderful guides, but no
names for them, Mrs. Chapman shook her head in amazement. "I
don't know anybody who has had such a reading as this . . . you

are getting so much help in your life from spirits, and they are all here. You seem to be standing very much alone at the present moment, but you know you are not alone."

Mrs. Chapman said that someone named Helen was going to be of great service to me. She was right in that, too, because it was Mother's friend from her Front Royal, Virginia, days, Helen Simpson Phillips who, you might say, launched my career. She was a head nurse at Mt. Sinai Hospital when I first arrived in New York and she helped me find my apartment and acquire some inexpensive furniture. While so doing she told me so many of her own interesting psychic experiences—some of which were verified by the other people involved—that I wrote an article about her. When it came out the next summer in *Tomorrow* magazine, it was my first published piece about the psychic field.

Among several other names Mrs. Chapman gave me, she mentioned William and Robert—my great-grandfather? Because these are common names, one cannot get too excited about receiving them. When they crop up as frequently as they do for me, however, there may be a reason.

"You are going to teach and preach immortality," she added. "You will relieve the fear of death for many. You are going to prevent several suicides. You are destined to help people. You have a world of work to do, in writing and investigating. Lots of research."

When Mrs. Chapman asked for a question, I suggested she try to give me my mother's name. "I'll work on that," she said. Then, after a pause, "It wasn't Elizabeth?" That was a direct hit, but I had hoped she would give me the name I liked better. I said, "Not quite." Then she said, "Betty. Didn't she die of cancer?" Again I replied, "Not quite," for Mother had cancer at the time she died and the doctor told me it would soon have caused her death if her heart hadn't given out first. Mrs. Chapman added, "Her heart was bad, too." Then she gave another prediction: "You will soon meet a professional man, a lawyer, who will be of help to you and play a big role in your life."

The medium finished my interview with a surprise that capped the whole thing. "James Anderson," she said. "He has given you some very definite things."

In a critical review of this one might say, "It was only telepathy involved here. Your own mind was the source of all the information." Telepathy is a genuine supernormal feat and nothing to be sneezed at. Much of what mediums get must involve it. Yet her prediction about my writing, with special reference to all the research and the teaching of immortality, has been realized on a long-range basis; and her statement that I would meet a lawyer who would be important to me came true almost immediately. Grant (as I will call him) was to become the one dependable individual who sustained me all through my time in New York, and he has remained the same good friend ever since.

Shortly after my visit to Mrs. Chapman I made a week's trip to Onset, Massachusetts with Miss Tubby and Mrs. Shelton, to attend an Arthur Ford seminar. I was eager for a reading from him, for even in 1957 the late great medium had a high reputation. I had told no one in New York any data about my family, hugging all personal information to my bosom because it might bring evidence from psychics. After our arrival at Onset, I attempted to arrange for a private sitting with Ford before he had any chance to learn anything about me from my two garrulous companions, who were his very close friends and might unwittingly reveal to him some of the few little things they had learned about me on our trip. I was to wonder about this later.

Almost the first thing Arthur said to me was, "Who's Ethel?" Then he went on with the following: "There is a lady who says you were named after her but you changed your name. You were named after your grandmother." Yes, Elizabeth. "She must have been Scotch. Annie and Jeannie, an aunt of yours." I greeted Aunt Anna. "She was very fond of you. She tells me that your life has been broken up into difficult emotional situations. You made an unfortunate marriage and got a divorce. 'On the earth plane,' she says, 'I was against divorce,' but you had to have it to keep your self-respect. For a while you built a cynical wall around you."

Ford also gave me the name Robert. He described Mother in almost the same words Mrs. Chapman had used. (No, there could have been no collusion between them, and nobody had heard the details of my Chapman sitting.)

Then Arthur said, "You were born with a great artistic ability. From the time you were a young girl you have liked to go off with paper and pencil and in later years a typewriter. You think better with a typewriter." I always maintain that, but how did Arthur Ford know it about a stranger?

He went on, "So far what you have been doing has been preparation, training, and in the next year or so immediately ahead of you, you are going to write some remarkable things. You are really a good writer."

"Do you know who Betty is? Was she Betty Smith? She says her fingers are straight now." (Mother had arthritis in her finger joints that had been very painful.)

Ford then focused on my current problem: "Right now you need to do very much about your financial situation. You have worked as a secretary. You are going to get another job, soon. You do have some remarkable psychic powers. They are slow developing. When the psychic flow begins to come through you, you begin to question and you defeat the flow." (How true!) "Don't try to analyze it as it comes. You have this objective way of dealing with things. Your big problem now is to settle down to serious writing and get yourself a job that will ease up on the financial situation."

Mrs. Shelton had been arguing with me about this on the way up on the train. While I had told her nothing about my past or my family, I *had* mentioned that I was living on an inheritance that had dwindled to the point where there was only a few hundred dollars left in the bank. It was also mentioned that I had done secretarial work but hated it and didn't intend to subject myself to it again because I was determined to make my living as a writer.

A wealthy woman, Mrs. Shelton was horrified that I should be so unrealistic. She began insisting that I get a job immediately. When Ford told me the same thing in almost the same way, I was certain that she had coached him to say it to me when she had made the appointment for me. I lost faith in him completely at that moment. Although enjoying his teachings at the seminar, I was quite reserved with him after that whenever we chanced to meet. I felt that my sitting with him had been a farce.

Reading my notes now I see that he made many hits he had no

normal way to know without a great deal of research about me—which he could not have done because he had not even known of my coming, much less who I was. And, for that matter, who was I? Why should it have been worth his while to try to investigate the background of this stranger even if he'd had the opportunity? Possibly he got the data by telepathy, but it is more likely that it came as it purported to come, from the entities in question. Ford was a medium of genuine talent who did not have to resort to such devious methods to get his information about his sitters. I am sure now that the personal information he gave me came psychically; and I observed a great deal in his life and experiences after I came to know him better that has altered entirely my first negative response to him.

Arthur Ford was no more impressed than I at our first encounter. Several years later after a Spiritual Frontiers Fellowship meeting in New York, I went up to him and identified myself. My first paperback, *ESP*, had just come out and he said shortly, "Oh, yes, Susy Smith. I've just read your book *ESP*. You're a lot brighter than I thought you were."

Arthur and I later became good friends and always had long and fascinating chats whenever we got together. I didn't hold that earlier remark against him, being willing to accept an occasional dirty crack, if it is constructive.

Chapter 30

WAS BEGINNING TO enjoy my New York contacts; and learning to be familiar with the big city was enchanting, if exhausting. My car had been sold after three days, because keeping it in the building was expensive and leaving it on the street required an unending struggle to find parking places. But waiting for buses and subways, and then usually having to stand in them when they came along, was no help to muscles and joints already made uncomfortable by the climate.

Junior settled into city routines, however, as if he had been born to them. He looked forward to his walks, when he could investigate the new and fascinating smells and commune with neighboring dogs also hiking along on their leashes. But he remained inside quite peacefully the rest of the time. He was middle-aged by then and not needing to be too active. Our Hungarian doctor friend who lived in the next apartment, kept an ear on him for me. He reported that when I was gone from home for long periods during the day, at about eleven A.M. he could hear Junior saying "Oooo" a few times; but that's the only unfavorable comment my pet ever made about New York living.

My big problem was continuously financial. My reluctance to apply for a job wasn't just a stupid refusal to give up and go to work. It was the understanding that I would never be able to tackle rush hour traffic, if I took a secretarial job, and the hesitancy to try to compete with experienced and established local newspaper personnel if I attempted to get work that would be interesting to me.

Upon selling the trailer for $1200, I accepted a deposit and monthly payments, and was trying to live on the $200-per-month checks that were finishing off that indebtedness. Then in September the final payment arrived . . . and the check bounced. There was, at that time, exactly $8.50 in my bank account, and the rent was due.

Having found that writing with Mother on the typewriter was almost impossible in New York—it is said that vibrations there are not conducive to communication—I had been almost out of touch with her. I didn't dare try to open my mind in order to hear from her mentally. Those intruders might still be lurking around and I wasn't about to give them the opportunity to penetrate my surrounding white light of protection. Now, however, in desperation, I sat at my typewriter and said, "Mother, what'll I do?"

Except to identify herself to my satisfaction, she didn't say much. But what she said was to the point: "Have you thought of your shell jewelry?"

I sat and thought of my shell jewelry for quite a while, getting out my few remaining pieces and looking at them. Were they anything sophisticated New York might appreciate? There was a little Christmas tree made of green shells and decorated with pearls and rhinestones and sequins. There were bell-shaped shells with red bows and green leaves, whose matching earrings were smaller bell-shaped shells. Actually, I decided, they looked quite high fashion—nothing whatever like the shoddy novelties one usually sees at the seashore. Certainly such things might be considered new and different in the city. I became enthusiastic and dressed myself up and carried them downtown to try to sell to some of the bigger stores.

The purchasing departments of large firms are something from which ordinary unwary citizens should be carefully protected. If one had to visit them often, he would be compelled to acquire a hard and aggressive veneer to survive the indignities he must undergo. Just getting in to see a buyer is an ordeal. After days of waiting for appointments, having them broken or postponed or ignored, and then sitting around with numerous hard-boiled salesman-type characters in anterooms for hours, I finally was permitted to interview the buyers for Saks-Fifth Avenue, Lord & Taylor, and Macy's Little Shop boutique. And from them I received orders for $500 worth of jewelry, to be delivered before Christmas!

Requests for a quantity of shells were rushed off to Lois in Florida; and while waiting for them to arrive I became acquainted with a woman in my building who had a horde of old costume decorations in her closet. She gave me strips of rhinestones and quantities of oddly-shaped sequins to embellish my Christmas trees, delighting me with my good fortune.

Unfortunately, Junior took that time to get excited over her dog and wet on the white carpet of her exquisite apartment—something he had never done since his puppy days. After that the relationship with my source of supply cooled somewhat. In fact, I didn't go back there any more, and never did get to thank her properly for all the lagniappe.

I spent October and November sitting at a card table in front of the television set making pins and earrings, working until two or three every morning. That was when Cupid shot his bee-bee gun at me and I fell for Jack Paar. His new Tonight Show became the highlight of my evenings, and I truly adored the lovable personality Jack projected at me from the screen.

He began urging people with interesting jobs or hobbies to come on the program, so I decided to try. On the telephone I bantered with a nice producer who then invited me in for an interview. Trinka Russell, another of my new friends in the building, loaned me her black diamond mink coat to wear for the interview and that sold me to them immediately.

Scheduled to appear the Thursday before Thanksgiving, I arrived all breathless (minus Trinka's mink) to meet my idol. To my disappointment they had decided that shell jewelry was women's stuff and so they had assigned my interview to Dodie Goodman.

Dodie is much prettier off television than on. She doesn't project that dumb personality either. What she does project is complete indifference to all and sundry. On the air she attempted to make so much fun at my expense that, although I managed to maintain my dignity, my shell jewelry became intertwined with my interest in the psychic into something spookily adrip with sand and seaweed. I left considerably discouraged.

Jack Paar's wife had seen the program, however, and wanted to know what it was I had been trying to say; so I was invited back the following week to talk about psychical research. The great man himself interviewed me on the air! He had no interest in any area of my field except dowsing—he'd personally had the experience of finding water with a forked stick; but he was an extremely gracious host.

I've been on numerous other major television shows since then, the interviews arranged by publishers of my books; but there has never since been the thrill, or the terrors, of those first two programs arranged for by myself because of my crush on Jack Paar. He couldn't have cared less, of course. Kings are bored by adulation!

I was paid $50 for each of my two television appearances. That "scale" they talk about is only given to professional performers. Most interviews to plug a book are entirely unpaid. I explain this because so many listeners think everyone receives fabulous amounts for television appearances.

The $100 obtained from TV, with the $100 Lex loaned me, the $500 that came in from the stores, and some help from my friend Grant, allowed me to exist through the fall and into the New Year. By then I had applied to the Parapsychology Foundation for a grant.

In Daytona Beach I had first read F. W. H. Myers' *Human Personality and Its Survival of Bodily Death*, a huge two-volume work published in 1903 that is a magnificent exposition of all kinds of psi events with beautifully written but excruciatingly wordy conclusions as to their significance. At the time, it occurred to me, "If only someone could cut down the tedious Victorian prose wherever it merely elaborates Myers' points, and integrate the numerous references into the text, this would be a fascinating book to introduce this subject to people who will never take the time to read that two-volume tome." So it seemed reasonable that Susy should be the one to make application to accomplish this endeavor. The idea also seemed reasonable to the late Eileen J. Garrett, the world-famous medium who was president of the Parapsychology Foundation; and shortly after the beginning of 1958 I received a grant to do this research. It only brought in $2000 a year for two years, but it was an incentive to do the work.

The time had come when I must finally break down and get a job. One was available in the Admitting Office of nearby Lenox Hill Hospital, and I stuck that out for three months. But being on my feet all day set my knees wild, so the doctors transferred me to a secretarial position in the Pathology Laboratory. All summer I took dictation while sitting beside the pathologists as they dissected and described the organs that had been removed in surgery, finding the work interesting, and even learning to tolerate a close acquaintance with rectal cancers and lungs ridden with bronchiectasis. But once, during a spell in August when the air conditioning was not functioning, a gangrenous leg that had just been amputated was brought in. I gave notice that day. Once again it had been revealed that my detached scientific objectivity could be pushed just so far and no farther. A doctor has to learn to tolerate such things, but my aspirations did not lie in that direction.

Learning that living close to my work was the secret of coping with New York wear and tear, I moved when my lease was up on 76th Street to a one-room apartment in a big Park Avenue building just two blocks from my new job as secretary to four Madison Avenue doctors. In the evenings the Myers condensation provided relaxation and challenge. No matter how exhausted I was, making the more enjoyable effort at night revived me and made it possible to endure the daily office grind.

I was sustained in my efforts with the Myers work by the moral support and suggestions of Martin Ebon, who was then administrative secretary of the Parapsychology Foundation and who has consistently been a rock of dependability for me. I have been so delighted that in recent years Martin's career has paralleled mine as an author.

In order to keep up with my personal psychic development, I realized the importance of sitting in groups. Here, too, in unity there is strength. When a few neophytes who suspect they have psi ability meet together, especially if an already matured medium is also present, a force is built up that helps everyone in the crowd to improve. Some of the best historical evidence for ESP and spirit survival has come from such home circles.

Although we attempted at first to eliminate anything of a religious nature from our meetings, we ultimately decided that it was wiser to include it. This was as much as anything in an effort to eliminate the possibility of the presence of intruding entities, who are said to dislike an aura of sanctity. Our procedure was to chat for a while, then turn the lights down low, have a prayer, and sit quietly and meditate for half an hour or longer. After this we would compare notes. We made it a habit to hold paper and pencil during the quiet periods and write down whatever thoughts occurred to us, or whatever we pictured mentally or saw externally. Thus we had written confirmation of what was experienced. This was wise because otherwise when one person, as she once did, said she had thought about something as prosaic as brown curtains and the girl next to her said she had visualized brown curtains, and someone sitting across the circle reported a concentration also on draperies of that same hue, we knew the confirmations were genuine. Although no one had any idea why a thought of something as lackluster as brown curtains had been passed around, there was written evidence for it on the note pads.

Some of my most interesting mental adventures have occurred in such development classes. Because it was easier for me to have my friends join me at my home than to go out to meetings, a custom began that was to continue for most of that eight-year stretch I was in New York. A group was formed that met regularly with me one night each week. Sometimes Betty Ritter or Mary Tallmadge were our mediums. We had one series with Ethel Myers. And occasionally we attempted to sit without any strong sensitive present at all.

I think it was actor Richard Kiley, who attended several of our meetings, who banteringly referred to us as the "Park Avenue Witches," and the name stuck to us, although if we were witches we didn't know it. Some pointed heads, maybe, but not a pointed hat in the crowd.

After the meditation period at one of our earlier sessions, Frank Bang said he had somehow sensed that I would become involved unpleasantly with glass. Frank, a quiet accountant, is another of those wonderful friends who have sustained me with his dependability throughout the years. I should have heeded him then. Someone else agreed with him, having had a vague premonition that I should be careful when washing dishes; and Lex had written down, "Warn Susy about cutting her hand on glass." Whether each one was reading the other's mind or they were genuinely predicting the future or what, I resolved to use a dish mop from then on.

One day the following week I absent-mindedly stuck my hand down inside a tumbler in the sudsy dishwater and the entire side of it came off, cutting a deep gash in my little finger. Because I'm such a noddy about evidence, I treasured that scar for years for its indication of something supernormal exhibited in my life. I can't find it anymore.

One night a member brought a friend to the meeting, a stranger to us all. During meditation I attempted to learn some facts about him psychically. I'm not able to produce a thought picture, as most people do. If I think about a thing my mind knows what it looks like, but there is no likeness of it produced in front of my closed eyes. Hardly anyone can understand why, when I think of a rose, it isn't immediately envisioned, because apparently it is for the majority. But a few of us are like that. From experience, therefore, I have come to know that when a picture shows itself to me clearly it has psi connotations.

It was difficult for me to make out what the scene that came for the stranger was all about. It looked like a wooden frame or perhaps half a bridge—against a wall. I decided it might be one of those little walkways around the side of a cliff in a natural park. There was a coiled-up rope hanging on the end of it. After the quiet period I asked the guest if those things had any significance in reference to him. He replied with amazement, "I'm a caulker by trade. All day I work on scaffolds on the side of buildings. The last thing I do at night before I leave is to coil my rope and hang it up."

My very most favorite telepathic event occurred shortly afterward. It has been written up in another book, but there are many incidents that will have to be repeated in order to make this present work a comprehensive survey of my psychic experiences.

Naomi Burroughs is one of those good friends who has endured through the years. A teacher of intellectually gifted adolescents, she is a woman of intelligence, charm, and a delightful wit. At one meeting I was attempting psychometry with her aquamarine ring. Psychometry is a means of reading the psychic vibrations from an object. As I mentioned earlier, there is a theory that all things have force fields around and interpenetrating them and these force fields are said to retain data. It is, you might say, a way of ESPying on a person by holding something which belongs to him. So I was trying to get mental impressions about Naomi by holding her ring.

We were sitting together on a couch; I was turned sideways facing Naomi with my eyes closed, holding her ring tightly and concentrating to receive what it was supposed to want to tell me. At first nothing came. Then I saw a picture that was delightful. It was the clearest psychic view ever to appear on my mental screen . . . a tiny, tiny tiger. He was a jaunty fellow, walking erect with his tail thrown over his arm, and he appeared in complete detail and living technicolor.

"Naomi," I asked, "what could this possibly mean to you? I see a very little tiger."

"You read my mind!" she shrieked. Then she told us that while she had been sitting quietly waiting for me to produce, her gaze had rested on an animal skin rug on my floor at her feet. It was a small ocelot my father had brought from Salt Lake City. Its little mounted head, with eyes glaring and teeth bared, had tripped me so many times that most of its molars had been kicked out, and I had learned to keep the head out of my way under the coffee table in front of the couch on which we were sitting. Naomi had been vaguely glancing down at it, and, not recognizing it as an ocelot, had mused mentally, "I wonder what kind of an animal that is. It has stripes . . . maybe it's a tiger. Well, if it is a tiger it's an awfully little tiger."

There were a number of witnesses to this. I wrote the incident down immediately after they left; but not one detail of it has ever been forgotten.

In New York I had my ESP gang, and then, by way of contrast and to make life more diverse, there were others who had little interest in psi with whom to go to the theater and play bridge. Pat Eells of *Shopping with Susy* days was one of these whose company was always most enjoyable.

On my second New Year's Eve there was a bridge game at my home, and we opened a bottle of champagne at midnight to lift our spirits appropriately for the occasion. By four in the morning Emmy Pontzen and Kay Jones were ready to brave the blizzard outside and try to obtain a taxicab. Corinne Allen, reluctant to face the turbulent elements, decided it would be more astute to spend the rest of the night on the second of my matching divans.

About five o'clock, as we were arranging ourselves for sleep, I said to Corinne, "Let me see if some kind of a psychic picture will come for you as a New Year's present." Then I tried to make a blank movie screen of my mind in the hope that something as intriguing as my little tiger might appear. It did. It was a minute peacock, in brilliant colors and exquisite detail. I told Corrine about it.

"I hope it means something to you," I said. "It has no significance whatever for me."

"Yes," she replied, "it definitely does. You know the new man I told you I recently met—the one who broke his neck?" Since we try to play a relatively serious game of bridge, we had not given Corinne the chance to say much about him, even though one seldom has a beau who breaks his neck right away and he sounded intriguing. Now she was excited about his connection with peacocks.

"When I visited him in the hospital just the other day, he didn't have flowers in his room; but he had two vases of peacock feathers. His brother runs a peacock farm . . . somewhere in New Jersey, I think . . . and so he brought him feathers instead of flowers."

As my friend thanked me for such an unusual and evidential New Year's treat, expressing her conviction that the bird was definitely more applicable to her than it might be to most people, I was able to keep on visualizing it. It has come to me occasionally since and has won for itself the appellation of my test pattern, for if it appears, then perhaps sometimes more pictures will follow.

Sometimes the ESP group attended circles held at the homes of others. Such a one met for a while on Sutton Place with Ethel Myers as the medium. Naomi Burroughs went there regularly, and I accompanied her twice. Naomi is such a strong psychic herself that she should actually be considered a medium, although she is so critical of all her results that she spends half her time attempting to understand the source and quality of them.

"I never want to allow myself to be deluded," she says, and her attitude is rewarding to me because it is rather a rare point of view among many who have such aptitudes.

Once at a Sutton Place meeting Naomi had a real milestone of an incident to report. She was sitting with several others on a couch that was about five feet across the room from the coffee table around the other three sides of which the rest of the group was clustered. On the table was a trumpet. (This is a cornucopia-shaped aluminum tube that is often used where physical mediumship might occur. It is so light weight that it could float around in the air easily, and is often reported to do so. Also, if direct voice purporting to come from spirits should happen to occur, the megaphone shape would magnify the sound of the voice.) This trumpet had luminous bands around its top and bottom dimensions so it could be seen in the dark room. During the evening it had been leaning itself over one way or another, as everyone sang vigorously to build up power in the room, hoping the trumpet might eventually sail through the air or do something equally as spectacular.

From time to time one person or another would exclaim over an unusual vision or something else that was of interest to him. Naomi had nothing at all to report, and it made her mad. Usually a most amiable soul, this night she became downright irritable. Not even singing with the rest, she was pouting instead. In fact, she told me later, she was mentally bawling out whoever or whatever might possibly be listening to her thoughts.

"Now look here," she said in her mind, "I've been coming here week after week and nothing has ever happened that applies to me personally. I don't think you are being cooperative with me. Unless I get some kind of a phenomenon that affects me specifically, I'm never coming again."

Naomi told me, "I really gave them an ultimatum. I felt deeply wounded because I was being neglected. I work very hard during the day and had to take a taxi to get to the meetings, so it was a strenuous effort in time and money for me to attend regularly. Yet other people were receiving messages and having all kinds of things happen and nothing was directed at me. I felt I had not moved forward in my development and that the whole thing was a waste of time. And so I sat there and fussed. Like a spoiled child I cried inwardly, 'I want it now!' "

No sooner had Naomi thought this than the trumpet leaped off the coffee table across the room and landed between her feet, its narrow end pointing straight at her. Everyone shouted, "Look, it went to Naomi," but they didn't know she had invited it personally. She checked with others afterward to make sure that what she had thought was purely mental activity on her part had not been unconsciously verbalized; but she was assured she hadn't said a word.

In analyzing the experience later, she conjectured that it might have been possible that someone had read her mind and then thrown the trumpet at her feet in answer to her plea. However, she says, "Even had that been possible, in that crowded room if anyone had made such a move and exerted himself enough to pitch the trumpet, the person next to him would have felt him or heard him moving and been aware of what he was doing."

The first night I attended a session on Sutton Place there was nothing of particular interest to me. The next time I went, however, a manifestation occurred that intrigued me mightily. We sat in the darkened room, with no light except for a thin reflection seeping in around the edge of the heavily curtained windows—but it was enough that you could see the bulk of a person beside you or in your near vicinity. We sang lively songs to build up the vibrations, and soon a loud banging on the coffee table began to accompany us. Most of the members of the circle were sitting around the table and in the dark one couldn't be sure someone's foot was not causing the noise, but, reasoning as Naomi had, I rather suspected that anyone's kicking vigorously enough to make that kind of uproar would have been evident to his neighbors.

I was in the same spot on the same couch where my friend had her experience. It was about five feet from the busy coffee table where the rest were gathered. The couch was exceptionally long, and the only other person sitting on it—the actor Rufus Jarman —was at the far end. He couldn't have reached me unless he had stretched almost full length; but, anyway, he could be heard loudly caroling from the same position all the time.

During a pause between songs I said aloud that it was all well and good for the force, whatever it was, to concentrate on the table, but I wished something inexplicable would happen to me personally. Never having experienced any kind of physical phenomenon, I would welcome it. Someone said not to ask for trouble, and I replied that one could even withstand blows on his person if it would bring evidence of supernormal activity.

Then we began rousingly to sing "The Battle Hymn of the Republic." (Such groups always assiduously refrain from singing the variation "John Brown's Body Lies A'Mouldering in the Grave.") And the rhythmic banging on the table resumed with enthusiasm. Suddenly I felt a powerful jab on the side of my right thigh. My hand instinctively and rapidly dropped down to grab anyone or anything that might be near, so quickly that nothing in my close vicinity could have eluded me, I'm sure, but nothing was contacted. The singing continued uninterrupted except by my shout of delight that I had finally achieved some kind of manifestation, slight though it was in comparison with Naomi's more important one. And, yes, I know a muscle spasm when I feel one. It wasn't that.

Certainly it couldn't be said that living in New York was monotonous. Not for anyone who moved in the right circles.

Chapter 31

AFTER THE PUBLICATION OF my Myers condensation I applied for and received grants from the Parapsychology Foundation for the preparation of other books, and I was able to give up my secretarial job and spend all my time researching ESP material and writing about it. With my first two hardcover books under my own name I acquired a reputation as a writer who attempted to be objective in handling her data. I cherished this reputation and tried to live up to it, although lately it has proved more interesting and more successful to write about contemporary, even if less scientifically verifiable, cases.

Because so many people think that to be a published writer is to be rich, it seems only fair to state that this is by no means true. Perhaps the achievement of a best seller and its possible subsequent conversion into a movie produces that kind of wealth; but ordinary free-lance writing brings only the merest subsistence. It is really shocking what a small proportion of writers earn a living at their trade alone. Almost all of them have supplemental incomes.* Because it is doing what I most want to do in all the

* An article in the *Wall Street Journal,* August 7, 1970, refers to economic survival among free-lance magazine writers as "precarious," adding that when free lancers turn to authoring books it "is a difficult way to make a living."

world, I do not complain; but for the record it should be stated that it has not been a high old living by any means.

Unless one has grants, even small ones, to help with his support, it is not possible to take the time to do any vast amount of research for a book. Eileen Garrett's foundation was wonderful enough to help subsidize my efforts for eight years, and this carried me so that after a time I could be entirely on my own; yet none of my early work ever paid enough to more than take care of rent and groceries.

When my first original paperback, *ESP*, came out in 1962, I took one look at the cover and bellowed with rage at what the publisher had done to me. Sabotaged my incipient career, that's what! The book was a sincere and factual attempt to give the lay reader a comprehensive understanding of this intriguing subject; yet the cover contained a drawing of the rear view of a hairy-looking monstrosity with one female breast peeking around its side and a big eye in the back of its head! An abominable snow-woman is the only way to identify her. Many have since mentioned to me their chagrin that such a hideous cover should have appeared on such a worthwhile book. Yet the publishers may have known what they were doing, for *ESP* received good reviews in spite of its cover, and apparently the snowwoman was at least one of the causes for its remaining in print ever since and going into, up to now, six editions. It was even translated into Spanish and published in Spain with the same iconoclastic illustration on the cover.

During these years of New York existence, while keeping at my typewriter constantly producing books, I had a spiritual relapse, seeming to forget most of what the previous few years had taught me and reverting to much of my former way of thinking. I didn't dismiss my Guardian Angels from my life, exactly, but from my thoughts, paying less and less attention to them. Well, when you can't see them or hear them or type with them and don't dare try to let them talk to you in your mind, you have to remain alert to remember that spirits are around at all.

A mind that actively creates words and ideas whenever one sits at a typewriter is not easily tamed into periods of quiet receptivity. Blanking in order to accept communication had always been difficult for me. Now, for years, it was impossible. Only when I was within the protection of a meditation group were there brief moments of relaxed mental chatter with Mother, and then the results were always so nonevidential that they could be ascribed to my own wishful thinking.

As time went on and the malevolent entities seemed to have disappeared, I even tended to forget my experiences with them—to put the entire episode out of my mind as a curious interlude of my past, no more pressing on my present thoughts than my unhappy marriage or my earlier illnesses.

If there is anywhere on earth that "the world is too much with us," it has got to be New York City. There one is so buzzingly active at all times that it is not easy to spend any hours in quiet meditation or passive receptivity. I was so busy trying to scrape out a living on the thin edge of insolvency that my thoughts naturally were occupied with that situation. The rest of the time my concentration was on my work, or on the evening's entertainment. (And increasingly on Grant, my lawyer friend.)

So, surprising as it may seem, I reverted, you might say, to my former ESP-less existence. Oh, there were *some* results of my past indoctrination. I was now more aware of the need to think positively and practice the brotherly love that had been so impressed upon me. This made my life easier. Friends always commented on the way I seemed to sail through all my financial difficulties and the depressing periods of waiting for publishers to make up their minds, always confident that everything was bound to come out right in the end—or at least not allowing myself to dwell on the possibility that it wouldn't. For me, a former leviathan of the negative, this was a definite, hard-won step forward.

In one of his wonderfully witty letters that helped with laughter to carry me over all my down spots, Bill Hanemann once wrote from Daytona Beach: "You keep at it no matter what the odds . . . and you *will* succeed, you're such a manly little fellow!"

But things were to become much worse before they got better. In fact, life was going to have to slap me down and tromp on me once again in order to get me back into my eccentric groove. This first evidenced itself as my little dog Junior became ill. He had begun to suffer from a chronic colitis that made it impossible for him to eat anything except an especially prepared canned dog food. I hated to serve myself steak and his other favorite meats without being able to share them with him; but then the point came where I couldn't eat much myself. For a time we both subsisted on pap and oatmeal and like gustatory trivia.

When I went to the hospital to have my gall bladder removed, a friend stayed in my apartment to care for my pet. She didn't believe in that foolishness about his diet, and allowed him to share her red meat as an animal should. I returned from the hospital just before Christmas to find a little dog psychologically more shook up than usual by my absence and physically in bad shape.

All during the winter of 1963 Junior ailed. Finally in March the vet suggested an abdominal operation which he said might be successful. When surgery revealed how ulcerated the intestines were, he told me that in a twelve-year-old animal it would only be a matter of extending a pain-ridden life a few more months if he let him live. I couldn't do that to him, so accepted the responsibility and the grief of letting him sleep away. It was truly one of the most traumatic experiences of my life, for Junior had been my only "family" for much of his lifetime.

People who belittle the way some individuals lean on their pets for love and companionship may be fortunate that they don't need them; but some of us do. It is true that Junior had been more or less allowed to take the place in my life that a son or daughter might have had. Since I did not at any time live in the ideal conditions for raising a child, however, it is a good thing one hadn't been forthcoming. I'm fortunate to have had such a wonderful dog to care for instead.

Bill Hanemann, in the beautiful letter he wrote in tribute to Junior, pointed out that he was always such a little gentleman. While loving and attentive to his favorite people, he never fawned over them as some dogs do, in the hopes of getting a belly scratching or a cookie. He had dignity, in other words, and that is as good in a dog as in a human being.

I have never been an overtly motherly type, yet watching my friends' children grow and develop has always fascinated me. From the James material it is evident that under the circumstances available to me, it is just as well for a child that one has not been born to me. James wants this world to be Utopia. He knows that won't come very soon, but he insists that it is inevitable, and that it will develop gradually through the efforts of those now on earth and their offspring for many generations. If we can learn proper procedures for raising our children and begin to follow them, all life will alter for the better and conditions for our descendents will be immeasurably improved.

"It will be your plan," he writes, "to try to make your child's earliest days as secure as possible. The way to do this is to love him so thoroughly and to devote yourself to him so completely that his first years give him nothing but peace and inner serenity. No matter what poor environment a baby may be born into, if both his mother and father love him and teach him to love others and to think constructively, he will not have all the character problems his playmates have. He will live relatively free of those insecurities that plague others."

It might seem that James is overlooking much of what makes up a lifetime—the harrassments, the unhappiness, the adjustments one constantly has to make in order merely to endure his existence. But he says, "Of course you will have problems." No life is so rosy that it can be without humiliations, irritations, exasperations, and even some genuine misery. How else can we learn? I was hoping he would say that the ultimate Utopia would be carefree but he says no.

"There is no reason for anyone to expect that it will ever be possible for man to sail through life without the striving, the effort, and the pressures which produce character. To expect to grow without seasoning is ridiculous; but if you have a good start you can overcome everything."

He maintains that raising your child wisely, with love and intelligence, and making a well-adjusted adult of him is the greatest contribution you can make to the human race. Disciplined parents who set an example by never speaking disparagingly of or to others, who raise happy children in harmonious surroundings, are happy themselves, however, so they don't need to feel that they are sacrificing if they attempt always to keep their homes free of discord for the sake of their offspring.

If a husband and wife cannot be contented with each other,

they should be intelligent enough not to have children in the first place. When you consider acquiring a family, think of the detailed amount of time and effort you will have to spend to raise it properly. If you do not feel equal to such a big expenditure of effort, do not even let yourself consider the project. Don't plan to have a family until you are sure that you, yourself, and your spouse are mentally and emotionally mature. If this sounds as if James is trying to reduce the population of the world, he says, "Why not? Overpopulation is a problem and babies should not be brought into a world which cannot care for them properly.

"You should never have a child just because he will be an adorable little extension of your own ego, to be cuddled while he is small and cute, scolded when he grows older and misbehaves, and then left to his own resources to develop into an ill-adjusted human being with the problems of adapting himself to existence. This has consistently been the custom of the world, but that does not make it right. If you are not able to raise your children under the best possible conditions, then do not give birth to them.

"Youngsters who marry because of pregnancy and then raise an unwanted and unloved child are not only pathetic but unkind and unthinking. Today there are prescriptions that make it possible not to have unwanted babies. In a culture (which I do not condone) where teen-agers are frequently thrown together alone in intimate circumstances before they have learned to control their passions, facing facts and being prepared for eventualities is an indication of intelligent forethought, not unrestraint."

Wow! Mr. James, are parents ever going to be after you! They don't mind leaving their kids to make out alone, but getting pregnant before marriage is still considered bad form in most circles. The only thing worse is being so bold as to take preventive measures when you're supposed to be too young and innocent to know about such things.

Others who won't be delighted with James's ideas are women who prefer to work and let others take care of their children, and philandering husbands, and married couples who can't get along and think having a baby might bring them into a better relationship . . . because James wants you all to stay home and mind the young or else not have any.

"Unless you are able to change your habits for the child, and can love him despite what you have to give up for him, then don't have him. There is no compromise."

He gives you a loophole for your love, though. "If you feel unfulfilled without a baby, but have a partner who is not responsible enough to assist in raising him wisely, then adopt one of the many who need any kind of help desperately. Take out your parental affection raising one of these poor little waifs, and you will be doing it, yourself, and the world a good turn, even though conditions are not ideal. Almost any family with one loving parent is a better place to raise an orphan than an asylum would be."

What are these ideal conditions James insists on in order to have a child of your own? "From the time that the small one arrives, until he is at least seven or eight years old, the parents should consider their own lives secondary to his. If this sounds impossible, stop and think what you have undertaken. You are giving personal identity to and raising an individual who will live forever. He has a great deal to give the world if he learns to cope adequately with life's problems. He will be unable to do this successfully unless you provide him with a firm foundation of character. Parents who have children needlessly, carelessly, and without considering the cost to them of inadequate training, who bring unwanted infants into the world without preparing themselves to give them loving care, are criminals! I do not say this lightly. They are perpetrating crimes just as surely as if they robbed or murdered. A personality which has been stunted because of improper upbringing is a life which should not have been started in the first place. Do you want to be responsible for the production of an earthbound spirit?"

You know, it does make a difference in our thinking, doesn't it, when we even suspect that life goes on forever? It could be worth giving up a few years of your time if you knew you were raising an individual who will ultimately become a permanent addition to that "Great Mosaic of Ultimate Perfection."

As an example of the lengths to which parents should go for their offspring James goes way out on a limb, saying, "In his earliest years the child should not be allowed to play with others who have a bad influence on him; and if you cannot keep unpleasant neighbor children away from him you should move. It is more important for the young to have proper associates than for adults. If your environment is wrong for your child, and if those with whom he plays are rude, impolite, undisciplined, and vulgar, by all means keep him away from them even if you have to move from the neighborhood to do it. Do not scoff at this. Do not say, 'His father's business is here and making a good living for the family is the most important thing.' It is not. A child does not absolutely have to be well-dressed, or have anything but the basic necessities to eat. He does not need piano lessons or dancing classes or any luxuries. He can work his way through college if you have not acquired the money to send him. But he does have to have agreeable surroundings in his earliest years, pleasant associates, constructive thoughts, and love.

"My last suggestion to parents is to begin telling your child about his spirit helpers at an early age. Let him know not only that there is a God in Heaven but that there are Guardian Angels who love him and want to help him, even though he cannot see them. If this rapport is established in youth between a child and his invisible friends, many of his biggest problems in life will be solved with their able assistance, and he will be able to avoid some of the misfortunes that could occur to him without the benefit of their far-seeing viewpoint.

"Be sure to warn him not to talk to his playmates about this subject, at least not until it is more generally accepted. It should be as personal and as little discussed as his other private habits."

"But, Mr. James," I interrupted him. "A child raised to know only love and compassion and Guardian Angels and all that will be absolutely clobbered when he gets with those little monsters at school!"

He disagreed. "By the time he is of school age he should be warned that his new associates have not been taught all the wonderful things he knows and that he must not feel badly if they do not understand. He should feel sorry for them instead. With his inbred warmth and loving personality, he will probably win over even the most arrogant; although he will be self-sufficient enough to be happy without their approval, if he should not gain it.

Don't anticipate any additional troubles for this individual who was indoctrinated correctly in childhood. His life will be an example for all to follow. He will have his share of unhappiness, unforeseen developments of one kind or another, deaths in his family, *et cetera*, but his backlog of personal security and harmony will carry him through anything."

James concludes his treatise on children: "If you do not care to live your private lives with wisdom, that is your business. But if you take on the responsibility of giving birth, then it becomes someone else's business—and this someone should be the most important person in the world to you, your child. He demands and must have the very best that is in you at all times. If you do not provide him with affection and wise attention, you are neglecting your duty, no matter how well you feed, house, and clothe him and how much money you spend on him. Money, I need not tell you, makes life more comfortable and easier to bear; but it does not provide instant character. That you must acquire for yourself through strenuous effort.

"The wonderful thing about it is that when you exert yourself wisely for love or someone else, your own character develops without your even being aware of it."

Chapter 32

ON THE MORNING OF June 30, 1963, eleven Italians walked into my hospital room in Sorrento, courteously shook my hand and said, "*Buon giorno.*" Some were obviously ambulatory patients in slippers and robes. The rest, I decided correctly, must be their sisters and their cousins and their aunts. What were they doing in my room?

They lined up around the foot of the bed and stood silently

gazing at this bemused *Americana* who had suddenly appeared in their relatively isolated *clinica*. Not knowing what else to do, I stared back for a while. Then, beginning to feel silly, I undertook to make conversation. I'd been in Italy three weeks and was fairly fluent with *bella's, bene's*, and *buona's* because of all my bragging to the natives about the beauties of their country. Now I also knew the words for pain, so I rubbed my aching foot and said, "*Dolore. Male* (pronounced mah-le—means 'bad!')."

The reaction was immediate. Everyone began to speak and wave his arms, either commiserating with me or explaining *La Signora's* discomfort to his neighbor. Then we all smiled kindly at each other. The ice was broken. We were fast friends from that moment, and seldom was my room free of at least one or two of them from then on.

This curious habit of the Italians of visiting their sick relatives in droves, packing a lunch and spending the day—and the night— was to my advantage because I became the recipient of candy, fruit, or pastry from every picnic basket. I was even served champagne once at a christening.

Champagne actually did little to help make festive my suddenly sidetracked glamour tour of Europe. (On $5.00 a day? Yes, someone had convinced me it could be done.) I had decided that summer to take the first surplus money ever achieved through my own efforts and do research abroad for the book on out-of-body experiences then in progress. I also expected to enjoy an extended European vacation. Instead, from the beginning the whole thing had been a complete disaster.

I had flown first to Italy, and shortly after my arrival had received a letter from a gloating acquaintance informing me that my friend Grant had been making a play for her. She included one confidence he was said to have told her which was so personally revealing that an uninvolved individual could hardly have learned it; so the information was more convincing than ordinary talebearing might have been. It shook me to small bits and pieces. Three months after losing Junior, I had apparently lost Grant; and now, on top of that, my foot was broken in a strange land where nobody spoke my language.

On the evening of June 29th I had returned from a trip across the water to the Isle of Capri and climbed aboard the sightseeing bus to take me back to Rome. The tiny, steep steps on these autobuses are three-cornered, so that if you don't plant yourself squarely in the center of them, you might miss your footing altogether. That's what happened to me. When my attention was momentarily distracted by the driver, my foot skidded off the top tread and I plunged to the ground—a good four feet. I ended up with numerous contusions and two knots the size of tennis balls—one on my left shin and the other on my right ankle.

As my foot slid off the step, there was a snap, which assured me that a bone was broken; but it was impossible to convince anyone else of it. After various delays I had finally been sent in a taxicab to the Catholic clinic, where not one soul spoke English. An outside doctor named DeLoro was called because, they assured me, he was familiar with my language; and, it is true, he could sometimes eventually grasp some portion of what I said if it was stated very slowly and very distinctly.

Ordinarily I let a doctor do the talking, especially one as distinguished looking as gray-templed DeLoro; but he was telling me to exercise my foot by walking on it as much as possible, since their X-ray hadn't revealed a break. It was important that he realize that my main difficulty was not the new indignities which had occurred in the fall but the old lameness involving the left hip. With the right foot now incapacitated also, how would walking be possible at all?

I thought perhaps crutches as a temporary measure would solve my problem and tried to ask him for them. That was the strangest procedure imaginable, since my little Berlitz dictionary had not anticipated a need for the Italian word for crutches. After Dr. DeLoro finally caught on, and we had settled on the compromise word "scrooges," he revealed that there were no scrooges available in Sorrento. Ordered from Naples, it was a long and uncomfortable week before they arrived. Yet it was not too tedious in another way because of the marvelous opportunity it afforded me to learn some Italian and to become acquainted with those pleasant *paisanos*.

My best buddy came to be a tall, thin-faced, broad-shouldered man with a big white patch over his left eye. Convalescing from his eye surgery, he had more or less taken over the leadership of the other patients. He had walked into my room on my first day there and said, "Mi name Orlando, mees, how old you?" Delighted to learn I was his exact age, he adopted me then and there. A shopkeeper with barely enough English to sell a magazine to an occasional *tourista*, he still could communicate with me better than anyone else, and so he became my interpreter and adviser.

Orlando knew everything that was going on. He even knew that you could buy a bottle of wine from the sisters for your dinner. He bought one for me one evening. Another time he brought me an orange and peeled it and fed it to me section by section. He discovered that I liked iced drinking water and after that he appeared each dinnertime with one ice cube daintily held between thumb and forefinger.

Orlando helped me while away the tedious days by sitting at the side of my bed, sometimes with one or two other men patients, playing cards. He taught me a lively game in which there was a lot of spirited competition. Our loud shouts of *"Cattivo* (thief)"* when one or the other of us thought we were being robbed would frequently ring out through the halls until a sister would scuttle in to quiet us.

The day my scrooges arrived was to be a celebration, but when the sticks were unwrapped my anticipation changed to chagrin. On one was the regulation rubber tip which prevents slipping. The other stick had *no* rubber tip. When I pointed out this problem to the intern who brought them, he said, "Sorrent." This obviously meant that another crutch tip could be purchased locally. It did not tell me whether he would buy one for me, send for one, or even tell anyone it was needed, and in truth he immediately forgot all about it.

Orlando came to the rescue as usual. He took the crutch up the hall and returned with the tip neatly bound in gauze and adhesive tape and perfectly usable for a tryout. He was followed by a crowd. The women drew up chairs in the hall outside the door and the men came in to help me get out of bed and onto the scrooges.

Now, I am as big a natural ham as ever came in a premium package, but it wasn't possible to put on a very good show for them after all. These crutches turned out to be the kind which fitted around the forearms and not under the armpits, thus one couldn't swing on them. With neither foot operational for balance, these gave no more support than the cane.

I gave them a try, but by the time the end of the hall was reached I was completely exhausted . . . and discouraged . . . with everything: the fact that the anticipated scrooges were no help . . . that my foot still hurt as much as it ever had . . . that I had no one to talk to about it . . . that I had no one at all, actually. I began to cry. Sitting down, I reached for a handkerchief but found none. I tried to explain what was needed to the sweet sister who was consoling me, but it was only Orlando who comprehended. He hurried to his room and returned with a large man's handkerchief, which was immediately moistened with my tears.

Soon I became embarrassed because these people, once more assembled in my immediate vicinity, thought the weeping was from pain. Orlando began pointing to his eye and to the bandages on other patients, indicating that others also suffered and weren't carrying on so about it. I couldn't find the words to tell him that my misery was for a wide accumulation of things, including largely a lost love. In fact, by then most of my tears were because I was in a strange, distant land and everyone was trying to be so kind and helpful. Does it sound incredibly corny to say that I was now sobbing in appreciation of humanity? Well, I couldn't say that in Italian, so just had to live with my reputation of having broken down because walking on the crutches hurt me.

Orlando, after half-carrying me back to bed, set out to entertain me back into a good humor. As he leered at me in his one-eyed fashion and teased me, I really was amused. It certainly never occurred to me to think of him as a lover, however; but it soon became evident that he pictured himself in the midst of a big romance. He started making frequent motions of throwing away his wedding ring, and the gleam in his eye as he looked at me became more and more pronounced.

Came then the morning when Orlando told me he was to be dismissed from the hospital the next day. He assured me he had lain awake all night. I wasn't surprised. With the heat and mosquitoes I hadn't slept well myself. If you asked for *Fleet* and made swish-swish motions the nurse would eventually spray a repellent, but its effects were brief because you had to keep the window open in order to breathe.

Orlando assured me this was not what he had in mind. He couldn't sleep for crying over leaving me. He made elaborate pantomimes of wrist-cutting, of stabbing himself in the heart. He put his finger to his temple, pulled an imaginary trigger and fell down dead. He even hung a noose around his neck and gruesomely seemed to dangle from it. I laughed heartily, but it was not the thing to do, for at that a few tears began to dribble from his eye.

Then I really felt uncomfortable. What fatal fascination had I that in a week's time I could inspire such soulful emotion? Remembering then that this was Southern Italy, where ardent romantic love is traditional, I cheered up. Nonetheless, after Orlando left, the head sister reported to me, also through gestures, that he had told her he had cried over me. She went through the same motions of shooting, stabbing, wrist-cutting, even throwing the wedding ring away. It was a bit disconcerting.

Orlando made a big ceremony of saying goodbye, but the next evening at dinnertime he returned. I then learned that his home town was only twenty minutes away by train. He had with him two paper cups of ice cream. Always thoughtful, he had remembered my complaint that my stomach was rebelling at all the fresh peaches from the hospital's orchard which were the only dessert ever served. He had something else for me, too. A clean handkerchief. I was to use it almost constantly before getting out of there.

After Orlando left for good, I was really lonely, not having realized how important to my well-being he had become. That same day a strange house physician came into my room and said, "*Buon giorno. Come sta?*"

I replied, "*Dolore.*" He pointed to the discolored bulge of my ankle and I said, "*Si.*" The elevation on the other shin had gone down, and its bruises, while as superbly decorative as a sunset over the Bay of Naples, were not particularly sore. But the right foot was still as puffy and red and hot to the touch as it had ever been.

This doctor now took his big thumb and pushed as hard as he could into the center of the swollen mass. I let out a yelp. He then, without another word, shook hands and walked out.

From then on Dr. DeLoro stopped coming to see me. I am not convinced it was entirely because he was told that he had made a wrong diagnosis, since my foot wasn't healing properly. More likely he was afraid he wasn't going to be paid. I had continued to insist to him that the bus company was responsible for all my expenses, even though it had made no effort to contact me since the accident. I was determined to take a strong stand about this. Even from my isolated hospital bed I felt the necessity somehow to make my point that those buses were dangerous. My complaint wasn't the fast and reckless drivers or the crowded, curving roads of Italy, for such were natural phenomena of the country. But those little triangular steps had to go. If the natives wanted to put up with them on their local transport, that was their business; but thousands of future American tourists must be protected. I had to win some money from the bus company to make my point. At the very least they must pay my hospital expenses.

When Dr. DeLoro stopped visiting me I suffered most because he had been my only source of reading matter, having brought me in a few old English language paperbacks from time to time. Now for three whole days there was absolutely nothing to read, and I was desperate about that in addition to all the other odds and ends. I played solitaire with a small deck of cards fortunately carried in my purse, and wished my neck instead of my foot had been broken.

Lying awake in the heat and mosquitoes every night, I bawled my eyes out over my predicament, my lost love, and my miseries in general. I was in such a disturbed state that there was no possible way for Mother to get through to me with a few words of assurance—if she were really there. I was even at the point of questioning that. All that foolishness about automatic writing with spirits had probably just been dreamed up. I was doubtless not only a physical mess but deluded mentally as well. That brought the tears again.

A couple of days later, in the midst of an exciting game of Canfield, it suddenly dawned on me that on top of everything else,

I was stranded. There I was, not more than a few miles from numerous popular resorts where many English-speaking tourists thronged, but it wasn't possible to get at them. When I asked the sisters to send for help, they replied with gracious smiles, "*No capeesh* (Neopolitan dialect for 'I don't understand.')" I couldn't even make a telephone call, although there was an instrument beside my bed, because the operator just hung up when he heard La Americana attempting her "*Uno, due, tre, quattro*, etc." What in the world was I going to do?

The next day a new patient, Rafaelle Botticelli, only slightly injured in a motor accident, moved into the room next to me. We met in the hall and attempted conversation. Rafaelle "*no capeeshed*" me as the rest did; yet it was possible to impress him that I had a very big problem and needed someone who spoke English to help me. The words "American Consulate" got through to him.

The next morning Rafaelle came rushing into my room and beckoned me, shouting "*telefono, telefono*." His niece in Naples was on his phone and she spoke excellent English. She assured me there was an American Consulate in Naples, and she said that Rafaelle's wife Dolores was coming for him the next day and they would take me there with them.

Then it was that I determined to break out of that hospital. Positive the bus company would never reimburse me if my bill was already paid, and still convinced of the need to protest those dangerous bus steps, I would be the martyr. I would go to jail if necessary to make my point.

All that night I conjectured about Italian prisons. Their beds couldn't be any worse than the swaybacked lumpy mattress I was on—or could they? And my bed linen hadn't been changed once since my arrival. Could jail conditions be dirtier than that? Did they serve anything to eat but pasta and fresh peaches? If not, I surely would die alone and unnoticed in this alien country.

I awoke the morning of my expected departure tired but still determined. A girl from the credit department arrived early with my statement. For my thirteen days of no treatment and slight care the bill amounted to $250. It is time the myth that things are cheap in Europe is exploded.

With Rafaelle attempting to act as interpreter, the clerk told me that Dr. DeLoro insisted I could not leave until his bill and the hospital's were paid. I replied that it was the bus company's responsibility. She said permission to go would not be granted without payment. I said I'd go to jail first; but that must have lost something in the translation for neither she nor Rafaelle reacted at all.

Finally after about half an hour of wrangling, it occurred to me to tell the clerk about my hospitalization insurance. She copied down the number of my policy, secure in the mistaken idea that the hospital would receive payment directly from the insurance company. Then she allowed me to leave.

For hours after that I waited apprehensively for Rafaelle's wife Dolores to come for us, painfully hobbling into the hall from time to time to make sure he was still in his room. He would always give me a reassuring nod, aware, as I was not, that citizens of his country are seldom on time for anything. Eventually Dolores arrived, and with typical Italian charm they all made room for me in the back seat of the car, squeezed between four other members of the family who had shared the adventure of the trip to the Sorrento hospital for Rafaelle and La Americana.

In Naples the Consulate put me into good hands at the Ospidale Internazionale, which is run by Swiss-German doctors. There, to my gratification, a more frequent word of English was spoken.

When my foot was now properly X-rayed, my suspicions were confirmed. The small bone back of the ankle was broken and the ankle bone chipped. I was told that if the foot had been walked on much longer in that condition, an operation would probably have been necessary. The surgeons at Ospidale Internazionale said they were accustomed to receiving many tourists each year who had been botched up by native doctors in Southern Italy, so no one was in the least shocked at my situation.

The only thing that bothered them about me was how to put my right foot in a cast without unbalancing me and causing strain to the left hip. They finally decided to take the chance, and my foot was placed into a cumbersome plaster casing. A few days later I could laboriously propel myself out onto my private terrace, which presented such visual splendor that it made me more forlorn than anything yet had in Italy. The hospital was on a mountainside overlooking the terra cotta roofs of Naples and the turquoise bay, with Vesuvius looming on the left and Capri capriciously appearing and disappearing on the horizon across the water.

My reactions to such beauty had to be communicated, yet there was no one with whom I could speak more than a few words. In Sorrento, at least there had been Orlando and the other *paisans* to keep me company. Here there was absolutely nothing to do but look at the view and suffer. Sitting in the sunshine and watching the busy little boats scuttling like bugs across the sparkling water, I fretted to be on them going somewhere to finish my vacation. At night when the moon lay its luminescent path across the bay, I ached for someone to enjoy it with me. Since the exodus of my Grant, I lamented, there was no one in the entire world who cared. I had so much love to give, so many songs to sing, but life seemed intent on tripping me up. I couldn't even have a decent European vacation like anyone else.

This was one of the few times in my existence that I contemplated suicide. Life was meant to be shared, I told myself. It wasn't possible to go on batting around alone except for the company of some invisible spooks who may or may not be real.

Still, it was the possibility that these entities existed that kept me from climbing over the rail of the *terrazza* and letting go. After all, no matter how far it now was from the events of 1955–57, I'd have to be some kind of a dingaling to completely forget them and deny them. Just because I was in such a mess now didn't mean that my Guardian Angels had deserted me. It was actually the other way around; I had deserted them. But what they had taught me hadn't really been forgotten. And in our communications there had been such strict admonitions against suicide that the idea could not now be entertained seriously for long. Just the fifty-fifty chance that there might be an existence after death that would be adversely affected if I chickened out now, was enough to deter me.

Once before in my life, when the possibility of surviving death had been completely remote to my way of thinking, I had actually attempted suicide.

Chapter 33

CANNOT OFFER A chapter devoted almost exclusively to suicide as very pleasant reading. Yet for those who may someday become miserable enough to contemplate it, what is said will be of value.

The subject is not an easy one to discuss. The reasons that any person might be tempted to kill himself are intensely personal and difficult to bring under the light of public scrutiny. They must inevitably be highly complex and involve an accumulation of depressing events. You could never say of anyone, "Oh, yes, he had an unhappy love affair and so he committed suicide," or "She was unsuccessful at her job and it just became too much for her." It is never that simple. Instead, over a time many worries begin to accumulate in your mind and as they enlarge there comes such a feeling of helplessness that you finally find yourself completely unable to endure it. The thing that finally touches it off has had a lot to build on beforehand. And as your personal anguish becomes so overpowering, you lose sight of the grief you will cause those who love you, to whom your suicide will also be a form of death.

One like myself who has so much resilience and resistance to life's pressures would have to be pushed by numerous agonies before such a final decision could be made. This had occurred to me in Baltimore, the year I worked for the hospital there and ended up back home convalescing from the mumps. That was a much more traumatic time psychologically than my interminable days in Ospidale Internazionale, for here, at least, I was receiving care and treatment and, since the cast was put on, was not in too much physical discomfort. In Baltimore I had an accumulation of aggravations that finally reached an unbearable point.

As medium Caroline Randolph Chapman was later perceptively to say of me, I am a person who must have a home, above all things. After I live in a rented room too long the walls begin to squeeze me, and eating in restaurants consistently gives me chronic indigestion. I chafe to get to a cookstove, to have space to put up my easel and do some painting, to have pots of growing plants around me, to expand into as many activities as is physically possible for me.

I need people. Although working alone is important, I am most happy when someone is near. If I have much pleasant companionship, I can get along for periods of time without romance, although that kind of a going relationship between consenting heterosexual adults is my favorite form of happiness. I didn't even have family or friends in Baltimore, but was determined not to give up defeated and return home to be dependent on Mother again. The people surrounding me at work were arrogant, rude, and consistently unpleasant because of the inspiration of that bitter head nurse for whom we worked. In addition, I was worried because I had not heard from a soldier friend in Germany for a long time. It was the pain, however, that finally did me in.

Although I have seldom been free of aching misery for long unless in a dry climate, when my life conditions are good I can put up with the discomfort. But when I'm unhappy the torment becomes almost unendurable. My weather veins always announce the news of impending rain or snow in a most emphatic manner, and in Baltimore that year it rained or snowed all the time.

As gloom deepened within me, I went to my doctor one rainy day for something to relieve the pain. When he could offer nothing more than aspirin—that panacea for arthritis beloved by doctors if not by their patients—something in me rebelled completely. I asked him for some sleeping pills. He must have sensed my latent hysteria, and so he wisely prescribed a liquid medication.

Clutching the bottle like a talisman in my hand all the way home, I debated any possible reasons for not imbibing its entire contents. Not one could be found. So on my return to my cramped quarters I sat at my desk and composed a letter which would have had no possible value to assuage Mother's grief:

"Mother dearest, forgive me for what I am doing. Life is just too unbearable. . . ."

Now that I was finally resolved, I went into the bathroom and eagerly began swallowing the medicine. Knowing better than to try to drink the bottle's contents straight down, for they would have come straight up, I took the potion spoonful by spoonful, secure in the belief that if enough of them were swallowed oblivion forever would result. I had not reckoned with the doctor's wiles, however. With each sip I became more and more nauseated, and finally it was impossible to lift the spoon to my mouth once more. I dragged myself into my room and threw myself across the bed for a few moments so that the malaise might pass and my deadly chore continue.

I awoke to a sunny morning with the birds singing merrily outside my window, and I never felt better in my life. I caroled with them, practically dancing around the room in glee to find myself alive and greeted by such a beautiful day.

The James material stresses the danger of just such an effort as this, which might so easily have been successful. James's admonitions against suicide are emphatic: There is no possible reason why one may be permitted to kill himself. If you do, whatever you have not learned on earth because of the shortened life experience must be made up in the etheric plane in ways so much more difficult that it is better to stay where you are and fight it out, no matter what terrible situations you may find yourself enduring.

The discovery that you remain the same person after death and are still living is a shock to you, and you find that you are still suffering the same mental torments until you learn to think properly about yourself and your situation. This is augmented by realizing the sorrow your death has brought to those you love and all others who were involved with you.

When you finally become aware of the fact that it is up to you to begin your progression, you will learn that you must make recompense to all those affected by your death, no matter how long a time it might take. Although it will require a great amount of effort on your part, you will eventually have to right all the wrongs you have caused. As you begin to understand your situation and let your new thinking techniques help you to change your own environment, you will work it all out; but not without much more trouble than you would have had if you had stuck to your natural habitat until your proper time to die.

No man escapes his problems by killing himself. He magnifies them instead. He has to make amends not only to those friends he would have been able to help while on earth, but even to some persons he had not yet met who might have been influenced for the better had he continued to live. His existence after death is considerably more difficult, merely because he took what he thought was the easy way out instead of remaining until his proper time to die and going over in the state of development he would then have achieved.

"Make no mistake," James wrote, "nothing good can ever come of suicide, and a terrible amount of unhappiness, misery, and misfortune is always caused by it. No matter how despondent you may become, do not ever allow yourself to take this way out of your difficulties. There is enough that is toilsome in the earlier stages of existence after death, without adding to the load. By no means must you let any possible argument cause you to take your own life. You will reach here soon enough, and you will be here a long time . . . forever."

There in Naples I relived my terrible time in Baltimore. Just think, I thought, if my life had ended there . . . all the unwritten books and the enjoyment of writing them, all the unspoken lectures and the fun of meeting wonderful audiences afterward, all the good food uneaten and the physical pleasures missed! And all those individuals I had been able to help who would not have had the "benefit" of my encouragement. What a fantastic amount of making up I would have had to do!

Now, here in Italy, it seemed that everything had gone wrong once again and I was as unhappy as ever before in my life. But now I knew, or at least suspected, that Guardian Angels hovered invisibly at my elbow, presumably actively encouraging me even though in my stirred up emotional state it was impossible to sense their admonitions against the desperate thoughts in my mind.

"Don't do it! Don't ever do it! It's the worst thing you could possibly do!" they probably were reiterating.

Even though I still argued with myself about the source of all my communications, I was intellectually aware that the information they brought was sound, that killing myself would only remove my physical body, that the spiritual body and the consciousness would continue to exist, and that suicide would give me a hundredfold more problems to work out eventually. Yes, I would have to stick with Planet Earth, no matter how wretched.

My mentors have said that it is not really important in the overall result of man's life on earth whether or not he is especially happy all the time. Although a cheerful existence is devoutly to be desired, and with proper effort on his part at positive thinking one should certainly be able to achieve it, happiness isn't the goal of living. What I must do with myself was to become complete and successful as an individual. Then contentment would be revealed in my life as a result of my inner serenity. If it were not possible for me to live in jubilance during my time on earth, it would definitely come later. That fact is always stressed.

James has since written a paean in praise of this anticipated bliss: "There is such great rapture in future planes of life that the small amount which can be enjoyed on earth is inconsequential. To live in a state of eternal overwhelming ecstasy is your destiny, and if you do not have it today you will not remember tomorrow that it was lacking. You already know this to be true. If you have been very sad for a period of time and then something wonderful like a new sweetheart comes to you so that you are glowingly happy, you spend no time recalling the last months during which you were sad. Because I know it is your ultimate destiny to be at all times joyously alive, vibrant, peaceful, and blessed, I cannot weep for you now if you feel that you have missed out on a few privileges and sensations during your earth life. Earth is your spawning place. For you to worry about not achieving happiness now is as if a young salmon were crying because he had no room to swim in the little stream where he was born, not aware that soon he would be cavorting in the magnificent ocean with all the space in the world at his disposal and scant memory of his early beginnings."

This particular bit of enthralling news had not yet been received as I sat alone on my terrace at Ospidale Internazionale and longed for someone with whom to share my view and my life.

Had hundreds of James's paragraphs on eternal ecstasy been available, they really might not have helped much. When you're as down as all that, the promise of a lot of beatitudinous bliss while floating around in the sky sometime in the future isn't likely to bring much encouragement. What I suspected then about the hereafter was not even much consolation. Yet, still, there was enough of a doubt, a possibility, which completely and entirely deterred me from suicide. The only thing for me to do, it seemed, was to delight in my lovely lonely vista and shut up about it— building character like mad, no doubt, but as far as I could see, doing nothing else of any value for myself or humanity.

One day during that most trying of periods, instead of the usual Italian nurses, a Swiss-German girl walked in to take my temperature. She queried me about my moroseness and I was able to make her understand that it was primarily because there was nothing for me to do. With a "Ya! ya!" she bustled out, completely comprehending my need to be busy. She returned a short time later with an armload of gauze and started teaching me how to roll bandages. After that I made thousands of them, sitting up in bed or on my terrace, manipulating the gauze into little folded packages until exhausted. Such work wasn't fun, but it was worthwhile, and it kept my fingers active, so my heart was thankful for it.

Finally, about the second week, a pleasant young woman from the Consulate arrived for a visit. After that she came regularly, bringing me books to read, and even loaning me a small portable typewriter. Later one of the doctors brought me a little set of watercolor paints, and I spent hours on my view, now able to enjoy it more because I was doing something about it.

After a while the head doctor asked me to be a sort of den mother for the occasional English-speaking tourists who were brought into the hospital. Hippety-hopping to their rooms, I would sit and entertain them with chit-chat whenever they felt the need of company. The time thus managed to get itself passed in a variety of ways and eventually a month and a half had dragged by. The cast removed, the doctors permitted me to resume my European travels—or what was left of them after the check to the hospital for $850.00.

The day before my departure the bus company finally granted

me an interview. The Consulate people escorted me there in an imposing black limousine, which didn't impress the autobus representatives at all. They assured me that I had absolutely no claim, with Italian law to back them up, because the bus had not been in motion when the mishap occurred.

There was no possible way to make my stand against those vicious little three-cornered steps. No one would even put me in jail about it.

Chapter 34

TOTTERED INTO LONDON in early September, exhausted from trying to struggle across Europe with no feet and no funds. It is not the way to travel.

The next morning I awoke early in my small hotel and then seemed to drift into a light doze. Suddenly I was with Junior. My dog saw me, perked up his ears, then leaped on me with his usual affection. Holding him in my arms as he joyously licked my face and expressed his happiness at seeing me, I just as delightedly hugged and petted his squirming body. And asked myself what the *hell* was going on.

"This is *not* a dream," I declared emphatically, and it wasn't. It was in no possible way dreamlike. Was it then an out-of-body experience?

I had written much about out-of-body travel, or astral projection, and had come during my research to realize that there is no doubt of its authenticity. Apparently astral projections occur to a great many people. While one is asleep, or in a completely relaxed state, or possibly when under anesthesia, or in various other conditions, his conscious mind may actually leave his body and soar up, up, and away. It could then happen that he may look down from the ceiling at his body on the bed and suspect that he might have died. If such things occur often, unless knowing that others experience them, he may begin to wonder if he is not a candidate for a straitjacket. Eventually, they say, one becomes used to such goings-on if they happen to him often enough. There are many persons who have learned that they can have such unorthodox adventures at will; even some of my friends do it.

The reason we can be sure these events are not merely subjective is that on occasion someone has been seen elsewhere while his body was, in fact, at home asleep in bed. He has been recognized and identified at this distant site, for the spiritual body in which his consciousness was traveling looked exactly like the physical. It may appear fragile and misty to the beholder; at other times it looks so solid and material that it is taken for the actual physical person. The consciousness of this astral traveler is usually aware of where he is going and what he is doing, and he sometimes returns with knowledge he could have no normal way to learn. There have also been reciprocal cases where the traveler was cognizant of being seen when out of his body and then later had this confirmed.

My friend Veryl Smith (now Mrs. Karl Romer) of Salt Lake City has kept up with psychical research ever since our initial efforts together and has read a great deal about out-of-body travel. So when she underwent a major operation in 1959, she determined to have such a flight. She kept the thought in her mind right into the operating room and even as the anesthetic was being administered. Over and over as she went under she kept repeating in her mind her intent to leave her body. When Veryl awoke after her surgery, she remembered nothing of having had such an experience, and she was disappointed because she thought her attempt to test her powers in this way had been a failure.

A few days later, however, when she began to have visitors, she learned that her friend Wally, who owned a photo processing shop, had been startled during the time of her operation to see her walk into his dark room and look around . . . rather stupidly, he said. He thought, of course, that she had died during surgery and immediately called the hospital to learn how she was.

A great deal of research has been done on this subject. It is the main interest of Dr. Robert Crookall, a well-known British psychologist, botanist, and geologist, who has written numerous books about out-of-body experiences. Of the possibility of making a firm conclusion about the genuineness of the phenomena, Dr. Crookall says:

"If our decision is based merely on the study of others' testimonies it cannot amount to an absolute certainty, but some laboratory work now in progress and the evidence of history make the reality of astral projection a good probability at the very least."

Lest one suspect that my experience occurred because I was so thoroughly aware of such a thing that it was inevitable to conjure it up for myself, this isn't necessarily true at all. It has happened more often to those who knew nothing whatever about the possibility of it. For example, an Englishwoman, Beryl Hinton, had been brought up a good Roman Catholic and had never read nor heard of astral projection. But suddenly during an illness she found herself out of her body. As she described it to Dr. Crookall, "There I was, above my body, around which were gathered the various people. I could not talk to them. I do not doubt that I was out of my body, and I was sure I was dead—yet I wasn't dead at all! That experience has gone further to prove survival to me than all the religious books I have read."

Phil Bentor of Baton Rouge, Louisiana, was relaxing in an old-fashioned Morris chair one afternoon in April, 1970. He assures me he was not asleep, but he began to realize that he was in a more or less numb condition, unable to move. He wondered if some unexpected illness had overtaken him. Debating what to try to do about it—he couldn't even call out for help—he found his consciousness precipitously up in the air looking down at his body in the chair.

"I must have died," he thought, deciding that it wasn't so bad to die after all if this was all there was to it. Being somewhat adventurous, he began to walk about—or it seemed to him that he was walking, even though he was high in the air. He went outside and traveled onward, looking down at the cars and people passing by, but aware that he must be invisible to them for nobody down below was panicking and pointing aloft.

After what seemed a short time, Phil saw someone coming to

greet him. It was his long deceased mother. Accompanying her was an unfamiliar man he was later able to identify from pictures as a brother of his mother's who had died before he was born.

After a warm reunion with his mother, Phil asked her, "Am I dead?"

"No," she replied, "but you'd better get back into your body before something happens to it, or you will be dead."

As his thoughts turned to that placid physical replica of himself sitting in the Morris chair, he suddenly found himself back in it. The numbness left him and he moved around—quickly, in fact, for he rushed to tell his wife what had happened.

The aspect of astral projection involving seeing a deceased entity is not commonplace, yet many people declare they have made just such realistic astral trips into the spirit world to visit with their long-lost relatives and friends, and sometimes pets. Similar travels were the basis of all of Swedenborg's vast information. Now it had happened to me!

I'd been told that Junior continued to stay with me since his death, because loved pets survive and may remain with their owners. Mother said she was taking good care of him for me. I had not doubted that someday the dog will be with me again; but a visit with him so soon was completely unexpected. Yet there he was, and there I was, and it was not a dream.

"I'm really here with Junior and we both know it," I thought. "I am awake and aware. There is no doubt about that either."

After a few minutes my experience turned into a dream, and it was obvious when it happened. My pet got down from my arms and began to move about. He pranced across a road, wagging his lively long tail, and I cried, "Watch out for the cars!" Then it occurred to me, "Nothing can hurt him now, he's already dead."

As one begins to withdraw from an astral projection, he frequently goes through such a dream stage. That was happening to me now, and I was conscious of it. Junior returned to me and I picked him up, then somehow had two dachshunds in my arms. One was a small puppy which dropped, and while reaching to grab him I awoke.

I lay there exhilarated, thinking about what had happened. Although it was possibly a hypnopompic dream, I rather doubted it. I'd had those experiences before where you lie in bed, not entirely asleep but dreaming. They were considerably different from this. Those half-awake morning dreams, called hypnopompic reveries, can be strangely real; but they are real in a different way. What had happened to me was instead what is known as a lucid dream, and that came only *after* my initial astral projection. A lucid dream differs from an ordinary dream in that one is aware he is dreaming. This had occurred to me a few times before in my life, but never since reading of the fact that some persons having lucid dreams can sometimes direct their attention at will and attempt various experiments. I conjectured that if my lucid dream had lasted longer, perhaps some testing could have been attempted.

"Enough of that!" I thought. "Nothing more is necessary. What has occurred is so exciting it will last me a lifetime!" It was, too. I now had a better understanding of a whole new aspect of psychic life.

Another rewarding English experience was my visit to the retired medium Gladys Osborne Leonard at her home in Kent. Because I was at the time writing the book *The Mediumship of Mrs. Leonard*, I was invited to spend the weekend as her guest, and she was a delight in every way. Mrs. Leonard was one of the two or three greatest mediums of history. She had been studied for over fifty years by the Society for Psychical Research and every word that came through her when she was in trance had been recorded and analyzed for the survival evidence it provided. In her late seventies at the time we met, this great lady looked and acted like a woman in her fifties. Her serenity was beautiful to observe, and we had an immediate rapport. I left her hoping that some of her tranquility and composure had rubbed off on me, but not suspecting that any of her mediumship had. Yet that very day my most profound psychic experience occurred.

Before I had left New York, Reneé Dubonnet had given me the name of a British woman to call to ask why she didn't write. She'd told me nothing about her friend, and I had been in England for some days and had not bothered to call her. After returning to my London hotel from Kent, an immediate urge possessed me to phone Reneé's friend. When her maid said she was out, I left my number.

That evening at five the woman returned my call, saying she would love to meet me but that she was leaving the next day for a vacation in Italy. Not really caring at all about seeing her, I nonetheless found myself insisting, "Oh, I won't take but a few minutes of your time."

"I have no way to entertain you," she demurred. "I don't even have any liquor in the house to offer you a drink." Nothing of the sort was in the least necessary, I replied, adding that it would be possible for me to come right over.

When I walked out of the telephone booth in the lobby of the hotel, the manager was standing near the front door. I asked him how to get to the address somewhere across London and he said, "I'm leaving now in my car and will be driving right by the house. I'll be glad to take you with me."

One thing you eventually learn is that there's no use fighting it! When a bunch of those etheric entities get onto something specific you might as well relax and go along gracefully.

Magician Aleister Crowley said in his *Confessions*: "It is impossible to perform the simplest act when the gods say 'no.'" This is a fact, and when one learns not to try to push ahead when it is obvious the "gods" are saying no, one can live much more successfully. This is also true in reverse. When the gods, or the spirits, or the Guardian Angels, or whatever it is who takes hold of your life at times, say "yes," your path is smooth before you. This was an illustration.

When I arrived at Reneé's friend's house, she almost immediately began pouring forth her woes to me. The pleasant woman, probably in her early forties, had recently had so many unhappy events in a short period of time that they almost overwhelmed her, and she was at the point of desperation where she erupted with them to anyone who would listen. As a captive audience I learned that she had lost her husband to another woman, and he had taken her family furniture and valuable possessions with him when they got the divorce—as he legally could do in England. Then her sister died of cancer, and to top it all off one of her beloved twin Siamese cats fell out a window and was killed and the other died of grief. This woman had troubles.

As I listened attentively, my head became very light and dizziness almost overwhelmed me. Since she hadn't been able to provide me with anything stronger to drink than sherry, I didn't know what was the matter, until a firm impression came that her sister wanted to talk to her. But would she be receptive to such a notion? Could I just say to this stranger, "By the way, your dead sister wants to speak to you?" She might take me gently but forcibly by my ear and show me to the door.

I went at it gingerly, saying first, "I don't know if you are at all interested in ESP and psychical research, but I write books about that field." She replied that she was very interested, and that helped. Then I tentatively offered that sometimes I became a bit mediumistic myself. Since that didn't seem to shock her, becoming bolder I said, "In fact, your sister would like to try to talk to you now. Do you mind?"

Grateful when the response was affirmative, I laid my head against the back of my chair and let the light-headedness take over. I remained conscious, and my actual thinking apparatus was very alert, sitting there inside my brain listening to the words that began to flow through my mouth. Monitoring everything that was said, I was horrified when statements were made that might or might not have been true. After all, I could have been making a terrible clown of myself; and yet my mouth wouldn't stop talking.

What was said at first went along with my thinking and could easily have been coming from me, for the lady was told to stop reliving her grief and talking so much about it. But then the words came, "When you are in Italy, try not to tell anyone about your problems. Be sure to take your oil paints and spend as much time as possible painting. That will be wonderful therapy for you."

Sitting there listening to this, I thought, "You don't know whether or not she paints." Certainly the walls revealed no amateur art, and she hadn't mentioned it.

As several other statements of a like nature were made, I became more and more apprehensive, but I was unable to take control of my mouth to apologize.

The finish actually startled me. The sister said, "Mother and I are with you all the time and love you very much and do all we can to help you. Trust us and make yourself receptive to us." Her mother might live right around the corner! "You don't know if she's even dead," wailed my mind. "This girl will think you're an idiot!"

Then everything cleared up suddenly. Not dizzy any more, I opened my eyes warily, prepared to be greeted by any kind of a dirty look. Instead, Reneé's friend was radiant. She hardly seemed to be the same person.

"You don't know what you've done for me," she exulted. "This is the nicest thing that's ever happened to me."

"But was it correct?" I asked. "Was what I said true? Are you an artist? Is your mother dead? Were there really any hits?"

"Everything you said was true, and the advice was so wise that I promise to adopt it," she declared. As I left, she reiterated her happiness at her messages; and it became evident that the profession of mediumship does have rewards which might be commensurate with the effort it takes to become receptive. I have since learned that others who do not go into deep trance have the same type of occurrences where the mind listens to the words being said. But the experienced have learned not to argue with them, knowing that when a spirit takes over and talks through them he will probably give correct information.

The sister urging her to spend time with her painting endorses James's similar suggestions. He insists we provide ourselves with hobbies that will improve our talents—anything that will add to our dimensions as persons. He says:

"The capabilities and talents one was born with are his for a purpose, for when he has ultimately perfected himself he is expected to contribute his services according to his particular competences. Those who do not have certain special capacities have others which are just as valuable; and all individuals are important because of the areas in which they excel. Each must therefore improve all his abilities so that they will be available for use for the overall good when he has finally progressed to Ultimate Perfection.

"It being necessary that whatever he is able to do he learns to do well, those who come into life with more talents must work hard to increase them. Yet those who have fewer capabilities will have to expend just as much effort to improve theirs. One who comes from fine stock and has inherited much in the way of background, position, and income, will naturally expect to make more of himself while on earth than one who has parents without pedigree or money. Even so, it may be the latter who achieves the most. If your limitations are many, what is required of you is within those limitations; and in areas in which you have few capabilities you need produce very little. Those who start with greater expectations must feel a responsibility to give more. Persons who cannot understand this while they are bravely enduring a life of hard work, will see the point after their progression starts. Now the one who seemed to have greater blessings on earth but wasted them away is far behind the one who lived wisely with his privations."

James put this in another way: your character is developed according to the pressures you work against. To illustrate this point he describes the son of a wealthy socialite who has three divorced wives and five or six children scattered about, whom he grudgingly supports but to whom he never allocates any of his time and attention. To this man he contrasts an Australian aborigine in primitive circumstances. This native loves his children well, gives them a thorough grounding in how to survive in the wilderness, and spends many weary hours hunting, or digging for roots in order to find food for them. His pressures are greater, but he learns from them and will be much farther ahead when he dies than the other man. If the aborigine has more to acquire educationally and culturally, the rich snob has much more to learn about love and compassion. So the native has not been discriminated against at all.

My first thought was that this ignorant native was going to have the devil of a hard time competing with an intelligent and educated man on the other side, no matter how much love was in his heart. Before I even had time to voice this objection, James wrote:

"You do not have to worry about the brain power of the native. All spiritual bodies have the same potential and all consciousnesses are alike in capacity. It is functioning through an inferior body, or in primitive circumstances, that causes a person to be unintelligent on earth. When the physical body is abandoned at death, all have the same capacity to learn. This also explains the situation with those poor little creatures called idiots or imbeciles. They are handicapped while in their physical bodies because illness or accident or lack of proper bodily elements in the mother caused the brain and sometimes the rest of the body of the baby to be so poorly constructed that its consciousness is not able to function through it properly to communicate adequately with the world. The mind imprisoned in this unfortunate body would not progress much on earth, it is true; but when liberated at death it is as normal as every other consciousness. It has a good deal of catching up to do, but with proper guidance that should not take too long. It will arrive at its ultimate heavenly destination exactly the same as everyone else. And this imbecile's time on earth was not wasted—think of the many lessons in love and helpfulness his parents and those who cared for him were learning while he was in their charge.

"Much insanity also comes from faulty, damaged, or under-equipped bodies. The conscious mind still retains its original qualities although it is consistently misled and confused by the problems encountered in attempting to cope with the world through a brain which is not performing adequately.

"There is no form of insanity which is not corrected after death so that the consciousness is eventually perfectly normal and able to begin its progression; although a badly deranged person has much effort to regain his natural personality. He needs a great deal of help. There are nursing homes in the spirit world just as there are in your world to take care of those who come over still influenced by having been disturbed mentally. They have to be retaught, just as a child is originally taught, how to think and learn and live normally."

Much about insanity is unknown to us on earth at the present time, and many of the ideas we hold are incorrect, according to James. Emotional problems are seldom the *cause* of insanity. It is instead the result of trying to cope with a body which is deprived of necessary chemical ingredients or in other ways is functioning inadequately. We all know that an emotional shock which will completely shatter one person will be taken in stride by another. The one who cracks up does not necessarily do it because of the trauma, but probably because his body is functioning so inadequately that he is unable to adjust when something difficult occurs to him.

"Another aspect of mental aberration will never be completely understood until the philosophy which I am discussing in this book is fully accepted," James went on. "Then your doctors will be able to account for many cases of insanity as spirit possession, obsession or intervention. The cures for this are twofold: first, for each person to be aware of the danger of it and consciously to protect himself against such intrusions; second, for people to be so enlightened that when they die they will not become the earthbound types who would attempt to possess others."

This reminded me of the really wicked people of the world. I asked James what happens to them. "I can't see why a Hitler or a Stalin should ever be allowed to progress to the same place where us nice folk go," I said, possibly indicating my lack of compassion but feeling righteously indignant about it nonetheless. James replied that they were not only evil but sick as well and that they were destined to be cured. Even so, when they eventually realize the enormity of their sins and begin to make an effort to redeem themselves it is a fantastically difficult job and takes them many eons of time before they can even be ready to start their progression. They will in the process suffer every kind of remorse and as much mental agony as they ever inflicted on others. Even such characters as those, no matter what terrible things they did with their lives, have, because they were once human, certain capabilities that can finally be made into something worthwhile.

"The reason talents and capabilities must be improved to their highest quantitative degree is simple, actually," James said. "It is because each individual ultimately has a major role to play and each must fit into a place where his capacities are used. Whatever you are capable of doing you must do. If you were born with the talent to become a great musician, it is your responsibility to practice the piano, the flute, the violin, or whatever instruments most appeal to you until you have mastered them. Then you should start on your other talents and perfect them also.

"If a child is born with the heritage of potentials which would make him, for instance, a musician, spirits similarly talented may choose him to help. Thus a Rachmaninoff has had vast assistance in his youth as he practiced his piano, and his progress was implemented in every possible way by spirit helpers. Now, today, Rachmaninoff is undoubtedly standing beside some person of great promise who is practicing, mentally giving him the benefit of his great experience. A truly dedicated individual has all kinds of invisible guidance. If he knew this his entire life would be less difficult. His guides could not, and would not, do his practicing for him, but they could give him much inspiration if he is receptive to it. Aid from the spirit world can be very advantageous to each of you, if you will allow yourselves to accept it. You do not have to fear that your own initiative will in any way be lessened because of it."

While improving your capabilities is important, James is aware that many who have great potential are forced to spend their lives on earth at mundane occupations in order to make a living or raise children or fulfill other duties. Because of the system we have, the necessities of existence have to take precedence, unfortunately. But if you are unable to realize your potential now, you will have constant opportunity to accomplish it later, so you who yearn to do things you are now unable to find the time for, take heart.

My mentor always maintains that there is no use to worry about what appear to be the inequalities of opportunity on earth. What we have here is not important in the overall picture—it is what we do with it. The earth is essential as the place where our personality and character start their development; but in relative value, I'm told, life here is equivalent, roughly, to the first mile in a trip around the world. So the actual events of our lives are not nearly as crucial as, in each instance, they appear to us to be.

What seem to be disadvantages here may actually be blessings instead, James says. So if we lived the life of a poor slum dweller and made the most of it, we have a head start on the rich kid across the tracks if he loafed through life.

Most of us would rather take the chance on getting our character development later and have all the goodies available while on earth and I told James so. He said he could understand that point of view, but he reminded me, as he so often does, of all that happiness ahead of us when our progression begins. He reiterated,

"It will all come out right in the end. That is an important point to be learned from this book. The universe is maintained by intelligence. There is a sensible plan for everything, and you only doubt it because you do not understand it. You have such great problems and so many worries and life at times seems so pointless that it is not easy for you to realize this. But all will end in success for you, no matter what your present aggravations. Every man whose life on earth is fruitless ends up just as highly advanced and just as happy and fulfilled as everyone else. The first faltering footsteps on earth will eventually become giant strides of progress in other realms."

Chapter 35

DURING THE REST OF MY three weeks in London I had sittings with two well-known mediums. Douglas Johnson is one of today's most respected sensitives because of his willingness to work with parapsychologists in their efforts to learn more about a psychic's abilities and talents. He and I have since become friends during his various trips to America. At the time of my first visit to him we were complete strangers and I went in anonymously. Yet Douglas Johnson told me thirty-five things that could be verified, beginning with a good description of Mother and a close approximation of her name—first the initial E and then later "Binny or Bitty."

He said, "She's showing me a manuscript. Have you anything to do with writing?" He told me there would be a lot of platform work in my future. Then he said, "It hasn't been a very lucky trip for you. Something to do with Italy." How true!

Douglas predicted that there would be an adjustment in my personal and material life when I returned to America—a physical movement of home and surroundings. "You may not be contemplating this at this time," he said, and I certainly was not, for there was a three-year lease on my Greenwich Village pad. Shortly after my return, however, Emmy Pontzen and I decided to share a larger place, my apartment was sublet, and we moved in together on East 36th Street.

The other medium I visited anonymously in London was Mrs. Elizabeth Bedford, and one of the first things she warned me was that I mustn't give up my home . . . not yet. She proved to be right, for sharing with Emmy turned out to be an uncomfortable situation for both of us. Her German firmness and my Southern casualness were constantly at odds.

Mrs. Bedford did not have too many hits for me, but she told me one more thing that proved out. She began to describe a man who was obviously Grant. "He is very kind to you and very fond of you and comes to see you a lot," she added to the identification. I acknowledged him rather reluctantly. Although always making every effort not to give anything away to a medium, this time I may have shrugged or made a face. My hurt was still too close to me for detachment.

"He's honest," she said, "and you can trust him. Don't give up his friendship. He hasn't proved sufficiently to you that you can trust him, but you can."

As it turned out, when I returned to New York the telephone was vigorously paging me. Grant was frantic because I wasn't home when expected, he hadn't heard from me all summer and he'd been worrying about me. When my coolness challenged him, he was able to prove that what I'd heard about him was malicious misinformation, and our relationship resumed on the same basis of mutual admiration and respect. But how did a strange medium in London know the worry in my mind . . . and know I was wrong about it? Unless somebody invisible told her?

There was one amusing psychic incident that came out of Emmy's and my effort to share the apartment. One Sunday afternoon we had a slight fracas. Determined not to let it grow into a full-fledged fight, I took a Miltown and went into my room, closed the door, and lay down on the bed.

Almost immediately words started flooding into my mind that

were so surprising they compelled me to pay attention to them. I had never once in my life dwelt on the subject of the discourse that now presented itself, yet what was said would have to be the result of some kind of genuine cogitation from someone.

I soon realized that what was coming was a poem, something for which I personally have no writing aptitude. In fact, since the age of ten I haven't ever written anything more poetical than an occasional dirty limerick. Yet here was an original free verse poem flooding into my mind.

After a few moments I scurried over to my typewriter to let the muse record his effort, which proceeded to the following total result:

INVOCATION TO THE PROPHETS OF OLD

Oh, great gray-bearded ones
With your visions of God and his glories
Help us to know you better.
For the needs of modern science
And research of the phenomena called psychic
Will you clarify for us the conditions surrounding you
At the moment of your startling revelations?

Do not corrupt the purity of your concept with naïve credence,
But project forthwith as upon a motion picture screen
The specific details of your supernormal happenings,
Making each succinct and to the point,
Unclouded by wishful thinking or childhood traumas.
Convince us, ancients, that imagination played no major role
In your accounts.
Rally for your defense observers of your grand experiences,
And if such be not forthcoming
Then submit affirmations from character witnesses
Who have known you from your youth
And found in you no bad or distrustful thing.

Think carefully, please, each one of you
And each one tell us true
If all events, on solemn reconsideration,
Were as awe-inspiring as initially affirmed by you.
Or do you now wish to change, perchance, your testimony?

Analyze your mental moods at the time of your visions—
Were you, perhaps, overwrought from contemplating
The beauties of your world, or the grandeur of God?
Had lack of sleep, or fasting, left you
In an exhausted and fanciful state?
Or, conversely, did an overindulgence in sweetmeats
Cause you restless dreams?
Is it possible that knowledge of the gentle body of a Hebrew maiden
Had left you sated, and susceptible?
Could native wine cooled in an earthen jar
Have gone to your head before your abdomen?
Or were you drunk only with love of your God?

Assemble, yet great prophetic scribes and orators
And with ringing rhetoric and resounding rodomontade
Apprise us of what took place in fact.
Was that wheel, Ezekiel, truly way up in the middle of the air?
Or had some curiously sublime cloud formation exalted you
And corrupted your senses?
And, Jacob, your ladder—
In the light of sober afterthought
Did it really extend all the way to Heaven?
Give us, Jonah, once again
The dimensions of your sacred whale,
Uncolored by fantasy
And uncluttered with desire to startle or impress your listeners.

You must know, gentlemen, that in this present day
Of science, psychology, and supreme conformity
Your unsupported testimony cannot be accepted
Without full corroborating details.

After my unusual psychic experiences in England, and now this evidence of what surely was genuine communication, I began to adjust once more to realities. The facts had to be faced that Susy was mediumistic, she believed in the existence of spirits, and she was going to have to use this knowledge intelligently to her advantage. No more would she ever allow herself to become so out of touch that she lost contact with her Guardian Angels, and, almost, her belief in their existence.

During that long period in which New York exigencies had been allowed to push this other awareness aside, my life was never controlled or purposeful. Eventually it had become the same kind of mess it used to be when I had nothing to depend on but myself. Now, once again, as I had in Durham after my helpful talks with Dr. Hornell Hart, I faced up to the fact that conditions or people could not be allowed to influence me otherwise; I must constantly keep in mind the existence of this other dimension of the universe and reveal my knowledge in the way my life was lived. Quite naturally, because of my makeup, there would always continue to be arguments about evidence; but I must stop questioning and fighting the rest of this inspiring philosophy.

After making this decision, I practiced it. From that time onward I have continually lived with the awareness of this other and more rewarding aspect of life.

Chapter 36

IN MY PARTICULAR CHOSEN field I unwittingly maintain a rather unique position . . . straight down the middle. This wins me the approval of readers of my books who find the subject matter interesting but don't want it pushed at them. But it sets me apart from many writers in the field who are either excessively captious or extremely gullible. And it causes many "believers" to think me so objective that I don't appreciate their point of view. Yet, because of the conclusions drawn from my years of research, I have become convinced by the evidence, so would not presume to call myself a parapsychologist. These persons with scientific bent feel that they must maintain their complete objectivity in order to justify their academic status. In opposition to them are the Spiritualists and others who have thoroughly accepted all phenomena as proved to their satisfaction and have no questions and no quibbles about authenticity.

Into neither of these categories do I fit, being a believer but not a credulous one. I still analyze every incident, keep careful records, quarrel with my findings, and sometimes toss out events as not being well enough substantiated for my satisfaction. Yet I don't arbitrarily reject an entire area of research just because fraud exists in some cases, being willing to allow that the persons of scientific repute who have reported what they consider to be factual experiences may have some grounds for their belief.

There are many of discrimination who claim to have seen materializations. These manifestations allegedly occur when certain gifted physical mediums are in deep trance and a substance known as ectoplasm extrudes from their bodies. Spirits then purportedly use this substance to cover themselves in such a way that they can appear before the sitters looking like real live—dead —persons. Early researchers found several mediums who were able to produce these phenomena; but it is seldom that anything of this nature that is genuine occurs today because it takes so much out of them—pun intended—that most modern mediums won't train themselves for it.

Now you know that such prominent scientists as Sir William Crookes, Baron von Schrenck-Notzing, and Alfred Russel Wallace were a lot brighter than I am. They were all convinced that they had seen genuine materialized human figures appear under controlled conditions at séances. They couldn't possibly have been taken in by the kind of fraud I've seen. No critical person could. So I'm willing to believe that there must, at least in the past, have been genuine instances of materialization. Yet my personal experiences in this area have been so disappointing as to be almost disillusioning.

What I have seen has been so fraudulent that the names of the mediums should really be exposed to public scrutiny. This is probably not wise because it might alienate many Spiritualists who are now my friends and who are convinced that on occasion, at other séances under more favorable conditions, these same frauds have produced genuine phenomena.

Although one knows better than to flash a light in the midst of a dark session or make a grab for the "entity" in order to prove it is the medium in costume, it doesn't hurt to attempt tests of various kinds when you participate in such activities. Naomi Burroughs spent a week at the same Spiritualist camp where I later saw such crooked materializations, and she ferreted out fakery by one simple little trick. When one registers at the hotel and signs up for a series of sittings with various sensitives, he is interrogated, and everything he says is written down. He is asked at that time from whom in the spirit world he would particularly like to hear. Naomi produced from her imagination an Uncle Fishel, and every message she received during that entire week included greetings from her Uncle Fishel.

A man of my acquaintance who visited this same place searched his memory for a name from his past, then told his interviewer he would like to hear from Susie Pridmore. He was surprised when various mediums brought messages from her during his stay; but when she materialized in purportedly human form and announced herself as Susie Pridmore he was more than somewhat taken back—for Susie Pridmore had been a pet chicken.

I was late in arriving at the materialization service I attended at this camp and had to give my name as a string-puller in order to get in. When I discovered fifty persons lined up around the walls of the room (at $5.00 a head) I had no hope that anything genuine would appear because no medium has the stamina to produce enough ectoplasm for half a hundred authentic materializations.

Identified, then, as the visiting author, I was asked to be the one to examine the area immediately surrounding the male medium's chair to make sure there were no secret entrances and no sites where any props might be concealed. The walls were bare, and a perfunctory glance around seemed to reveal no hiding places. I did not attempt to lift the rug from the floor, thus probably exposing a trap door through which costumes, and possibly even additional personnel could be brought into the room. After my brief inspection, heavy velvet curtains were pulled around the sides of the space, secluding the medium in a rather large "cabinet," as such an enclosure is called.

After the medium entered his cabinet, all the lights were turned off in the room except one tiny red bulb high on the wall at the end opposite the cabinet. The room seemed pitch black until our eyes adjusted, but after that we could make out the forms of the people across the circle from us; and it was easy to see the manifestations when they appeared.

I must say it was all very stimulating at first. Ginger, the friend who accompanied me, and I clutched each other in a delicious dither as a white figure slid out from between the curtains of the cabinet, wavering and fluttering about with unearthly effect from a distance. But when it passed near us, it didn't look ghostly at all. It was obviously a human being draped in cheesecloth with a mask over his face.

"It's Mother, dear," the entity said to the woman who had been asked to go to the center of the room to receive her visitors. "Don't you recognize me?"

"Oh, yes," was the reply, and it seemed to be sincere. As the evening wore on it became evident that at least some portion of those in the audience really did believe they were truly seeing their deceased relatives.

The phenomena came in two assorted sizes: medium size and smaller-than-the-medium size. The smaller one must have been a woman confederate who had come up through a trap door inside the cabinet. White gauze was worn for the role of women spirits, and black for the men. The faces of every visitor, when one was close enough to observe them well, confirmed my original impression. They wore rubber or plastic masks, or possibly stockings over their features, which hid any definite outlines, yet showed a vague indication of eyes, nose, and mouth. The same two voices were always heard, with variations as to the age and sex of the spirit impersonated, and the figures undulated their arms and bodies in such a way that they looked truly ethereal. Their shod feet, which occasionally showed under the robes, had a much more solid and well-cobbled appearance.

They had a way of backing up to the curtains of the cabinet, then ducking and pulling the curtains around them with one quick gesture that actually gave the illusion they had dematerialized right in front of your eyes.

Ginger was rather amazed when her mother, who had been a fairly small woman, appeared before her, for she was at least two feet taller and had a man's large frame. The fact that she also wore the medium's shoes did not add to her impressiveness.

I was saved for last, and three entities came for me. When the woman who was acting as gatekeeper, ushering the spirits on and off stage, called me to the center of the floor and asked whom in the spirit world I would particularly like to see, my act was great. Stanislavski himself would have approved the quaver of deep emotion in my voice as I said, "Oh, do you think it might be possible to see my dear sister Marie?"

"We'll try to bring her," said the woman doubtfully.

My first visitor announced herself as my grandmother.

"Susy, dear," she called to me, "it's so wonderful to be with you again." Grandma Anderson, my great-grandmother, was the only one of all my grandmothers who had lived to see me, and that imperious Scotswoman would have died before referring to me as anything but "Ethel." So I didn't greet the white-robed figure with any special enthusiasm.

Then came a tall, masculine figure draped in women's white. "Don't you recognize me, dear? I'm sister Marie," she said, fluttering around in front of me, but never letting me touch her. It would have been difficult to recognize her as real, even if she had taken me in her arms and waltzed me around the floor, because there is no sister Marie. I never had a sister. Mother never even had a miscarriage which could have been interpreted by an ardent Spiritualist as a baby sister who had been raised in Spiritland. Marie was presuming that she was welcome, however, so I went along with the gag and talked to her about how well she looked and such drivel. But I was not happy.

My last guest that evening was an author who said he came to a fellow writer because he admired her work. He wore a top hat and a stock around his neck to characterize him as a gentleman from the past. We were apparently on such intimate terms that he introduced himself to me as "Ralph." Seeming chagrined at my purposeful obtuseness in not recognizing him, he said indignantly that he was "Ralph Emerson," quite unaware that the famous essayist always insisted on being called by his middle name of "Waldo." He stated that he stayed very close to me, assisting me by inspiring my writing.

Still in my role of guileless gullibility, I thanked him and admitted that he'd probably been most helpful with my passementerie, and he nodded in complete agreement. "Yes, indeed," he said, not catching on that my test word "passementerie" had to do with old-fashioned bead or braid trimming instead of writing —but the real Emerson certainly would have known the term which was quite commonplace in his day.

Although it seemed wise to make no scene about all this, I was inwardly fuming at the insult to our intelligence this medium thought he was perpetrating.

Several years later in Miami I was equally as infuriated at a materialization séance held by another man from this same organization. He did not even attempt to produce anyone specific, satisfying himself with generalized manifestations who flitted about giving healing to the members of the audience. He was not aware that the red light reflected through his gossamer gown and showed his trousered legs.

I was so disgusted with the crudity of this performance that I had no compunction about reaching out and grabbing a handful of the alleged ectoplasm as he stood beside me and gave a healing to my neighbor. What was in my hand proved to be a soft material, not gauze or cheesecloth but something plush, more like mousseline de soie. At the price he charged for his séances, the medium could afford to be robed in silken luxury.

Some years later in San Diego, California, a group of us who had a private séance with a "Reverend" in nearby Jamul, California, held an indignation meeting afterward, debating what could be done to stop such manifestly fraudulent performances. We finally settled on sending him a letter which we all signed. It read:

Dear Reverend —:
We decided to write you and let you know that we were not taken in by your fraudulent materializations last Thursday night. We pretended while at your home in order that there would be no unpleasantness; but we were all incensed that you should think you convinced us by such an inept performance as you gave.

This is not to recommend that you improve your techniques of "materializations," but that you discontinue them entirely. A man who can mouth such pieties as you do in your extremely lengthy preamble, should have the spiritual awareness not to try to perpetrate fraud. If you truly believe in a life after death, you should know that you are making for yourself a tremendous amount of work in the future, for you will someday be held responsible.

Why don't you straighten up and fly right and stop putting on such fake acts for the public?

God guide you on a righteous path,

Sincerely,
(And we all signed our names.)

Chapter 37

║N THE SUMMER OF 1965 I signed a contract with World Publishing Company to write *Prominent American Ghosts,* with the understanding that a complete circuit of the United States would be made to acquire the data. I planned to store my furniture and take perhaps a year for my touring. Having previously met and become interested in the medium Keith Milton Rhinehart of Seattle, I expected to fly first to that city to investigate a local ghost, then to lecture for his Aquarian Foundation in late September or early October, if it was possible for me to get away by then. Emmy, too, wished to leave New York, so we attempted to sublet our apartment, hoping to be out of it sometime early in the fall.

In August, when all arrangements were completely up in the air regarding my leaving, I anonymously visited the psychic JoAnne Chase. I carefully told her nothing about my situation, yet she gave me a reading so applicable to my past and present that it encouraged me to hope that her precognition might also be dependable.

JoAnne told me I was contemplating a change soon, and that on the fifteenth of September a new era in my life would open up. She spoke of a dark young man with the initial R, who was identifiable as Rhinehart, and said that he would have something to do with this change that would come up on the fifteenth. Then she said, "San Francisco, Seattle, Portland are just ahead of you." She added that I would not be coming back to New York City to live, although that was definitely my plan; yet it is true that it has never been my home since.

On another tack, JoAnne Chase said, "Your relationship with a man that you like very much disturbs you. Release yourself." This was what I had in mind, to break off with Grant by leaving because increasingly I had begun to realize that there really should be no future for us together.

Two young men who lived next door to Emmy and me planned to take our apartment if they could sublet theirs, but they had no immediate prospects. However, shortly after the first of September they acquired a tenant, and events went so quickly that they were able to move into our place on the fifteenth. Through no precise design of my own, it came about that I left that day for Seattle; and, as JoAnne had predicted, a new era of my life opened up.

My investigation of Keith Rhinehart's mediumship, which was undertaken for the Psychical Research Foundation of Durham, was fascinating. Also, my own psychic abilities developed promisingly in the classes at his church, so I remained in Washington State for over three months. I would have been quite willing to spend more of my time outdoors gazing at Seattle's beautiful mountains and waterways had the weather only cooperated. But it rained instead, whenever it wasn't snowing. Even the white-capped grandeur of Mt. Ranier, which should dominate the scene there, only occasionally popped over the horizon. So it was not any inconvenience to spend most of my time inside the darkened sanctuary, attending development classes or séances.

Keith had his thirtieth birthday while I was there, although he appeared much younger. An article about him in the *Seattle* magazine describes him as looking less like a pastor than a "country-and-western singer." Perhaps they were right, because he invariably dressed for his church services in one of his expensive, brilliant, well-tailored, Liberace-type jackets. Whether wearing gold lamé or turquoise shot with silver threads, he carried them off with first-class showmanship.

Slim of figure, Keith has a large head with unusually high and broad forehead, wide cheekbones tapering to an almost pointed chin, black hair, and bright blue eyes. Clean shaven he looks boyish; with a goatee he looks like a beatnik (or the devil! See next chapter); and when he wears a beard that outlines his face, he is a beautiful and inspired prophet. His intensity of delivery when he becomes inflamed with one or another of the many causes he espouses with vigor makes him appear like a fanatical demagogue of olden times. There is nothing old-fashioned, though, about the "New Age" services he conducts and his sermons on many of the most modern problems—man's inalienable privilege to believe and behave as he pleases about homosexuality, prison reform, human rights, religion . . . even bare-topped waitresses.

I became very fond of this young man, but I always argued with him because he was scattering his talents much too widely. If he had concentrated on his mediumship and the wonderful philosophy that it could help to provide, his existence would have been more than justified. Instead he insistently and sincerely wasted his enthusiasms and his ability to sway audiences on areas whose value could as easily be propounded by those without his psychic ability. So he invariably disappointed me.

He occasionally produced phenomena, however, that were challenging.

On my very first night in Seattle, a service was held in my honor at the Aquarian Foundation. As I was a newly arrived guest, it did not seem proper to ask to be allowed to examine the church, the podium, or even the cabinet of the medium; but on many later occasions I went over them very thoroughly and never found anything in the least indicative of fraud. There were no trick electrical devices possible, according to the very responsible person who had done the wiring, and there were no hiding places for props or gadgets. Sometimes trickery must have occurred, but I am rather inclined to feel that sometimes it did not. Still, the church room was always pitch dark at all séances, and there is no way for any investigator to be positive that some kind of skull-duggery may not be going on under such conditions.

At that first meeting I was somewhat uneasy sitting in pitch blackness surrounded by fifty or sixty complete strangers; yet they were all such kind and agreeable individuals that it was soon possible to relax in their presence, even when startling events began to occur. As we sang numerous religious and metaphysical songs to build up the power, I acquired a feeling of rapport with this group that has never been lost.

Suddenly three aluminum trumpets began to bang back and forth from one wall to the other, hitting each time with a resounding smack. Then one trumpet with luminous bands around it whirled in a large circle at the ceiling. On this occasion, I presumed that someone in the dark was levitating them by means of rods and wires; later the same thing occurred when I had carefully searched the podium and found no paraphernalia of any kind.

The medium was ostensibly in the cabinet all this time. In order that his audience will not think he is practicing ventriloquism or fraud when voices are heard coming from the cabinet, Keith always has his mouth filled with water or milk and then taped shut before going into trance. Marks are made on the tape extending onto his skin, so that if the tape were removed it would be evident. After the session is over he spits out the water or milk to indicate that he has held it in his mouth all the time. I have learned from experimenting that it is possible to loosen the center of the tape and talk without disturbing the correlation of the markings; one can also do a little bit of talking with water or milk in his mouth; and some persons can swallow a fluid which they later can regurgitate. But would it be possible under these conditions for a variety of voices to be produced, ranging from very deep, sonorous tones, to childish prattle? And can conversation be sustained for hours on end under these conditions, as it often is at the Seattle services?

After the uproar caused by the banging trumpets, the childish voice of Susan, Keith's control, was heard coming from the cabinet, welcoming us and giving messages. Then other persons allegedly spoke through the medium. None who claimed to be for me were in the least identifiable by voice or inflection, although the information they gave about me, while not intimately personal, was factual. Later in the evening a famous deceased Hawaiian singer announced himself and was greeted warmly by the congregation, to whom he was a familiar guest. He began to sing loudly in a beautiful baritone—unaccompanied—responding to requests. I was to learn that Keith's own singing voice is a mediocre tenor, and so this performance was more convincing to me in hindsight than while it was occurring.

From time to time the trumpets would tap us on the shoulders or on the head. Toward the end of the three-hour-long service I was asked to reach into a trumpet that presented its open end to me. In it were several dewy pink rosebuds. The last thing before the lights were turned on, I was told to extend my arms to receive a gift, and about twenty-five fresh white carnations were tossed from somewhere and fell across my arms. Not even one dropped, they landed so neatly. Considering that my seat was in the second row and the flowers would have had to be thrown over the heads of the persons in front of me, this was quite a trick—even if the tossing had been done by someone who was wearing the kind of glasses with which you can see in the dark. Since we had been for three hours in that sealed room, those flowers were surprisingly fresh.

I won't go into detail about much of the rest of Keith's manifestations observed in Seattle. I have written about them for Martin Ebon's book *True Experiences in Communicating with the Dead*.

My own psi improved while I was there, because of sitting in every development circle offered at the foundation . . . sometimes as much as three and four nights a week. Fortunately, I have somehow managed to have at least one personal sample of each of a wide variety of psychic experiences. This makes it possible for me to understand the similar reports from others. One is naturally more skeptical until personally seeing or experiencing something unaccountable. When someone in a darkened séance room says, "I see a red light over there" or "there's a white mist in the center of the room . . . it's coming nearer" or "I see a figure standing back of your shoulder," it is easy to suspect that he is hallucinating or deluding himself with shadows. Yet it is certainly possible for some individuals to have psychic episodes that others in the same group do not share. It may occur because they are ready for it at the moment, or they may have a particular ability that others present do not have.

If everyone in the crowd sees the same thing it might actually be more sensible to question it. Once in a session where KMR (as Keith is called by his intimates) was not present but one of his students was the medium, on various occasions during the evening everyone observed a small light in the shape of a cross flitting about over the walls and ceiling. Since it is possible to prepare a flashlight to show only such a small cross, this was not impressive to me.

Another time, though, when in the dark, sealed, and guarded room with about a dozen others, I saw something that did stir me. It was an occasion when a group of us were sitting without a medium present. I was in an aisle seat. After some time there appeared about shoulder high at the end of the aisle toward the podium a slightly luminous, but rather hazy, cross. It was elongated to the extent that it was perhaps two and a half feet long and the horizontal bar was only about eight inches wide. There was no possible way that any ray of light could have entered the room, so perhaps it was a hallucination . . . at last! I didn't want one, but nonetheless what it was easy to suspect of others might now be happening to me. Without verification I certainly could not claim to have joined the club of those able to see visual psychic manifestations. In order to check myself, I did not call out a description of it. Instead, in an effort to gain confirmation I asked quietly, "Does anyone see anything unusual right now?"

The woman sitting directly behind me said, "I do."

"Will you please describe it?"

"Well," she said, "what I see is a cross in the air right at the end of the aisle. It is much longer than it is wide, and is not sharp and distinct, but rather misty." No one else spoke of seeing this, so I tended to suspect it must be a genuine psychic phenomenon.

While in Seattle, I dated John L. Metzgar, a tall, rugged man with a frosting of white hair. He is an artist by profession, but also a great hunter and outdoorsman. One night during a period in my psychic growth when the ability to go into trance seemed to be developing, I did "go out" for a brief moment during class and had a short vision or dream. In it I turned around and looked at a man in the seat behind me, where in reality no one was sitting. He had white hair and thin-rimmed glasses, and actually he answered the description of John Metzgar, although at the time I did not associate him with John. During my brief dream of him, this man leaned forward toward me from the seat behind, staring at me fixedly, and then suddenly he snapped his teeth at me. He just opened his mouth as if to take a large bite and then snapped his teeth together, like a hungry lion grabbing at a piece of meat. I came to, startled, and spent some time afterward wondering what in the world such a peculiar action could mean. If that had been a genuine trance, what was seen should have had some significance, but there seemed to be none. No one to whom I spoke about it could deduce anything from it; I mentioned it to John but he didn't identify it either.

Several nights later John and I were sitting side by side on a couch when he impetuously leaned toward me and snapped his teeth at me.

"That's what the man did in my vision!" I screeched.

"It's just a silly habit of mine," he explained. "I often do it to my children . . . playing as if I'm going to bite them." He had not thought of this when he heard me talk about seeing it; but he now mentioned that on that night he *had* been trying to send me some kind of a message, or hoping to make me aware of his thoughts. He had not entertained the idea of snapping his teeth at me, however.

Of particular interest to me while in Seattle were Rhinehart's Sunday morning message services, because there seemed to be a certain amount of evidence for genuine mental mediumship exhibited there.

Keith's blindfolding procedure is unlike that of most other mediums. This is because certain precautions are taken which should make his billet reading as nearly fraudproof as possible. Shortly after the meeting starts, the medium, standing at the altar, closes his eyes, jerks his head a few times, and goes into trance.

Then the deep voice of his main control, Dr. Robert John Kensington, speaks through him. Dr. Kensington introduces himself and asks that some skeptical individual in the audience come up and bandage the eyes of the medium.

I volunteered several times for this duty and observed the entire procedure carefully. First Keith's eyes and face were wiped with a dry paper tissue to make sure there was no oil or grease that would allow the bandage to slip so that a peephole could be achieved. Then a strip of adhesive tape two inches wide and about eight inches long was placed over his eyes. It was pressed tightly against his skin, below the eyes particularly. After this a wide white cloth bandage was tied around the medium's head, but it was not so wide as to hide his face. It would have been observable, therefore, if he had twisted his facial muscles so as to maneuver the adhesive tape in such a way as to form a crack or crease through which he could see. He never did this.

I took the same roll of adhesive tape used by KMR home with me after a service one day and practiced employing it as he did. When it is pressed tightly against the skin below the eyes and over the cheekbones there is no possible way to see out of it. It is quite uncomfortable to remove, and it's no wonder that strips of adhesive pulled off Keith's eyes during my stay in Seattle frequently contained one or two of his eyelashes.

Before the audience went into the auditorium for the message service, each person wrote a question on a card and signed his name to it. It is easy to suspect right away that some kind of skullduggery might be afoot because the request was made that each billet be signed, but in reality the cards lay openly in a basket on a table in the foyer until the service began. Anyway, subsequent events often tended to preclude the possibility that anyone had looked at the questions and passed the information on to the medium.

I always try not to reveal anything of a personal nature in my questions. Years before, in my first experience at a billet service at Camp Cassadaga, Florida, I had given so much away that the message received was of no value. My billet read: "To my mother, Please state what we discussed last night via automatic writing." This was a loaded question—loaded with information, which the blindfolded medium proceeded to hand right back to me. After calling out my initials he said, "Your mother is in the spirit world. Why, you and she have communication via automatic writing, don't you? And you were communicating with her only last night!" The audience gasped when I admitted the veracity of these statements, which were probably being read off my card. They did not know that my actual question was never answered.

That experience made me realize how easy it is to give away too much information in one's question on a billet. So I watched that carefully from then on. I also always take down in shorthand everything that is said to me by a medium; thus there is a complete record in my files of all the information I received at the services at the Aquarian Foundation. There were various answers over a period of weeks that correlated curiously, making me feel that interesting cross correspondences occurred.

A cross correspondence is some portion of the message which may be carried over from week to week, or answers to questions asked one medium which may be given by another, or corroboration of information by one sensitive which has previously been stated by another. These occurred in the sessions I am discussing.

At Keith's message service, after his eyes were bandaged, a monitor brought the basket of billets and placed it on the podium. The control, Dr. Kensington, now quickly began to give messages to members of the congregation. It was frequently his habit to ask for a certain person, or to start making a statement, before he had ever placed his hand into the basket. Then, as he gave the message, his hand rummaged briefly among the thirty to fifty or more cards, and he pulled out one billet. He usually twisted this in his hands as he talked and when he was finished with the message he gave it to the monitor. She then returned it to the person who had acknowledged the message. It was invariably his own card. This occurred once when John Metzgar had written his question with a ball point pen which was out of ink. It barely made a few indentations on the card and was almost impossible to read; yet Kensington asked for John, answered his question, and commented upon the unusual spelling of his name. He had used his professional signature "Jonel."

Week after week cards were returned to visitors, strangers, and members of the congregation alike, and little gasps could be heard as they identified their own come back to them from the blind-folded medium.

One Sunday when I was present Dr. Kensington called for a certain woman, who answered from the audience. He gave her several bits of information and names which she identified. Then he asked her if she had ever been to a service in that church before, and she admitted that she was a complete stranger, there by chance.

"Did I answer your question?" he asked, and she nodded. Then, and only then, he reached into the billet basket and pulled out a card which was handed to her and she claimed as hers.

On another occasion a man named Steve was asked to rise to receive a message. He proved to be a large, ruddy-skinned lum-berman in a red and black checked shirt, whom I had never seen in the audience before. Steve was told that Anna was asking for him and that she loved him. She was reported to state that a candle must be lighted for her at the table on Christmas, because she would be there. Then Dr. Kensington began to describe a dress, with red flowers and green leaves and dashes of yellow in it. Steve by this time was shedding tears, as he was told that he had very recently had this dress out because it was his favorite of his wife's, and that he had been sitting cradling it in his arms, weep-ing bitterly.

After the service I checked on what this man had asked, won-dering just how much information he had given away by his ques-tion. He showed me the card that had been returned to him. It read, "To Anna, please talk to me, I love you." It was signed "Steve." He told me that his wife had died a few weeks earlier. He said he was a lumberman from Canada who had just hap-pened to come to Seattle and knew no one there connected with the Aquarian Foundation. He also told me that the night before he had taken out his favorite dress of Anna's, which answered the medium's description, and had sat and held it and cried over it. Needless to say, he had not told anyone of this.

As a part of my development of my own psychic talents, each evening after returning home I sat at my typewriter and en-deavored to communicate. I discussed this with no one, and not a person in Seattle knew the name of James Anderson, with whom most of my automatic writing was done. Neither did they know the man in spirit I suspected him actually to be.

Anderson had earlier told me that I would not believe it if it was revealed who was really writing under his pseudonym. I knew that my psychic abilities were not powerful enough for me to be able to receive anything of an evidential nature that could prove who he was if he told me, so I made no effort to try. As time went on, however, several mediums told me that the great American psychologist William James was with me as one of my guides. I put this down to possible unconscious wishful thinking on my part and mind reading on theirs.

It is true that William James had been extremely interested in psychical research during his lifetime. He said of it in *Psychology*: "But if, as has been asserted, we have to deal with genuine phenomena of an unknown, transcendental origin, the study of these facts is one of the most important tasks ever imposed upon science. For it must bring about an unexpected widening of the knowledge of the processes of human life."

James is often reported by various mediums still to be active, trying to help prove the possibility of communication with the spirit world. I was nonetheless reluctant to claim him.

When I finally sat at my typewriter one day in 1964 and deliberately asked James Anderson who he really is he typed "William James." Even so I have made no effort to get anything substantially evidential from him, fearing it might not be successful and not wanting to flub it. Certainly there is no great evidence of his style in the James material received through me, yet it is not too unlike him either. I do occasionally find signs of William's delicious wit, such as in the "Ode to the Prophets of Old." As to whether what James says through me agrees with what William James believed and wrote while on earth, why should it? He knows a great deal more now from an entirely new perspective. (Interestingly enough, William James's father was a Swedenborgian, and he was raised as one.)

It is true, also, that what James Anderson originally told me about himself when he first began communicating and I wasn't suspicious he was really someone else, applies to William James.

He said he had lived in Massachusetts, had children, and had died in the early part of this century.

Now, in Seattle, I was given one name as often as another for the signature of my private communications. Then one day, after the entity had written an entire page without signing it, he typed at the bottom, "Take this to your medium and ask him to try to get a psychic impression as to who wrote it." I did this, and Keith, after holding it to his forehead for a few moments, said, "William James? Is he one of your guides?"

I decided this was perhaps enough evidence to end my arguing. I nonetheless make it a point to refer to the material allegedly received from him as nothing more spectacular than "the James material" because of not wanting to have to argue with anyone about its source. I can only let his wise counsel stand or fall on its own merit; I do not attempt to proclaim that the eminent William James is bothering with me.

It was before I had shown the page to Keith and before anyone at the church knew anything about my efforts at communication or the possible names of any of my guides, that my series of cross correspondences occurred. They began on Sunday morning, November 14, 1965. I still have all my billets, dated and safely tucked away, with their tiny bits of evidence intact.

Before the church service that morning I had written on my card: "To W.J.: A message please." I signed it with the initials "S.S."

The medium said to me: "James Anderson is here." I acknowledged him happily, especially because he was not the "W.J." to whom my appeal had been made. Then Dr. Kensington reported, "Mr. Anderson says you have lost or misplaced something recently. Some little inexpensive object." This was true. It was a pencil-shaped typewriter eraser that had disappeared and I had been looking everywhere for it for several days, even carefully sifting through all the wastebaskets in case it might have fallen into one; but this had not been mentioned to a soul.

"James Anderson says they have apported it away," said the control. An apport is an object that appears somewhere that it had not been the moment before, or that disappears suddenly under curious circumstances and then reappears somewhere else that it should not normally have been. When such acts are genuine, they are said to occur by a process of dematerializing the object so that it disappears and then later rematerializing it in a different location. There is substantial evidence that on occasion some cherished possession that a sitter knew was safely in his home has been brought to him in a sealed séance room. On other occasions, of course, less dependable mediums have secreted something on their persons and then produced them as apports.

The attendant invisible spirits take full credit for being able to produce apports when conditions are right. I had always thought if they were going to try to do something of this sort for me it would be nice if they apported me a diamond bracelet or a million dollars. Now, however, as my first experience of this nature, all they were doing was fooling around with a typewriter eraser. "Anderson is laughing," Dr. Kensington went on. "He says it is too small a thing we are discussing to sign the initials W.J. to." Then the control chided me for giving only my initials on my billet, and my card was returned to me.

During the week after this I found the typewriter eraser. It was way at the back of a file folder lying on a table near my typing desk, tucked in so carefully that it did not seem possible it could have arrived there by chance. But neither could one be sure it had not. The question is why, if it had been apported away and then returned, it would not have been brought back to a more conspicuous place, such as the center of my desk or the seat of a chair that had been examined for it previously. In such an event there could have been no question in my mind about the supernormal quality of the return, as there was now. I had mental references to this argument when writing my billet the next Sunday, November 21st. It read: "To J.A. Please explain situation regarding last week's message." It was signed properly this time with my full name.

My message began with the statement: "W. G. is here for S.S. (Remember that my previous week's billet had been directed to W.J. and signed S.S.) I said with a question in my voice, "W.G.?" He replied, "No, it is W.J." (If the medium had been consciously trying to impress me by trickery, would he have made this error?) He then gave me my parents' initials and told me they were associated in the experiments. He said they were pleased with the way my mediumship was progressing. When he didn't say anything definite that would explain the apport situation, I asked him for more data regarding my question. He replied that I would start having so many experiences of that nature that I would wonder what in the world was going on.

After he had concluded my message, the medium paused, then came back to me, saying, "An unexpected change of plans is coming through a letter within twelve days." I made a mark on my calendar twelve days ahead and resolved to watch for a letter by then which would alter things for me. I suspected this might have something to do with a prospective visit to Hawaii. My arrangement with the Aquarian Foundation was that for a series of lectures and classes in Seattle and Honolulu I was to be paid with round trip plane fare to Hawaii and ten days at a leading Honolulu hotel. The date for the trip had not been set, but KMR had written to his Hawaiian members asking them if my lectures could be scheduled for the week of the tenth of December. Perhaps Dr. Kensington's prediction might mean that, instead, some other date would be set for my Island trip. I did not mention any of this to Keith, or anyone else.

About that time a non-professional medium of the congregation, Bep Diefenberger, attempted to give me a book test at a week-night meeting. She said: "At another place, not your own library, you will be drawn to a bookcase. On the second shelf, pick out the eighth book from the left. Turn to page seventy-two. The twelfth line from the top will contain a message for you."

I was at that time a guest in the home of Marguerite Dolch, author of a well-known series of children's books. I randomly selected her bookshelves for my test, discovering that the eighth book from the left on the second shelf was *William James on Psychical Research* by Dr. Gardner Murphy! The page and line Bep mentioned seemed to have nothing with personal application to me, however. Bep did not know of my special interest in William James, but even if she had, she had never been in Mrs. Dolch's house.

I seldom dream anything which later comes true, and only a few of my sleep escapades seem to have special significance. Still, when I dreamed one night that William James had a dog named "Blackie" I endeavored to verify it by automatic writing, getting nothing satisfactory about it. The next Sunday my billet was worded: "To W.J. Who is Blackie?"

Dr. Kensington said: "A gentleman is trying to show me an animal. Your question has something to do with a name you don't know. I'm not saying that this is the name of the animal, however. What I am saying is that this gentleman is trying to give you cross-connective messages through different mediums . . . a series of things. I feel the time will come when you will come across information somehow that will add to what is available through the main sources about this person you seek information about, and then all the pieces of a jigsaw puzzle will come together so that there will be greater proof than ever before. Some of this material cannot be verified. This particular name may be a place, a person, a friend, or animal. I get only an impression. I don't get the direct answer."

On the night of December 2nd, just twelve days after the prediction about my delayed trip, I returned home from a date at midnight. My telephone was ringing as I walked in and it was Keith, terribly upset.

"Where have you been? I've been trying to reach you all evening," he cried. "Susy, I'm desolate. They don't want you in Hawaii."

Knowing that Keith was having trouble with his Hawaiian membership, I was not too surprised that they might rebel against his directives.

"That's all right," I told him. "I don't need to go."

"Oh, they want you after Christmas. But they won't take you on the dates I suggested."

"It's O.K.," I said. "After Christmas would be even better."

"But I was planning on your being there for the tenth," he said, still resentful at their having thwarted him. "I received the letter from them this morning, but didn't get around to reading my mail until this evening. I hate so to disappoint you."

"You're not disappointing me. Twelve days ago Dr. Kensington told me my plans about a trip would be changed within twelve days and I've been expecting this," I reassured him.

"Dr. Kensington told you? What do you mean?"

When I explained, Keith, an extremely emotional individual, sounded miffed. "Why didn't you tell me?" he raged. "Here I was, all upset. I've been frantic ever since I read that letter for fear you would be hurt and think we didn't love you!" He really seemed so sincerely chagrined that it is difficult to believe he was faking his lack of knowledge about the message while he was in trance. I was glad the communication had arrived on the date it did because it proved the prediction correct.

On the night of Saturday, December 4th, I lectured to a large group of people interested in psychical research in Olympia, Washington. After the talk some of us were invited to the home of one of the members of the organization for coffee, cake, and conversation. A man named Sam Miller, who was unknown to any of these people, apparently having attended the lecture by chance, accompanied us. He came with us, he declared, because of a mission he felt he must accomplish.

"I have something important to tell you about yourself," he advised me. So I sat down to talk with him about one of my favorite subjects, me. He asked for a deck of cards. The host didn't have any, and so, while my attention was turned to someone else, Sam Miller left for a moment. It was later learned that he had made the host take him next door, where they awoke the neighbors to borrow a deck of cards!

When Sam returned he had me cut the deck several times, then he laid out some cards in front of me. After that, hardly looking at the cards, he began to rattle off the following statement, which I recorded: "Something completely different is going to happen to you. It will be good fortune for you and for others. It will put you in touch with forces and things of great moment and will concern large groups of people. It will change your entire life. Unusual forces are surrounding you. They have been gathering for quite some time.

"This thing that will happen to you is completely unusual. It will be the turning point of your life. It has been building up. Watch for it and don't be frightened when it happens. Follow through on it. A man will be associated with it."

To this day I don't know of any especially exciting and wonderful event in which a man was associated with me—well, actually, I do—but I mean one that could be the answer to this prediction. The message itself, however, was confirmed in an interesting cross correspondence the following day.

I arrived back in Seattle about 2 A.M. The next morning I awoke late and just had time to rush to church for the service, at no time talking to anyone about my message of the night before. The couple who had accompanied me to Olympia was scientifically oriented in their thinking and did not attend Aquarian Foundation services. Between 2 A.M. and 10 A.M. they were not at all likely to have spoken of my personal experience, least of all to anyone connected with KMR's church; and they have assured me they did not.

The prophecy was exciting enough that it was still in my mind, and so my question on my billet involved it. I happened to pick up a pencil with exceptionally light green lead, and the card, which is still in my possession, is almost indecipherable unless held very close to the eyes. My question was: "To my Guides, Explain Sam Miller's message."

My answer, when it came, began: "There was a change of plans in connection with a prophecy."

When I confirmed this, Dr. Kensington added, "In twelve days. Your guides are happy about it. An amazing opportunity will open up in the Islands for you. A contact so strong you will be returning there over and over again." (The mighty contact was the beauty and peace of Hawaii. I would quite willingly return frequently; but no amazing opportunity opened up for me there.)

Then the good spirit doctor who used KMR for a sounding apparatus turned to my question. He said, "I sense as though the thing you have wondered about from your guides is very unusually accurate. There is a message you have received only within the past twenty-four hours and you couldn't believe it because it is too good." This is right, of course, in all details.

I asked, "Is it true?"

"Of course it's true and a wonderful thing," the medium replied, adding, "You sometimes doubt too much."

Chapter 38

HADN'T FORGOTTEN that the initial reason for my being in Seattle was my ghost hunt for the book then in progress. The fame of a haunting at the Burnley School of Professional Art had reached me in New York, and that was one of the reasons for choosing the State of Washington to begin my tour. I did not intend to investigate it under any circumstances as potentially powerpacked as having four mediums with me, but that is how it turned out.

For about six years, until it somewhat abated in the spring of 1965, the Burnley School had loud creaky footsteps on the stairs and locked doors that opened themselves in the night. On the evening of October 4th I kept an appointment to learn about this from Jess Cauthorn, the owner-director of the school and one of the Pacific Northwest's best known watercolorists.

After our chat I interviewed several of his students who had heard unexplainable activity in the building. It was planned to have Keith Rhinehart and one or two of his followers join us later and see what psychic impressions he received there. His arrival accompanied by three of his student mediums would have been vetoed had it been anticipated. At least, it would have been vetoed had I known what I know now! Four mediums in one haunted building create so much power that anything can happen!

I enjoyed my chat with Jess Cauthorn, who has himself heard the manifestations in his school. He had never believed in ghosts until then. But now?

"I'm a realistic person," he said, "but there are some things you just can't ignore—like the sound of desks being moved in an empty room behind locked doors."

John R. Nelson, a tall young student, illustrated for me the sound the ghost made on the stairs. He went down and clomped up the wide flight leading from the first floor to the third. The steps are very creaky, and each footstep squeaked in its own specific way. There was no possible doubt that the sound was just that—a footstep on the stair. John said that when he had been working on a big art project and didn't want to stop, he had sometimes painted most of the night. When he was all alone in the building, he would hear at any moment between eleven o'clock at night and three o'clock in the morning, footsteps mounting those stairs. He would naturally go to see who was arriving, but nobody was there.

"Can you ever get used to a thing like that?" I asked.

"Not really," he replied. "You just learn not to work here alone at night."

Jennie Miller told me a similar story to John's, and then several other pupils verified her account. They had even devised tests to catch the haunt. With masking tape they fastened thread across the stairway and various doorways about three feet off the floor, and some of the threads were broken by the invisible spook. On other occasions they heard him climb the stairs, but the threads remained intact. They had also perceived the sounds of groans and rustlings; and they had been totally unable to keep the doors to the school locked at night.

Dr. Keith Milton Rhinehart then arrived with his retinue, Judy Crane Ballard, Kenneth Bower, and Helen Lester. Judy's new husband was also along, and Clyde Beck. Clyde was an Aquarian member who had also belonged to the American Society for Psychical Research for years and attempted to be quite critical in his evaluations. These people all united with the group of art students, Jess Cauthorn and me for a tour of the building. After traveling all over it, even into the dank, dark and unpaved cellar, we settled down for a séance in a small room on the second floor, just large enough to hold the ten of us. We put opaque screens over the windows and turned out all the lights. Just enough glow came in around the edge of the screens from the streetlight outside so that we could dimly see what went on in the room. Keith and I sat together on a short couch, and the others milled around in the dark for a while.

In order to learn if there might be any spirits about who wanted to make an effort to be known, all those in the room except Keith and me put their fingers lightly on the top of a tall stool. Almost at once it began to move so fast that they kept up with it only with difficulty. Then the stool banged itself with great force against the floor and the wall. Asked to answer questions with a code, one rap for "Yes" and two for "No," it gave a few comments. But whatever was propelling the stool had no real interest in such attempts at small talk. It preferred to show off its great force by banging itself senselessly against the wall.

To Keith and me, sitting on the couch, this was all very boring. I became sleepy, and he became . . . possessed? The others finally settled down in chairs and sat quietly. After a few moments while the full impact of the silence and the darkness crept over us, I glanced toward Keith—and discovered that he was staring at me fixedly with the most malevolent expression I have ever had directed my way. He was at the time affecting a moustache and goatee, and, the way his eyes were now glittering, he looked positively devilish. We all decided that he had been taken over into trance, possibly by the entity who was haunting the school. If he was earthbound, he must be convinced that he should stop his uncanny practices, so I began racking my brain for suitable phrases with which to interrogate him and make him aware of his condition.

"Who are you?" erupted suddenly and uproariously from the medium.

I leaped into the air, as it is my custom to be slightly unnerved by an abrupt loud verbal attack in the dark. An experienced hand at such things is presumably imperturbable, but I'm a very female person and tend to react like one. Anyway, that glaring face was too close for comfort.

"We're here to help you," I quavered, beginning to explain to him that he had passed through the experience called death and that he must adjust himself to the fact and go away and stop bothering the school . . . that there were helpful spirits around him who would give him assistance and advice if he would but listen to them. . . .

"I'm not dead," he screamed, interrupting me. Then he lunged in my direction, waving his arms and shouting, "Get out! Get out!

all of you!" No matter what was said to him, he kept roaring this refrain, with the appropriate motions.

It was coming to my attention that we might have here an entity harder to convince than those who had pestered me so long ago in Daytona Beach. And I didn't have Mother's Chapter handy to read to him. A hidebound haunt inside the body of a man might be a totally different situation to contend with, for that matter. How could one talk sense to him or try to persuade him when he refused to listen?

Then this intruder began to murmur about what must have been his murder. "Blood all over everything," he said, supplying numerous other melodramatic details that seemed to be involved with his sanguinary demise. Even as I sat there participating in this drama, it sounded overplayed and amateurish to me. In retrospect the whole evening seems a trivial travesty of a bad B movie or a television turkey. Yet even now I am not entirely persuaded it was a put on. It might have been; but it might more probably not have been.

While the events were going on and I was participating in them, it was rather necessary to take them at face value, which was not in the least reassuring when the allegedly entranced medium kept jumping my way threateningly from time to time. Finally he lunged and waved his arms in my direction just once too often and I got up and moved over to a bench just opposite the couch. The Thing, whatever it was, by then was muttering irresponsibly to himself, and he glanced down at my expensive camera which was on the floor beside where my feet had been. Lest he be inspired to break it, I reached over and picked it up.

As I did, the maniacal look on the medium's face made me think, "That would make a great picture for the book." I began sighting the camera on him, but wouldn't have snapped it because there is a theory about a sudden light being dangerous to an entranced medium. Whether or not it is true, it would have been stupid to take the chance. The possible occasion for my snapping the picture didn't come up, anyway, for at that moment Keith cried, "What are you doing?" and made a leap straight at me.

"Don't touch me!" I shouted . . . and kicked him. It was just a little kick—it barely connected with his thigh; but he plummeted to the floor as if a hatchet had landed on his skull. I began to quiver then with a new kind of fright, because he was lying prone, breathing as if each gasp might be his last. Maybe I'd killed him! My foot had no more than touched him, but this had apparently dislodged the ghost, causing it to lose its hold on him.

Finally, as we all sat with eyes glued on the medium, we heard the sonorous tones of his control speaking: "This is Dr. Robert John Kensington, and we have things in hand." KMR, still entranced, but now by his proper guide, got up and sat back on the couch, Dr. Kensington apologizing all the while for having allowed him to be taken over by such an irresponsible entity. He said he had not realized that the spirit was actually insane until it had gotten into Keith's body; and that the number of mediums present acted as a battery that gave it more power.

Keith then came out of his trance, asked for a drink of water, and sat holding his head, complaining of a violent headache. He questioned us about what had happened, and someone began to tell him. I was doing a lot of thinking, meanwhile, all of it very negative. If this had been an act, it was such an overdone performance that it was hardly worthy of Keith's histrionic ability . . . yet if it had not been, perhaps the entity really hated me for telling him he was dead. Good Heavens! I'd been in real danger!

I turned and said to the people with me, possibly a bit sarcastically: "How did it happen, may I ask, that all of you sat there so calmly while I was being attacked by a maniac?"

The Aquarian mediums informed me that touching an entranced person when he was in such a state might have injured him. They were a bit put out at me for having dared to kick their beloved.

"But what if I'd been injured?"

"You didn't have a thing to worry about," they assured me. "We were surrounding everyone with protective thoughts, so everything was completely under control." Under control? I almost had a camera wrapped around my head!

Then Jess Cauthorn revealed that things hadn't been as orderly as the foundation members hoped, for he and John Nelson had been sitting on the edges of their chairs, signaling each other, and ready to spring if the medium got one inch closer to me. They had been considering the entire affair to be a clumsy hoax; but they wondered why, if it were a hoax, Keith had not known he was going too far and would be in danger from them if he got rough with me. This was part of the whole big mystery. If he was putting on an act, why didn't he realize the possibility of being physically restrained by those two men so much larger than he? There were many mysteries about this evening that have never been resolved; and this was one of them. Yet the biggest enigma of all occurred after we left the séance room. It put a slightly different light on the whole performance; but it did not solve anything. It only made the confusion worse.

Rather depressed by the episode that had just taken place, I had gathered my wits, my nerve and my camera and walked out of the room to try to get another picture or two of the building. I was accompanied by Keith and Clyde Beck. The rest spread out, eventually going downstairs.

The three of us walked back down the hall and into the auditorium, around a corner and about fifty feet from the séance room. After discussing the possibility of getting a photo there and deciding it would be useless to try with my lighting equipment, we started to walk back up the hall. Hearing a funny sound from Keith then, I turned to look at him. His eyes were getting that glassy, glittery look again, and he began to mutter incoherencies. Along with other phrases that weren't particularly intelligible, he mumbled, "I told you there was something I could do you couldn't."

"It's got him again!" I called out, rushing up the hall away from him. "Clyde, *do* something!"

Clyde did something; he watched to see what was going to happen next. I moved on as quickly as possible, hollering to the people downstairs. Aquarians and students came bounding up, and as they did the medium began to speak once more in the healthy tones of his control.

"This is Dr. Robert John Kensington," he said. "The entity got back in once again because there was something he insisted on saying. Will you please call the owner of the building?"

Jess Cauthorn was just arriving up the stairs on a run, and he said breathlessly, "I'm here."

"Do you recall if there was a rock about the size of a brick in that room where the séance was held?" Dr. Kensington asked.

"No, I don't think so," answered Jess. "I'm almost sure there was not."

"Well, the entity was trying to say that he had the power to bring apports," the voice went on. "Now if you will go into the séance room you will find a rock there close to where Miss Smith was sitting."

We all rushed into the room, and sure enough, right where my feet had been, there was now a smooth, oval rock as large as a brickbat. It could not have been there when my feet were cringing in that spot a few minutes before.

I went home that night disturbed by the possibility that a Thing who had wished to bop me with a rock might follow me and try to take me over. What I had been through in Daytona had not favorably prepared me for anything of this nature. If the spook could entrance Keith, with all the protection *he* had, it certainly could give me a vast amount of trouble if it wanted to try to move in on me. This was one time to be grateful for the band of Indians who had been rallied to my defense so long ago . . . presuming they were still there. I was truly relieved when the night passed with no further incident that might be considered untoward . . . untoward me, at any rate.

Although my experience at the Burnley School was effective enough to be somewhat disturbing, it could not have been permanently convincing, and I continued to argue that the whole thing must have been an act. Jess Cauthorn, his students, Clyde Beck and I were never to come to any firm conclusion about that. As we thought about the apport and tried to explain it, we realized that neither Keith nor Kenneth could possibly, without being observed, have hidden so large a rock on their rather slight frames in order to bring it up from the basement. If one of the women mediums had managed to secrete it in some oversized handbag, then how did Keith, down the hall with me, know about it?

The only answer, except one really crediting ghosts and apports and other supernormalities, is that the whole event was an extravaganza put on by the entire group of mediums in collaboration, to show the visiting author a good time and give her something to write about. But Keith and all the others knew that I was prepared to write scathingly about them if they were discovered in anything manifestly fraudulent, or even anything particularly suspicious looking. Why, under those circumstances, would they play stupid games with me? Why also would Keith have run the risk of being clobbered when he leaped at me knowing full well that the large, healthy male non-Spiritualists in the group would certainly defend me, with blows if necessary?

Of all the questions raised by this incident, the biggest that remains is this: If the Aquarians *had* decided to put on an act, why wasn't it a *better* act? These were presumably intelligent adults, not children; they couldn't have been stupid enough to have produced such an overblown, overacted melodrama and expected it to be believed, could they?

But an earthbound spirit so dumb as to hang around a school for years without knowing it was time to graduate—he might have acted just the way he did that night. After all, we *were* in a building in which a great many genuinely inexplicable manifestations had already occurred. Maybe this was just one more in the series.

Chapter 39

‖ TOOK LSD in Hawaii. The realization that having psychic experiences of my own made me much better able to understand the incidents described to me by others caused me to believe that I should know more about psychedelic drugs in order to write about them intelligently. At the time, before it was generally known how dangerous they are, and before they were illegal, they were often experimented with in an effort to have psychic experiences.

Also, I had come under the influence of several persons who were convinced from their own results that if one took the hallucinogens under proper conditions he could have a truly awareness-expanding experience that would make him feel closer to God in every way. With this goal in mind, I was determined to make the attempt at the very first chance that presented itself. Wiser heads warned against it, for even then there were those who were aware of the dangers; but I could not be deterred.

A friend in Los Angeles had bought two capsules of LSD from a pusher and used one of them. He had such a magnificent mental adventure that he couldn't talk about it enough. When I made a quick trip from Seattle to L.A. to lecture for the Southern California Branch of the American Society for Psychical Research, this man gave me his other capsule, with his assurance that I would surely have an experience as mind-blowing as his. Awaiting the proper occasion to take it, I kept it with me until after my series of lectures in Honolulu in January. Then I took the acid under the guidance of a doctor who was experienced at handling psychedelic drugs.

I wished I hadn't done it almost from the first minute afterward.

My reaction to many things is nausea. Although loving boating, and automobile riding on curvy mountain roads, I often become seasick or carsick. Now I got LSD-sick, and remained that way the entire morning, almost on the verge of throwing up all the time. Apparently the pusher's dose had been the right size for a man, but was too strong for a woman. This is one of the main problems with taking psychedelics, of course. You don't know the proper strength for your constitution, or for your brain.

Besides keeping me physically miserable, the acid showed me colorful pictures, nothing more. I had read Jane Dunlap's book *Exploring Inner Space*, and had been interested in the fact that she had experienced a whole evolutionary cycle during her LSD trips. Now, I, too, followed evolution in a return to my origins and back up to the present. I would live in a world of brilliant visual imagery for a while and then rouse back up to conscious awareness of myself again, striving for rationality and proper orientation as well as fighting nausea.

"Promise I won't stay this way," I'd implore the doctor who was monitoring me. "It's interesting to look at the pictures, but I'd rather die than have to live like this. I'm completely insane.

Promise I'll come out of it soon!" He'd reassure me, and then I'd submerge again, my mentality completely fused into the pictures of prehistoric monsters appearing on my mental screen.

Once when I became conscious, the Dunlap book was recalled with the realization that Jane's path was being followed.

"Maybe I'll even run into that white cobra she saw," I thought with revulsion, never having been in the least enamored of snakes. "Hope it doesn't take me over as it did her." But it did. I identified with it in order to understand how it feels being a snake. Not too bad, actually. It was a nice, well-meaning white cobra with none of my problems upon surfacing, when I was always aware of being insane.

What then began to bother me most was the fact that I was doing no more than traveling this evolutionary route I'd read about, not showing any originality of my own and definitely not soaring into any ethereal spheres.

"What's wrong with me?" I'd wonder during my conscious periods. "Others reach out in spirit and have beautiful God-experiences. What's happening here is nothing more than a bunch of pictures out of any movie." Was my soul too low in caliber to deserve an illumination? Obviously this was my trouble. I was a person of negative spiritual values, not worthy of anything better. On looking inward, all that was exposed was trash. Now, because a searching of my innermost being disclosed nothing of worth there, when I submerged all the pictures were tinselly and tawdry, the colors neon-signish, fluorescent, and garish.

At the next surfacing, the picture show was over, having obviously, to me, performed its function of revealing me for what I truly was . . . nothing. The depression was complete, and it stayed with me when the doctor and another couple took me to the beach for the afternoon. I talked constantly all the way there, but what was said seemed unpleasant. Positive that my companions were judging me as shrewish and cheap, it seemed necessary to justify myself for having such a bad trip. Yet also, on a deeper level, I was perceptively aware that they were sorry for me because I hadn't been worthy of better. It is true that those who have had illumination or any deeply spiritually enlightening experiences always and forever afterward tend to be a bit patronizing toward those who have not. I'm sure they don't mean to, but they let their consciousness of superiority stick out all over them. I was sensing this now in the people with me, for my acid trip made me able to see into the minds of those about me to an unusually perceptive degree all that day.

At the beach I lay on the sand all afternoon, looking at pictures of Chinese dragons in the wispy clouds, totally oblivious to the effects of the sun, which caused a somewhat uncomfortable burn. I was taken to dinner at a cafeteria that night but had almost to be spoon fed. I told my friends that people must think they had their moronic daughter out with them, for indeed, that is exactly how it felt. Pictures appeared in my mind again at bedtime; but only a hangover was evident the next morning, as if from some big alcoholic binge.

The depression was to stay with me for months. I had gone to Hawaii a well-adjusted individual, happy in my work, loving the traveling and meeting people, completely at home in my universe. It is to be wondered whether the despondency would ever have been thrown off if I had been less harmonious at the time of taking the drug. What if I had been a possibly neurotic teen-ager completely at odds with the world? Hospitals are full of unfortunates who had just such bad trips and did not readjust at all. Apparently for everyone who has a beautiful experience there is another who reacts negatively. I can only thank God for coming out of it sane, for I know now the horrors of insanity.

Life was hardly worth living in that state of miserable depression, and I fought it all winter, mulling my situation over and over. Having worked so hard and long on my constructive thinking and spiritual enlightenment, surely I had deserved some kind of inspirational adventure, yet all that had resulted was this feeling of complete unworthiness and inadequacy. So what if I had learned how it feels to be a snake? That was hardly compensation for all the misery afterward.

If my spirit guides were really trying to help me, shouldn't they have aided me into something successful and inspiring? Why didn't they? I was evidently not a person of character, after all, or something better would have occurred when the opportunity came to expand my awareness into illumination.

The beauties of Hawaii were not as enchanting to me now as they had been; but I finished my tour, particularly loving "The

Big Island"—Hawaii, and Kauai, which are much more unspoiled and less touristy than Oahu. Then I flew to Los Angeles and remained there until April. During that time, although not feeling bright enough to scintillate, I made several lectures and numerous television and radio appearances publicizing a new book; and it was while on the air in March telling about my LSD debacle that the insight came that finally pulled me out of my depression.

On KABC radio Paul Condylis was discussing with me what I had learned from personal experimentation with acid—how dangerous to one's morale it might be to fool around with hallucinogenic drugs—when suddenly it dawned on me that having the bad trip was the right thing to have happened to me, the only possible perspective for me to have achieved! What if mine had been the kind of rewarding experience Aldous Huxley had! I'd have undoubtedly written and talked persuasively about it, and eventually might have had many acid heads on my conscience. To think that even one or two young people had started on the dangerous drug path because of anything I might have said or written sent more chills through me than any contact with ghosts ever had.

Obviously, I now realized, if my spirit associates had had anything at all to do with it, my bad trip had been deliberate. Then, grateful for my narrow escape, I relinquished the God-experiences to those who could acquire them legitimately without the use of drugs, and went on my way rejoicing.

Chapter 40

AFTER VISITING ghost houses in San Diego and San Jose, California, I flew to New Orleans, bought a small car, and drove up the East Coast. In the early American Bishop Huntington House in Hadley, Massachusetts, I was to see the only manifestation of a possible ghostly presence on my trip. It was a rather feeble effort, a hazy kind of substance peering at me out of an attic. But it was at noontime on a sunny day, when no proper haze should have been in evidence, so I gave it a bit of credibility —especially when afterward learning that the attic was the most haunted area of that house.

A woman who is probably the most prominent citizen of the Hawaiian Island of Kauai told me she believes ghosts are in some way affected by electricity. She bases this conclusion on the fact that before she had electric service installed in an old home she owns in the most inaccessible part of the island she used to see ghosts there regularly. Now they appear only rarely. Perhaps that helps to explain why an attic of an ancient house might still retain its haunt while the rest of the building, now electrified, does not. It's an idea, anyway. I offer it herewith to parapsychologists for possible research.

On Friday, July 1, 1966, I drove to Albany where I met my friend Leah Exon of Syracuse, New York, and Naples, Italy. Leah is the sister of Dolores Botticelli, who with her husband Rafaelle had rescued me from the hospital in Sorrento and taken me to Naples. Leah contacted me when I lived in New York and fascinated me with her stories of her personal ESP experiences. You never know where you're going to meet a psychic any more; the woods and the towns and the villages and the cities are full of them.

Leah was to accompany me on part of my New England haunt hunt; but we detoured over the Fourth of July weekend to visit with Rafaelle, who was then working in Montreal while trying to learn English in order to come to the States. The next day Leah and I drove to Quebec and the Gaspé Peninsula, spending the night at the small town of St. Jean Port Joli. The following morning we came through New Brunswick to Edmundston and reentered the United States at Madawaska, Maine.

I am going into detail about the touring in Canada because it is important to the story about to be related to establish that we had been away from American contacts for several days. We seldom heard anything but French spoken while in the remoter regions of Quebec Province. Deciding to try to show how cosmopolitan we were, we endeavored to use our own shaky French to communicate even with those who might have spoken English to us. We read no newspapers during this time. There was no radio in my Corvair, and the only broadcasts we heard on occasional stops were in French.

From noon until evening on the Fourth of July we drove along U. S. 1 in a very rural part of Maine, seeing little traffic and few people because of the holiday. We enjoyed ambling through the wilds, stopping to eat the tiny delectable wild strawberries growing alongside the road, and scaring a bear cub into the bushes to his mamma when we muscled in on his luscious lunch. Another time we shared the highway with a large, many-horned stag for a few brief moments. Altogether it was a pleasant day as we meandered along, and our mood was practically euphoric.

As we approached the Maine seacoast and the town of Machias, our destination for the night, I told my friend the story of Nelly Butler, the famous Machiasport ghost of 1799, whom I planned to investigate on her home grounds the next morning.

The more one knows about a thing, the less intelligently he seems to practice it on occasion. I had certainly by then had enough experience with intruding spirit entities to be able to accept them at face value without too much fuss. I also knew to protect myself, and certainly not to issue a blanket invitation to anything that wanted to barge in. Yet blithely oblivious to any possibility of danger from an unseen source, I sent out call after call to the spirit of the late Mrs. Butler of Machiasport. I spoke aloud, broadcasting to the invisible world the word that we would be receptive to a visit from this spirit if, after all her years of inactivity, she should care to attempt to make herself evident to us in any way. Leah and I planned to hold a meeting as soon as we were settled for the night, in the hope of contacting this oldest ghost in the United States or any of her friends and relatives who cared to drop by. It never once occurred to us that any undesirables on our wave length might intercept our message and accept our invitation.

We arrived in Machias around 8:30 and found a large room in the pleasant, modern Bluebird Motel. Then we went out to dinner and returned at ten o'clock. The moment I entered the motel room I began to feel light-headed, exactly as I had in London and various other times when going into a trance-like state. I hurriedly prepared for bed, quite uncomfortably tired and dizzy. Lying down on one of the two full-size beds in the room, I felt as if trance might come very easily and quickly.

Leah put all the lights out at my request and then retired. But she jumped up immediately, walked across the room, and turned on the lamp in an alcove where the dressing table was. Then she draped a towel over it to darken the room and returned to bed.

Aware that I was ready to go into trance, Leah suggested we arrange a signal—that I would return to myself immediately if she touched me and called my name. She then said a prayer and asked that we be protected in whatever might occur. After that we lay quietly in our beds and waited.

My head spun as if it were being pulled forcibly into a whirlpool, and a condition of semiconsciousness was approaching, when suddenly I became as chilled as if somebody'd dropped an iced iguana down my back. My whole body was cold inwardly as well as externally, and my stomach began to tremble with fright. With a strong effort I opened my eyes and sat up in bed, crying out, "No, this isn't right! I can't do it!"

Leah jumped up, eagerly agreeing with me. "I'm glad," she said. "I feel nervous, too. That's why I wanted the light on."

"Something evil is here," I said.

My friend's response was vehement. "It's a bad influence of some kind, that's obvious. And I'm chilled to the bone."

I had not yet spoken about being cold, but had experienced it before she mentioned it. We both felt some kind of negative presence in the room so strongly that we were alarmed. We began wrapping ourselves in protection, repeating all the aphorisms for routing "evil spirits" that we could recall, and praying and invoking the forces for good. Also, always the practical party, I turned on the Johnny Carson Show, sure that laughter would bring me back to normal quicker than anything else.

Soon I was calmed down, but it took my friend a while longer to regain her composure. She said that inwardly she kept hearing a voice saying, "It's all right. Why are you fighting it?" Yet she knew it wasn't all right and that she must fight. She walked up and down the room repeating protective statements. Finally she felt relieved of the apprehension and went to bed and was slumbering very quickly.

I watched television until 12:30 and then, leaving lights on in the alcove and the bathroom, finally managed to get to sleep.

Sometime later in the night I sat up in bed terrorized by a nightmare, having dreamed that both Leah and I had been taken over by intruding malevolent spirits and were yelling and acting most peculiarly. As I awoke—and here's the really scary part— an entity who had been bothering me and with whom I was myself somehow confused or identified, was talking to me or through me. I didn't know whether it was a man or woman, but it was a wretched voice saying urgently, "I did *not* kill my children! It's all a mistake. I didn't do it!"

I now had the same frightened feeling in my viscera and the identical cold chills of earlier that night, having to fight again to control them. It took me quite a while, but eventually I slept, not awakening until perhaps eight o'clock.

As Leah and I dressed and packed the next morning, I told her of my nightmare, and we discussed the happenings earlier in the night. Although we had no special reason to think there might be anything particularly significant about them, we decided they somehow were worth noting down. I wrote a complete report of the events and our reactions to them and signed my name to it. Underneath, Leah appended an attestation that the facts were true as they involved her and as I had reported my experiences to her.

Then we left our room and went to the motel office to settle our bill. I told Mrs. Barbara Manchester, the manager's wife, that we were going to the nearby hamlet of Machiasport to try to learn more about the early American ghost, of whom she had not heard. She kindly offered to telephone several members of the local Historical Society to ask them to help me. Then, not finding anyone at home, she began giving me directions for locating Machiasport.

Just then Leah, who had been glancing at the paper while I was talking, came over to me with it in her hand.

"Not now, Leah," I said, "I'll read the news later."

She insisted. "Look at this front page item. I think it has some-thing to do with our experiences."

The information contained in that newspaper and others since procured was startling in the light of my nightmare. I immediately gave Mrs. Manchester the handwritten account of our adventures of the night to read. Then I wrote out another statement and asked her to sign it. It read: "I am witness to the fact that Miss Susy Smith has shown me an account which she had written prior to coming into my office at ten o'clock this morning. While in this office her friend discovered an article in the Tuesday, July 5, Bangor *Daily News* that she felt applied to her dream of last night." Signed, Barbara Manchester, July 5, 1966.

The newspaper article to which I refer told that Mrs. Con-stance Fisher, age thirty-seven, was being held without bail for the murder on Thursday, June 30, of her three children by drowning. This same woman twelve years before had drowned her first three children, had been placed in a mental institution, and had later been released to return to her husband. She had borne three more children and now had also killed them. On each occasion Mrs. Fisher had been found unconscious with the dead children. The first time she had written a note saying: "God told me it was the only way to save them." Now a note read: "I'm sorry to have to do this. I haven't done a proper job in raising the children. They will be better off in Heaven."

Both Leah and I could not help but be sure that the agonized cries in my dream, "I didn't kill my children" were somehow connected with Mrs. Fisher's pathetic case. How, we have tried and tried to analyze, considering almost every explanation and alternative. Several prominent parapsychologists with whom the experience has been discussed found it exceedingly significant and thought it should be published, but they had no explanation for it. All suggestions, until we discussed it with those who have strong Spiritualistic leanings, provided only tentative answers.

First we naturally try to discern how far the subconscious can be credited in an instance of this kind. Although I had not read or consciously heard anything about this case, which had been a *cause celébrè* in Maine over the Fourth of July weekend, could I have glimpsed a headline without being aware of it? Perhaps I had overheard something in French about it and my meager knowledge of the language had translated the thoughts in my unconscious mind.

Yet again, might it not have been telepathy? Perhaps I had somehow tapped the mental climate of the State of Maine in such a way as to know telepathically in my dream about this tragedy that was in the minds of so many citizens. If the explanation is either of the above, though, why the chills and feelings of horror that accompanied the nightmare and the earlier experience?

Certainly the case represents more than merely two hysterical women trying to hold a séance and scaring themselves silly. We are both old hands at this sort of thing and have had no such reactions with our past experiences. And our moods, as I have stressed, were blithe and cheerful as we went into the situation.

After all the experiences I have now had with earthbound entities, I am inclined to accept them as the explanation for this as well. I suspect that Mrs. Fisher was an unconscious medium who was occasionally possessed by a highly confused and miserable earthbound spirit . . . perhaps even one who had killed his children. Not understanding her condition, she had no defenses against him on the two occasions when he decided to entrance her and then commit a horrible deed using her body while she was asleep. Naturally she would not then be aware that she had personally been involved. And thus she would continue to utter her pathetic cry, "I didn't kill my children!"

Then who was it who had troubled Leah and me earlier? Was it the entity who had left Mrs. Fisher now that she was in prison and was trying to extend his influence elsewhere? When we made ourselves receptive and sent out calls to Nelly Butler, were they intercepted by this desolate soul, who answered and came to us? In that case, if it was this entity who had attempted to take me over earlier, how should my dream be interpreted? Was it he with whom I identified in the dream?

I can't help but think it might have been Mrs. Fisher herself. The poor woman was probably in intense turmoil in her jail cell. Great emotion can be conveyed telepathically to a receptive person. Since my thoughts were tuned in this general direction because of the advent of the malevolent entity earlier in the night, perhaps I was broadcasting Mrs. Fisher's inward reaction to the crimes when someone in my dream cried out in anguish.

Whatever the explanation, for a long time I continued to cringe whenever I recalled that agonized cry, "It's all a mistake! I didn't kill my children!"

Chapter 41

FOR A LONG TIME after the Machias episode I said protective statements, just in case that unhappy spirit was still on my trail.

As we drove on down the enthralling coast of Maine we were particularly charmed by the towns with their tall elm trees and huge white sea captains' mansions. If Maine had Arizona's climate I'd have located there forever.

As we pulled into Saco, where Leah was to leave me and take a bus home, there was such a deep, penetrating fog that all traffic was halted. There was nowhere left for us to sleep but one last lonely falling-apart tourist camp, depressing in its gloom. There I prayed very hard for guidance that night because I was at a crossroads.

My problem was where to go to write my book. What I really wanted to do was to return to California—there were several interesting men there—but my furniture was stored in New York, my car wasn't up to such a long drive, and starting out on a long cross-country jaunt alone again would be dumb, anyway. But I had to go somewhere, so the question was put into the hands of God and my Guardian Angels.

The next morning I phoned Shirley Harrison, a medium friend who lives in Saco; and she met me and took me to the Old Straw Place, where there was an excellent ghost story for my book. Then she invited me home with her for lunch with her guests.

Among them was author, astrologer, and yoga teacher Marcia Moore.

Being familiar with my work, Marcia gave me an unusually warm welcome. Then during our conversation I mentioned my impasse.

"I'm ready to settle down now and write *Prominent American Ghosts*, but where?" I asked. Marcia responded with a brilliant idea.

"Come home with me," she said. "My husband and I live in a big house on the coast near York Beach. We could let you have a suite of rooms for as long as you like."

Marcia was so charming, her husband Mark Douglas so nice, her home so inviting, and her invitation so sincere, that I accepted, and roomed and boarded there for nearly three months. The house was one of those huge twenty room "summer cottages" that were so often built on the seashore in the early part of this century. The empty servants' wing alone was larger than most modern dwellings. Marcia and Mark lived and wrote their books in this large abode, rattling around like seeds in a maraca when her children were away at summer camp or boarding school.

I settled down with delight at such a favorable spot in which to work, sitting most of each day at my typewriter before a window overlooking that famous rockbound coast. It was ideal! Except for one thing. I was still spooked by my Machias experience.

As I sat at my desk in front of the window looking down on the rolling waves, all was well . . . in daylight. As the tides went out at dusk, my back, exposed to the large bedroom and the larger hallway beyond my open door, began to chill. I didn't want to be rude and close myself in, but the huge dark hall opened into a stairwell that was at least fifty feet across and extended from the front foyer up to the gaping third floor and yawning attic—an expanse that could have been inhabited by any number of ghastly ghouls at night. No matter how much I worked to control my mind, flurries along my spine were inevitable as I sat and wrote ghost stories.

"What a profession I've got," I bemoaned frequently. Why did publishers always insist that I must write about such icky ilk?

My only companions in the house—Mark and Marcia—spent

most of their time working in their bedroom-and-office suite at the far end of the hall, a good half block away. Mark, an excellent editor who was helpfully reading my manuscript as it was produced, had a habit of walking softly up the hall and then abruptly saying, "Susy!" just outside my door. My tendency to leap out of my skin had considerable practice until I trained him to jingle the chandelier in the hall or hum a little tune to announce his coming.

Daytimes the massive mansion, charming in sunlight, was really enjoyable. The ocean was too cold for swimming but I sunned on the rocks every warm day, and attempted to learn some yoga for exercise. I almost got my fill of Maine lobster, caught in the little pots bouncing on the billows outside my window. I made pastel sketches of the Nubble lighthouse on York Point way across the bay. And my book was written under what might be considered ideal conditions. Except at night.

In September came time for another big decision. My work was finished and sent to the publisher, now where did one move from Maine? With no family to return to and no established home because of all my traveling, I'm always having to ask, "Where do I go now?" It is frequently necessary to have special help about this. Even though I now try to live my life as if God had me in His pocket, sometimes when a big decision must be made, more prayerful effort has to be expended in order to get specific results.

Again the answer came so promptly as to be miraculous, for in just a few days I received a letter from Margaret Sanders Adams who was planning a trip around the world for about six months and wondered if her friend Susy would like to live in her Miami apartment while she was away. My response was immediate; Margaret joined me in Maine; I sold my car; and we drove to Miami in her Mercedes Benz, which was then at my disposal until her return from her round trip.

Yes, my friend had done well since our days in Salt Lake City. So had her finger lickin' good father. So the elegant penthouse apartment I moved into in Miami was filled with expensive antiques as well as Margaret's sculptured heads. My time there until January was spent working on two new books, then after her return I took an apartment of my own and remained in Southern Florida for over three years.

Brief mention should be made of a few interesting psychic experiences that occurred during this time. Shortly after my arrival in Miami, I attended a meeting at which medium Eunice VanWyk gave a talk. Afterward she had a message for me from someone named Gertrude.

"She died this summer," Eunice said. To save my life I couldn't at the moment think of any Gertrude who had died. "She died while you were in New England," Eunice said, and how did she know I'd been there? Then she gave a date in July. When I disclaimed any knowledge of this Gertrude, Eunice insisted, "Yes, you do know her. Gertrude Tub . . ."

"Of course!" I interrupted her with an exclamation. "Miss Tubby. How nice of her to come!"

I had read in the Spiritual Frontiers Fellowship magazine that Tubby had died in July. Eunice may have read that magazine, but there was hardly any way that she could have known that Miss Tubby and I had been acquainted long ago in New York.

Two other mediums, Harry Levy and his wife Marjorie, were said to have physical phenomena at their home, so a group of us met there a few times with high hopes of seeing trumpets fly in the air or anything else sensational. We didn't have that kind of luck, but once a table levitated while we were sitting around with our hands on it. As it was quite dark, it was not easy to be sure just how the table lifted—whether alone or with some judicious prodding from underneath—but it did rise up into the air to the height of our shoulders and there was no evidence of any kind of trickery that I could see.

My surprise was not at this, but later, at a response which came when the table began to tip in answer to our questions.

Before the tipping started, Marjorie said she saw a woman bringing me a rose. This may perhaps have been that same flowery female that the psychic in Los Angeles in 1955 had mentioned. I was still sure it wasn't Mother, and so asked Marjorie to describe her. When she mentioned the long brown hair, parted in the middle and pulled back smoothly over the ears into a bun on the neck, and the beautifully serene face, I recognized my Aunt Ivy.

After this, while we sat with our hands on the table and repeated the letters of the alphabet, the table rose up and stood on one leg with the other three up in the air. It would come down flat on the floor with a rap when we reached the letter it wanted. In this way several names were spelled out and messages were given for various persons.

When it came my turn I asked, "With whom have I had communication at home?" In my mind was the James Anderson-William James controversy. Perhaps the table might spell out William's name and thus give me one more in the series of confirmations of his identity.

My first response was quite satisfactory. The table spelled "Mother."

"Who else?" I asked, increasingly eager to get the desired verification.

"Harvey."

It had been ten years since Harvey was last with us, and he was seldom recalled. No one in that group had heard of my experience with him, and the Levys knew nothing personal about me. Was Aunt Ivy sending me a message in this unusual manner? Was anybody? If not, where did it come from?

When I lived in Coral Gables, an acquaintance dropped in occasionally who had no interest whatever in ESP or related areas. He stated firmly, "My rabbi says there's no life after death." That was enough for him.

Once when this man happened by I got out the Ouija board to entertain him, and he endured it out of curiosity as to how it worked. He soon had it all figured out. "You push it," he asserted.

My, "No, I don't," was to no avail, so I invented a new technique of Ouija board operation—placing my hand lightly on top of his hand which was on the planchette. The little pointer began to race across the board and indicate letters, but as I had purposely sat at the back of the board so that he could see what was going on, I did not observe what was spelled. In fact, I just presumed it was making nonsense as it usually does when getting warmed up. After it stopped writing, the man took his hand off the planchette and sat and stared at me. Finally he said, "Do you know what happened?"

"No," I replied, "did it spell anything that made sense?"

"It only wrote the name of a dead uncle of mine and gave me greetings from him," he said. He didn't want to work the board any more after that. He seemed a bit disconcerted, actually. Before he left, however, he had arrived at an explanation that satisfied him.

"You pushed it," he said.

On the night of January 21, 1969, I was being interviewed on Alan Rock's talk show on Miami's Channel 23. At midnight when the program ended I was handed a sheaf of telephone calls from people who had not been successful in getting through while we were on the air.

When I returned Mrs. June Witlin's call the next day, she said she had wanted to tell me that a tall woman had been standing back of me during the program. Since nobody was in the camera's view but Alan and me, I suspected she had seen a ghost, but didn't get excited until she began to describe it. What she had seen, she said, was a pleasant-faced woman about sixty years old who looked good-natured and full of fun. She was large but not heavy and wore a simple, not fussy dress.

"You look like her," she said, then added the touch that completely eliminated the possibility that she could have been referring to just any old apparition.

"Her hair was smooth at the sides, and its most outstanding feature was a beautiful wave."

Mrs. Witlin thought this might be my mother, and who could doubt it? The wave she portrayed had been Betty Smith's only vanity, and so I was most impressed to hear about it.

Was this an actual ghost Mrs. Witlin saw, or had she just psychically sensed Mother in a vision? I called every psychic person I could think of, but none of them had happened to see the program; so it was not possible to gain verification. I rather suspect, though, that if Mother had appeared as an actual overt ghost, there would have been more repercussion than that.

Yet June's description had been proof enough to me that she had somehow had some kind of a glimpse of Mother. After all, no picture of Mother has ever been published; and Mrs. Witlin did not know me nor I her. She told me she was in the habit of seeing things that brought evidence of her psychic ability. Who could doubt it?

Chapter 42

T WAS IN JANUARY, 1967, that my first poltergeist experience occurred. I have written about this in two books, so only a brief resume of the case will be given here; but it was truly the most exciting period of my life while it was going on.

I had heard and read that such weird manifestations have happened throughout history, and I put as much credence in them as in any other well-attested phenomena. But instinctively one is not likely to admit to himself that objects can really fly through the air when not propelled by some kind of human mechanics.

Parapsychologists have come to the conclusion that this unseemly activity is caused by what they call psychokinesis, an unusual force in the mind of a person who has a good deal of repressed emotion. Spiritualists admit that this force may exist, but prefer to believe prankish spirits are using it and directing the flow of the energy.

I hardly suspected or even hoped that an opportunity would occur for me to see such things for myself. But while I was being interviewed by Bill Smith on WKAT's Talk of Miami program on January 12th, a woman called saying that glass beer mugs and boxes were flying from the shelves of the warehouse where she worked. What did I recommend they do to stop this annoyance?

Stop it? If a poltergeist had gone berserk among their bric-a-brac, I wanted to see it in action.

"Just hang on and keep calm until I can get there," I told her. And they did. Or rather, it hung on to them. It was to remain with them for twenty-three days altogether. During this time I managed to be right in the midst of much of the action, starting the next morning—Friday the thirteenth—an ideal date on which to begin such a singular enterprise.

"I don't believe in ghosts," said Al Laubheim, one of the two managers of Tropication Arts, the locale in question. "But something we can't see is making a shambles of our warehouse." Just then there was a thud somewhere in the building. Everyone, with me trailing, rushed to the large back room where ten cent store souvenirs were stocked. There we found two young men and a girl pointing excitedly to a box lying on its side in an aisle between two tiers of shelves. From it were spilling a number of plastic pencil sharpeners.

"It just fell all by itself!" the girl said.

I wasn't about to be railroaded into instant enthusiasm about something anyone could have knocked off a shelf. Still, I took out my notebook and started to ask each person in the room where he had been standing, what he had been doing, etc. They all corroborated each other's statements that nobody had been near when the box dropped from the top shelf to the floor.

All the other employees who gathered around sounded the same refrain as they told me about the things they had witnessed there during the two days since it all began: "I don't believe it, but I saw it happen!"

This was catching, for very soon events just as inexplicable were occurring near me, and "I didn't believe it, but there it was!" During the whole period of the manifestations, undoubtedly in a few instances some kind of trick could have been perpetrated; but on the whole, hundreds of objects fell or flew about, and they very seldom could have been caused by normal means.

The first day, after I had interviewed all the people there, I stationed myself at an observation point at the north end of the thirty by fifty foot warehouse. There are three tiers of heavy wooden shelves down the middle of this room. Sitting at the end of the center tier, I could watch Glen Lewis, Al Laubheim's partner, and the two stock room boys as they busily worked at the shelves. At 1:50 P.M., when all three of the men were close to me and directly within my line of vision, we heard something fall in Aisle Four near the west wall. It proved to be a box of rubber daggers. While the four of us—the only persons in the room—were gathered around the daggers, examining them and the shelf from which they fell, there was a crash over in the first aisle, some twenty-five feet away. There we found a china sailfish ashtray smashed to bits.

By the time I had settled back into my chair and begun making notes about these incidents, a box containing imitation leather coin purses fell into Aisle Four. Moments later, as stock boy Julio Vasquez, intent on cleaning up the remains of the ashtray, walked past me up Aisle One with a broom in one hand and a dustpan in the other, a shot glass fell to the cement floor behind him with a loud retort, but without breaking. Julio realized that my first reaction was to suspect him of trickery, so he took my hand and placed it over his heart so that I could feel its wild thumping with fright.

It was soon revealed that most of the poltergeist activity in some way followed or was centered around this handsome, likable nineteen-year-old Cuban refugee. I was often to note his fright, and even to feel his paradiddling heart occasionally when some suddenly crashing item startled him. This, to me, offered a certain amount of evidence that he wasn't consciously playing games with us. During the many occasions later when he was under careful observation, it became definite that he was not causing the activity by trickery of any kind.

The following day, Saturday, things were just as exciting, and Al Laubheim began to fear that someone might get hurt. So he did what any other normal red-blooded American male would do in a similar circumstance—he summoned the police. After the law, came the press, then swarms of television and radio people. From then on the public also tried to take the place over, almost breaking down the plate glass front windows with their pushing to peer.

After observing the exotic activities in the warehouse for only one day, I realized that my training and experience did not sufficiently qualify me to give them a proper scientific investigation, so I phoned my friend W. G. Roll, the project director of the Psychical Research Foundation of Durham, with whom I have worked on several occasions. Bill Roll and Dr. J. Gaither Pratt of the Medical Department of the University of Virginia visited the warehouse very soon. They both had investigated many previous poltergeist cases, including the "House of Flying Objects" in Seaford, Long Island, of fleeting fame in 1958. In Miami they staked out watches that proved to their satisfaction that neither Julio nor anybody else was physically causing the curious contretemps. They believed that it must undoubtedly have been some psychokinetic force emanating from Julio's mind that produced the phenomena.

To the rest of us there was never any doubt, either, that an intelligence of some kind was behind the poltergeist, for it played the kind of tricks that an invisible juvenile delinquent might delight in. It never manifested in a specific spot where anyone was watching, but when our attention was directed elsewhere, an object fell right where we had just been looking for it to happen. Thus we almost always missed seeing the action while it was going on. I once turned around in time to catch sight of a box in the act of falling off a shelf; but only two or three persons ever actually saw something start its flight.

The haunt definitely preferred to work without supervision. It was willing to dash any dishes and crash any crockery in the place—it dearly loved the crackling, splintering, spine-chilling crunch they made as they hit the cement floor—but it would never cooperate as long as an area was watched. One afternoon a CBS television man trained his lights and camera on Aisle Four for several hours. I told him nothing would happen while he was there, and nothing did. But as soon as the camera was folded and the lights tucked away, beer mugs banged with their usual assurance, right in the spot that had just been under surveillance.

An example of this occurred when a police officer and I attempted a little experiment with an empty Coca Cola bottle one day. Expecting the cooperation of the geist, we carefully placed the bottle far back on the second shelf of Tier Three and then moved away from it—but not so far away that anyone could have reached the shelf without our observing his every act. No one even approached it, but within brief minutes, as soon as our attention was momentarily distracted, the bottle dashed to the floor.

Patrolman David J. Sackett and magician Howard Brooks had one of the best-observed incidents to report. Brooks, a professional magician for some thirty-five years, had been a friend of Al's for even longer; but their relationship nearly broke up over the poltergeist. When Al began to talk about the crazy happenings at his business, Howard taunted him unmercifully.

"What kind of gullible fool are you?" he asked. "You obviously have an employee who's playing tricks on you. I can make things crash from shelves, too, when nobody is near them. Just a little piece of string and some spirit gum will do it easily. Or some dry ice. Any magician can do this."

While Howard Brooks was still in his truculent mood, one day when I was away because of a previous commitment, he and Police Officer Sackett experienced something that convinced them both of the genuine supernormality of the occurrences. Sackett had brought in his wife on his day off to see in person the curious things he'd been telling her about. They happened to be standing at the south end of Aisle Four and Howard Brooks was at the north end of the warehouse, looking toward them. At that moment two boxes fell from the top shelf into Aisle Four. Although nobody saw them actually leave the shelf, both Sackett and his wife and Brooks observed them in flight and watched them land on the floor, one neatly on top of the other as they had fallen. The only other people anywhere near, Julio and the other stockroom boy, were in completely opposite directions from the area, attending to their own business.

When Brooks and Sackett rushed to the shelf there was no evidence of foreign substances of any kind which could have caused the boxes to move, without themselves remaining on the shelf afterward. No string and spirit gum, no dry ice, nothing small enough not to be obvious could have moved objects so large. The two boxes, which, as Sackett noted, "remained curiously together as they fell," weighed four pounds.

"Any paraphernalia," Brooks said, "which would move that

weight would have to have been visible when we arrived there immediately afterward." After that, Brooks admitted himself completely sold on the supernatural explanation for the phenomena. And Officer Sackett told me later that he knows that nobody was near enough to that shelf to move those boxes, and he knows that boxes don't propel themselves from shelves alone . . . but he also knows what he saw.

How our invisible playmate must have been laughing at us as we worried and wondered and tried to explain, and he continued to produce his phenomena almost under our noses, or at least as soon as our backs were turned.

My best proof of the genuineness of the phenomena occurred one noon when Julio and I were alone in the warehouse, for objects fell under conditions just about as controlled as you're likely to get. Officer Sackett had decided to try an experiment and had wiped one of the amber glass beer mugs clean of fingerprints and placed it as a decoy on the second shelf at the north end of Tier Three on the Aisle Four side. He then stretched a rope down the middle of Aisle Three and said that no one was to go on the other side of it past Tier Three into Aisle Four. Julio and I, then, were outside this roped-off area, talking at the front desk in the warehouse. Just at twelve o'clock, glancing around and realizing that everyone else had gone to lunch, I said, "There's nobody in here but us. Now's the time for something to happen."

At that very second a pop was heard, and we discovered that a shot glass had fallen into Aisle Three at the north end, just inside the rope. It had not broken. We left it there without touching it and returned to the desk; but I had hardly sat down when a loud crash sounded from the same area. It was a beer mug, just outside the rope at the same end of the same aisle. I wondered if it might be the decoy mug that was on the far side of this shelf so crawled under the rope and checked to see it that was still in its original place and condition. It was . . . at the moment. By the time I returned to Julio and the desk, a smashing retort announced that it was in Aisle Four in a thousand small pieces.

Since I had been talking to the Cuban boy and looking at him during every one of these events, I certainly knew he had not made any of them happen—not consciously by manipulation, at any rate.

After the poltergeist quieted down at Tropication Arts, I remained in the Miami area, as much as anything to keep an eye on Julio, the potential source of further book material. I was never present at any more of the unusual activity that followed him to two more jobs before it abated; but reports from the managers indicated that phenomena had occurred even when Julio was standing right beside them and under careful observation. I finally got the lad to go to Durham to be investigated by parapsychologists and psychologists there. While he was in Dr. J. B. Rhine's own laboratory, being tested by some of Rhine's assistants, a vase fell off a table outside in the hall and broke. Need it be noted that there was no one else in the building at the time except Julio and the men closed in the room with him?

It is no wonder that this has gone down in the records of parapsychology as one of the more interesting poltergeist cases, particularly of value because it was possible to put the involved youth under controlled conditions and still observe the violent supernormal activity going on around him.

Chapter 43

By FEBRUARY, 1957, books of mine were ready to come out under the aegises of several good publishers; I was living in a small, easy-to-care-for apartment in Miami's salubrious climate, with a swimming pool outside my front door for exercise and relaxation, and I was not unduly pressured either for time or money. I was sitting regularly once a week with a development circle, but was not aware that my psychic abilities had improved to any great extent. In fact, I had no idea what my current capabilities were, having been unable to try communication for some long while due to the excitement of chasing ghosts and poltergeists and such.

On Wednesday, February 22nd, I had dinner at the home of my friend Anne Fansler, a highly educated woman who is a librarian at the University of Miami. During the evening we decided to meditate together for a while. When we were sitting quietly and making ourselves receptive, we both began to have an unusually elated feeling as if something wonderful were about to happen. I almost burst from my skin with the joy that took hold of me.

Then a voice began to speak through my lips, not of my own volition. It did not identify itself, but spoke most kindly of the work we both were doing to help promote an understanding of psychical phenomena. As in my London experience, I was listening quietly as my mouth spoke the words, remaining quite conscious but not instigating what was said.

As the message of commendation and inspiration continued, I began to feel embarrassed. After all, one didn't know just who or what was speaking, and if it was subconsciously originated then I was revealing myself to be an egotist and a braggart.

Finally this statement was made: "You are now ready to begin receiving a book by automatic writing, and if you will sit at your typewriter at nine o'clock tomorrow morning the communication will start."

When my voice was returned to me, I promised to keep the date and did. Every day from then on for a week I sat at my typewriter most of the time, and in that one week the entire James book was written through me. I have as witnesses to this fact the friends who eagerly gathered evenings to hear me read the new material that had arrived each day. Since I take a week or sometimes longer to write one chapter on my own, the speed with which this came seemed quite extraordinary, to say the least. Although it was extremely tiring to sit and allow James to use my mind for such long hours of work, what was coming through me was exciting enough to be worth any effort on my part to produce it. Yet when the entire manuscript had been written, I realized there was a great deal more effort ahead, for it wasn't really in any great shape editorially.

"I hope you don't mind," I said to James at the end of the week, "but it seems to me we should go back and make some revisions."

"I hope *you* don't mind," James said to me, "but we are going to write a whole new book." So the same procedure was repeated in the following weeks—although this time he went considerably more slowly.

His newer effort dealt with the identical material, but it was now better organized, as if the original had been gone over and carefully edited and rearranged. Apparently he had found it easier in the first place to allow the words to flow through me when I was in an especially receptive state, even though everything had not been received entirely as he wanted it. From then on we continued off and on for a long time to edit it even more scrupulously. He would work a week or two and then let me rest for several weeks or even months and then resume. Thus I came back to it each time refreshed.

The way our editing is done is interesting, and to me somehow evidential in itself. As we are writing the machine may stop in the midst of a sentence. I will wait for a few seconds, wondering what is wrong. Then I'll say, "Did we make an error?" In my mind a "Yes" may be heard at this point, and so I will move the typewriter carriage back to the beginning of the sentence. Then I use the space bar and move along word by word until the typewriter stops again. I xxxx out that word and let him write in his correction, then we go ahead with the forward flow.

Of course, I would never presume to change his text without his permission. If anything is not quite clear to me or is too wordy or difficult to understand, I tell him and then he rewords it. Unless, as he sometimes does, he remains adamant that he has written it exactly as he wants it. Often he is willing to accept my suggestion that he should more fully elucidate some obscure point. Sometimes I have asked questions raised in my mind by his statements and he has given a good bit of new data in order to clarify things for me.

Some people think that any entity attempting to communicate from the spirit world is omniscient and thus all his sacred words must be left intact. Because of the difficulties of getting immortal thoughts through mortal minds, however, even the very best mediums may color the material unwittingly, and anyone who receives should be wary of this at all times. James indicates by his way of writing just how human he is, and this is actually part of his aim. He wants us to be aware that he is still a man, only now a man invisible, who has a certain amount of information to impart about little-known and little-understood aspects of the universe.

Some have wondered why, if he is the spirit of a man who died in 1910, he can now talk intelligibly about television, radio, jet airplanes and such. It is because his interests have been close to earth interests and he has seen from his special vantage point everything that is going on here. This confirms his statements about how close he and his companions actually are to our plane of existence.

Early in 1956, my first year of attempted typewriter communication, my hands used to be picked up from the keys before we started to write and held for a moment in the praying position. At that time I definitely did not believe there was a chance that there was any kind of a God who might be paying personal attention to me if I approached him through prayer, so the significance that sign was supposed to have escaped me. I finally decided it was probably an identifying signature of the communicant.

Now when I sat down to start receiving the material for James's book, my hands were first lifted from the typewriter keys in the same praying position, and now I understood it. During the years since, my indoctrination in the wisdom of approaching God for loving assistance was complete, and I knew that prayer was the best way to protect myself from any unenlightened entities who might try to intrude their thoughts upon me. So I was willing to cooperate, and thanked James for reminding me to clear the air before making any effort to communicate. I immediately started a regular habit of asking Divine Consciousness for help before each typing session, and then stating firmly aloud that nothing could come near me or in any way influence me that did not come from God in love and peace.

I also insisted that contact could only come with wise communicants who would give me the truth. The sincere desire to transmit only *facts* about conditions after death has been very strong in me as the writing flowed through me.

Whether all that came is truth or not, there is no sure way of knowing. There is, of course, a great deal more material explaining conditions after death than was possible to incorporate into this text. That will undoubtedly be supplemented with additional information by my mentor and used for future publication.

As I am concluding this book James has made his last contribution:

"I find nothing to add to what has already been stated except to stress the importance of continued personal striving for self-improvement," he says. "For much too long your psychologists and behaviorists have attempted to convince you that man is a mere machine, or even an animal. It has been forbidden by your intellectuals to discuss man as a soul or spirit living in a physical body. One has been looked on as naïve if he believed in a life after death, in a soul that could continue to live forever.

"It has been evident in recent years that this idea of man as a mechanical unit has given little harmony to the world, no peace and much dissatisfaction to men, for a theory so nihilistic cannot bring happiness. Now you are beginning to realize that in order to survive as individuals it is necessary to have a philosophy, to know that you are of importance in the scheme of things. There is no way that you can achieve true happiness and peace of mind until you once again return to the old concept of man as a spirit inhabiting a body. Then you can allow yourself to conjecture about the ultimate destiny of this spirit and its reason for existing. When you become aware that the plan of the universe is a perfect plan and that you are a fundamental aspect of it, you will recognize your worth and that of all others.

"No one who knows that all men are destined to return to Ultimate Perfection can ever belittle himself or his fellow men. No one with such knowledge would be able to use his authority to declare war, to kill, to in any way deliberately harm another, to do anything which will hinder the perfect growth of all other human beings and the world in which they live. When one thinks of himself as one with Supreme Intelligence he will act in a responsible manner at all times. In all things such men are peaceful, loving, kind, wise, and responsible. No such concerned man will make his own causes more urgent than those of another, nor his own needs more important. Your ecology problems will resolve themselves when each man thinks more of his neighbor and his neighbor's property than of his own. Your pollution situation will be remedied when care for all the world's beauties and bounties is more important than gain for any individual or group. Overpopulation will recede when all people learn not to have children until they are able to raise them properly under ideal conditions. There will be no racial injustices, no inhumanity to man, when all are known to be kindred with the identical beautiful destiny."

Christians will say there is nothing new here, and that is true. There is not even anything divergent from Christ's example in this book's discussion of continued existence after death and of "evil spirits" who possess others. But the theme of self-improvement, the use of free will, and the enrichment of the whole through the perfection of each individual part is still being ignored as it has been ignored, or only halfheartedly accepted, since the days when Jesus and the Buddha lived it and taught it. James insists that the time has come when it must not be dismissed so lightly; and I believe he feels that his explanation of why we must follow these steps in order to die in such an enlightened state that we won't become earthbound should clarify the reason for it.

"When more and more persons attempt to use these precepts, it will quickly be realized that all life is changing for the better, not only on earth but in the first dimension after death as well," he says. "Do not think of this as just another collection of platitudes. I have told you the exact techniques for the successful accomplishment of the ends here advocated. Basic to their use is the information that no one who answers this challenge will be working alone, for he will have the help of progressed entities. If he accepts this knowledge and practices it, his life will be easier, and as he becomes more and more peaceful his happiness will project itself onto those around him. As he takes personal responsibility for his own development he will be an inspiration for everyone else, an actual step toward ameliorating conditions for the rest of the world while he is improving his own personality and character."

This circular process by which each man helps himself and in so doing sets an example for others is supposed to catch on like miniature golf or hula hoops and soon everyone will want to get into the act. I told James he must pardon my natural skepticism about that, human nature being what it is. Those of us who have written our Congressmen regularly, yet nonetheless have seen laws we felt urgently about pigeonholed in committee and bad laws passed because of self-interest lobbies are not so encouraged about all this good one man can do. But my communicant insisted that even legislators are going to want to participate when they see everyone else doing it.

"Look at the effect your present day young people have had on conditions in your country, just by making a strong stand for what they believed in," he said. "They are the ones who are most likely to take the precepts in this book seriously. In a way they have been working on ideals for some time. All their talk of Peace and Love and Brotherhood has not been empty words and has been very fruitful. They are truly representative of a generation where self-interest is much less predominant than it was previously."

Because I'm an arguer, it was natural to be a Devil's Advocate with James, even while agreeing with him for the most part. And so I pointed out all the subversives who have been causing much of the campus riots, leading well-meaning students into strife and violence in the very name of Peace.

James passed this off more lightly than I had suspected he might. "Most young people are catching onto the troublemakers among them," he said. He was like Mother with that constant reiteration of the positive thinking bit. He was *positive* that an acceptance of the idea of spirit survival and continued existence after death was going to make everyone think differently about himself and change his living habits. Practice in constructive thinking, trying to love those who make it difficult for you to love them, attempting to understand and have compassion for ideas less sensible than your own and for people less wise, all this will take effort. But, James says, "It has been proved time and time again by those who tried it to be the only really enlightened way to live."

The more I have practiced this since they've been bugging me so about it, the more I realize how difficult it is—even though James is right that it does bring much happiness and enough peace of mind that it is worth any amount of hard work.

Sometimes, however, you feel almost silly when you're in a

crowd where everyone is running someone down and the only thing you can allow yourself to say is, like the kind old lady, "Yes, but he kin whistle good." I commented on this to James, mentioning that until each individual gets on this kick of being personally responsible for his own character development, most of the world is going to continue to be just as ornery as ever. Most people already think they live pretty decent lives and don't need to make all that effort to change themselves. And those of us who are trying are going to stick out like sore thumbs.

"I'd put it differently," said James gently, topping my cliché with another. "You'll stand out like beautiful blooming roses in a weed patch. And when the weeds come to realize that with work they too can become as triumphant, they will begin to follow your example."

Quite astutely, it seems to me, James is not hopeful that this will come in a generation, or even ten generations, but he is sure that it *will* come eventually.

"It is the inevitable destiny of your world," he says. "Not self-annihilation, death from overpopulation, or any of the other fears you are constantly bombarded with . . . but peace and love and perfection."

Chapter 44

LIVED IN MEXICO most of the time from August, 1969, to March, 1970, having fallen in love with the beauty of the country, the charm of the people, and particularly the stimulating climate of Cuernavaca, a city forty-five miles south of the capital.

It was in Cuernavaca that my friend, author Ruth Montgomery, made the suggestion that resulted in this book. She read James's manuscript and then told me what friends had told her before she wrote *A Search for the Truth*—that a large amount of philosophy is more easily assimilated when broken down into smaller units and incorporated into a book of personal experience. James concurred that Ruth's idea was a good one, and this is what came of it.

In Mexico City in September, when I lectured for the American Club, host Lee Nichols introduced me as "the Auntie Mame of psychical research." Although surprised at this glamorous and amusing designation, I told the audience it was gratefully accepted and that I would be delighted to live the role to the hilt, so if anyone knew any millionaires . . . any *single* millionaires . . . please to bring them around and introduce us. They didn't, of course. Nobody ever has any of those to spare.

The following Sunday I was sitting with Lee and his wife Grace in front of a large open fireplace, relaxing and basking in the glow of the flames. Lee, who loved to tease, said, "Just look at you, sitting there being Auntie Mame."

"I'm not anti-anything," I replied. "I'm too blissful."

Well, this book started with a pun; it might as well end with one. Especially one that so presents my attitude toward life. It isn't just when sitting in front of a fire glowing that I think and feel and act that way, but much of the time now. And when a joyous feeling is not present, I try to discover what is keeping it away and how conditions can be improved so that it will return.

I sometimes talk such situations over with Mother or James and benefit from their wise counsel. Just as often I don't, the communion seeming adequate without resorting to actual conversation.

Many who have not developed their psychic sensitivity to the point that they can communicate, or who, being warned of the possible dangers, do not wish to try it, have asked me how they can become conscious of the presence of their Guardian Angels. Nothing better can be offered than what Hornell Hart and Mother originally suggested: expansion of your awareness with a mental reaching and surging that will almost invariably be successful if you don't give up too soon. Most people do not have much patience for this sort of thing. If they don't get results immediately they doubt if anyone who loves them is really there. I can only say, don't despair. Everyone has someone there, who comes from God in love and peace.

In *The Child from the Sea** Elizabeth Goudge wrote that when asked, "How do the dead speak?" Old Parson replied: " . . . They may say nothing. They may merely forgive. But if it is knowledge you need then what they know can touch your mind like fingers on a keyboard. Then your mind may perhaps give you words and a voice, but perhaps not. It is no matter if you have the knowledge."

And if you persist you will have the knowledge.

Shortly before he died, Bill Hanemann wrote to me, "The reason the study of psychical phenomena appeals to so many people is because it exalts the human ego, making a man feel that he's something beyond his ordinary crummy self."

"That's absolutely right," I answered him. "It does this because he *is* something beyond the ordinary crummy self he usually allows himself to be. If he would recognize that he is actually a spiritual being with a soul he would live accordingly, and be exalted."

Bill's reply was a few complicated sentences which added up to the total comment of "Oh, yeah?" He was never one who could have been convinced without definite scientific evidence. So many people are like that. I was once that way myself, and my cherished hope is still that science will one day support religion in the certainty that man survives death. I'm not sure that idea seems as ludicrous today as it might have several years ago, when psychical phenomena were considered to be so far outside the scientific scheme of belief that they had to be categorically denied in order to protect the system. Yet even then one of the country's most prominent philosophers, the late Professor C. J. Ducasse, of whom I was very fond personally and for whom I had great admiration because of his wise and open interest in psi, once said, "If the facts do not fit our logic, it is time to reexamine our logic."

It was exciting to learn recently that the Parapsychological

* New York: Coward-McCann, Inc., 1970.

Association has finally been accepted for affiliation with the American Association for the Advancement of Science. So now the simple investigation of ESP—telepathy, clairvoyance, precognition—and also psychokinesis, is attaining a certain amount of scientific recognition.

But it will doubtless be a long time before any parapsychologist will even so much as dare suggest the possibility of doing any research about the survival of the human spirit. He knows this would be a self-destruct for his academic career. I wouldn't be surprised if it may not be physicists and chemists who first attain some kind of achievement in soul survival research, they now seeming to be so much more open-minded about the subject.

A friend of a friend of mine had the unusual psychic experience of seeing her spirit father when she was at the point of death after an automobile accident, and she was suddenly and miraculously healed. Later she went to a Harvard professor of psychology for an explanation and his reply was, "I'm sorry I can't help you. Unfortunately, we're still working with white rats and dogs. We won't get to incidents like yours for a hundred years."

Actually, that might be an unusually pessimistic statement for these times, with the mental climate of the world what it is now becoming, for more and more people are looking for answers to life's questions and a fantastic number are finding that psi opens the way to philosophical discoveries.

The kinds of things I have discussed in this book do occur frequently to a great many people. And they don't necessarily happen to those who are neurotic, up tight, ill-adjusted or under pressure. I hadn't been boozing or tripping on dope . . . wasn't living on happy pills or pot or sleeping tablets or speed . . . only took LSD once under fairly clinical conditions . . . didn't even smoke straight cigarettes or dip snuff.

No, I had these experiences by deliberately inviting them, feeling myself to be making a systematic investigation of a new field of challenging interest. I knew from the first that it would be difficult to be impartially objective because I wanted some rational scheme of life after death to be true . . . even when not consciously admitting it to myself. That's why such a point was made to observe all events critically, to read more of the "con" than the "pro," to have frequent discussions with those who did not believe, and to argue with myself over each new manifestation.

As revealed by my efforts recounted in this book, such personal research takes a tremendous amount of patience; but it is fantastically rewarding. I don't claim that the incidents which occurred to me are necessarily convincing of spirit survival. Many of them, taken individually, would surely indicate coincidence and nothing more. Yet collectively there is such a large volume of curious happenings of what must surely be a supernormal nature that coincidence can hardly be the answer. As Camille Flammarion, the famous French astronomer and psychical researcher, said: "When well-observed incidents multiply, coincidence disappears."

One thing that can be said about these episodes is that they *have* been well-observed. And if they didn't want to get themselves itemized, classified, labeled, and written down in a book, then they shouldn't have started happening to someone trained for newspaper work.

It is only when you make the effort to learn more about this subject personally that you really are likely to begin to accept it. Most people who look at it only superficially reject it completely —as I did before beginning my study. I had resisted for years the idea that those who die, if by chance they still continued to exist at all, might have any possible interest in earth people and their affairs. I'd hoped they'd have something better to do. And yet after learning about the system from Mother and James, it is easy to understand the idea of gradual transition as part of an intelligent development program after death—Evolutionary Soul Progression, as they call it. A new kind of ESP.

Certainly existence for all of us would acquire greater magnitude if we could believe what James has been telling us. How grand it would be if, while enjoying the present to the fullest, we could be secure in the knowledge that life goes on, that there is no death, that what we have accomplished on earth does count for something, that we are not living just for today but for eternity.

Then we would be aware that existence doesn't have to be a mere struggle for bread and butter or mink-lined Cadillacs, or for recognition, power, and fame. We would know it is not merely an endurance of a span of time begun by accident and ending nowhere. We'd be sure instead that there *is* a reason; there *is* a goal; that it all makes sense after all.

It would mean that as we live on earth, so our progress is determined in the next plane of existence. That the mean grubby little individuals who acquire only money or only physical sensations are doing themselves little good, but if there is enough love in the heart any life can be a brilliant success.

To those who hate the thought of mental effort, this entire picture may have a somber cast. To some it has been consoling to believe that halfhearted church attendance or deathbed repentance will carry one through eternity effortlessly, or that death is the end and it doesn't matter how life has been lived. For them it would be disheartening to learn that there must be self-discipline on earth and endeavor even into future existence until all their capabilities and talents have been built to their highest degree.

But actually the picture is tremendously inspiring. To feel that through your own strivings you will one day achieve unity with God is overwhelming. It makes more sense, doesn't it, to believe that it must be done by your own consciously applied effort? You wouldn't want to think, would you, that you could just lie back and languidly go cloud-floating and harp-strumming to the heights without even having learned the lesson of love which has been urged upon us since time began?

If you could find yourself able to accept the idea of Guardian Angels, you might begin to receive assurance of their presence from your invisible partners. There is always the chance that if you tried mental receptivity you would soon sense that a guiding spirit is with you. He will help you, if you'll let him, toward happiness and greater accomplishment during your lifetime on earth.

You will then have joyously stepped onto the escalator leading to that magnificent destiny that awaits you. And perhaps you will find yourself agreeing with Walt Whitman, who says in his poem "Starting from Paumanok":

Nothing can happen more beautiful than death.